BLACK PERFORMANCE ON THE OUTSKIRTS OF THE LEFT

SEXUAL CULTURES
General Editors: Ann Pellegrini, Tavia Nyong'o, and Joshua Chambers-Letson
Founding Editors: José Esteban Muñoz and Ann Pellegrini

Titles in the series include:

Times Square Red, Times Square Blue
Samuel R. Delany

Queer Globalizations: Citizenship and the Afterlife of Colonialism
Edited by Arnaldo Cruz Malavé and Martin F. Manalansan IV

Queer Latinidad: Identity Practices, Discursive Spaces
Juana María Rodríguez

Love the Sin: Sexual Regulation and the Limits of Religious Tolerance
Janet R. Jakobsen and Ann Pellegrini

Boricua Pop: Puerto Ricans and the Latinization of American Culture
Frances Négron-Muntaner

Manning the Race: Reforming Black Men in the Jim Crow Era
Marlon Ross

In a Queer Time and Place: Transgender Bodies, Subcultural Lives
Judith Halberstam

Why I Hate Abercrombie and Fitch: Essays on Race and Sexuality
Dwight A. McBride

God Hates Fags: The Rhetorics of Religious Violence
Michael Cobb

Once You Go Black: Choice, Desire, and the Black American Intellectual
Robert Reid-Pharr

The Latino Body: Crisis Identities in American Literary and Cultural Memory
Lázaro Lima

Arranging Grief: Sacred Time and the Body in Nineteenth-Century America
Dana Luciano

Cruising Utopia: The Then and There of Queer Futurity
José Esteban Muñoz

Another Country: Queer Anti-Urbanism
Scott Herring

Extravagant Abjection: Blackness, Power, and Sexuality in the African American Literary Imagination
Darieck Scott

For a complete list of books in the series, see www.nyupress.org.

Black Performance on the Outskirts of the Left

A History of the Impossible

Malik Gaines

NEW YORK UNIVERSITY PRESS

New York

NEW YORK UNIVERSITY PRESS
New York
www.nyupress.org

© 2017 by New York University
All rights reserved

References to Internet websites (URLs) were accurate at the time of writing. Neither the author nor New York University Press is responsible for URLs that may have expired or changed since the manuscript was prepared.

ISBN: 978-1-4798-3703-8 (hardback)
ISBN: 978-1-4798-0430-6 (paperback)

For Library of Congress Cataloging-in-Publication data, please contact the Library of Congress.

New York University Press books are printed on acid-free paper, and their binding materials are chosen for strength and durability. We strive to use environmentally responsible suppliers and materials to the greatest extent possible in publishing our books.

Manufactured in the United States of America

10 9 8 7 6 5 4 3 2 1

Also available as an ebook

CONTENTS

ACKNOWLEDGMENTS

This writing has been accomplished with the insistent support of many tremendous people to whom I wish to express my gratitude.

I started discussing this book with José Esteban Muñoz, who brilliantly and generously organized the field this publication enters. I am grateful for the extra life Ann Pellegrini, Tavia Nyong'o, and Joshua Chambers-Letson granted this project. Nyong'o has been a generous advisor, offering important mentorship, even though I am a little older than he. Jennifer Doyle and Francesca Royster gave fantastic feedback and welcome encouragement, and thanks to Eric Zinner and Alicia Nadkarni for their support. Great jobs and inspiring colleagues in the Department of Performance Studies at NYU's Tisch School of the Arts and Hunter College's Department of Art and Art History have made it possible for me to get to this acknowledgment.

Sue-Ellen Case advised the research from which this book was developed. Her rigor, clarity, and years of attention kept the train on track, and her own scholarship has served as a queer inspiration. I was fortunate to work with a number of consequential professors during my time at UCLA, including Susan Leigh Foster, Steven Nelson, Janet O'Shea, Joseph Roach, Carol Sorgenfrei, Frank Wilderson III, and Haiping Yan, who each helped me think. Before that, while I was studying writing at CalArts, Mady Schutzman planted several seeds that bore colorful fruits. In this list of instructors, I am compelled to mention my high school German teacher, Dorena Kehaulani Koopman, who taught me a lot about order and ambivalence.

Alexandro Segade, gifted facilitator and interrogator, boyfriend *par excellence*, has much to do with anything that is produced from that which might be construed as my "self" and cannot be thanked enough. Along with Alex and our collaborator Jade Gordon, as the group My Barbarian, I have been able to pose in performance the questions of representation, action, collaboration, influence, and location that instigated this study. I remember once leaving a graduate seminar on transnational theory in Los Angeles, flying to Munich, taking a train through the Italian Alps, arriving at an old castle, performing a short musical adaptation of *Titus Andronicus* that asked the audience to decide whether or not a black baby could be the emperor of all of Italy, then taking a train back to Munich, flying back to L.A., and going to a graduate seminar on theories of representation. While scholarship and practice are different, they have plenty to say to each other.

In what follows, I describe the year I was born as the end of the excessive sixties, and in some sense, this book interrogates that primal scene. My parents, Barbara Gaines and Charles Gaines, with their various boldnesses, are behind the pages of this labor. My in-laws Gustavo Segade and Irina Kaplan Segade add their own influence to the politics and unstable raciality through which I emerged. And much support has come my way from Joseph Rosato and Roxana Landaverde.

The diversity of these chapters reflects very different archives. Special help negotiating these came from Rumi Missabu, Daniel Nicoletta, Pam Tent, David Weissman, Irwin Swirnoff, Lawrence Helman, Joseph Zaccarella, Emory Douglas, Sam Durant, Wenzel Bilger, Christina MacMahon and the University of California African Studies Research Group, Emeka Ogboh, Alicia Hall Moran, Jason Moran, Isaac Julien, Mark Nash, Thomas Lax, and David DeWitt. Thanks to Yasmeen Chism, J. M. DeLeon, and Ethan Philbrick for their assistance in the final stretch. Much of chapter 1 appeared as the article "The Quadruple-Consciousness of Nina Simone" in *Women and Performance: A Journal of Feminist Theory*, July 2013, and elicited excellent feedback in that process.

This project began with the artists who are the subjects of these chapters. I have only met one in person, the gracious, witty writer Ama Ata Aidoo; the rest are deceased by the time of this acknowledgment, which is perhaps telling. Their enduring works, in a certain parlance, give life still. One must only consider the present ubiquity of Nina Simone's music to think of generation in a generative way. Despite her lifetime of difficulties, I hear her songs played regularly these days, in all sorts of settings. On a trip to the Middle East, I heard recordings of Simone in cafés in both Ramallah and Jerusalem, and as I hummed along I thought this must be an instance of transnational imagination, in all of its possibility and impossibility.

Introduction

A Legacy of Radical Differences

Summer is coming with bursting flowers and promise of perfect fruit. Rain is rolling down the Nile and Niger. Summer sings on the sea where giant ships carry busy worlds, where mermaids swarm the shores. Earth is pregnant. Life is big with pain and evil and hope. Summer in blue New York; summer in gray Berlin; summer in the red heart of the world!
—W.E.B. Du Bois

Yet I have hope for the Black people. . . . First of all, all the peoples of the third world are increasingly conscious of the revolutionary necessity; secondly, the Whites, and even the Americans, and even Johnson and what has come after, can transform themselves.
—Jean Genet

Imagine this, please, for a new world around the corner.
—Gayatri Chakravorty Spivak

Difference, embodied and spectacular, is a poor condition out of which to construct subjecthood, but can be an effective position from which to perform. This book argues for performance as a radical act, and pursues the possibility that performances of blackness have been capable, sometimes, provisionally, and contingently, of amending dominant discourses that manage representation and constrain the lives they organize. In considering the works of the American singer and pianist Nina Simone, plays of Ghanaian writers Efua Sutherland and Ama Ata Aidoo, performances of Afro-German actor Günther Kaufmann, and the activi-

Figure I.1. Reggie (a.k.a. Anton Dunnigan) of the Cockettes holding Dusty Dawn's baby, Ocean Michael Moon, 1971. Photo by Bud Lee.

ties of San Francisco's Cockettes troupe—in particular of Sylvester—I read these artists' performances against the archives of three complicit registers, each of which engages a history of radicalism.

The first is blackness, a famously contested force that is fundamental to the coalition of capitalist, imperialist, and democratic orders loosely understood as modernity. I use blackness to describe both an Africanized experience of race and the discursive regimes that have racialized the Euro-American sphere of influence. While the former instantiates a sense of subjectivity or a claim to a historically situated self, the latter have persistently denied subject status to blacks, and demonstrated the rightness of that denial. In terms of cultural production, blackness operates a theater across the border from modernity's privileged territory. A spectacle of difference, the insistent demand for blackness' reenactment points to a powerful performativity, founded in negativity, but which, in performance, may be deployed resistently. Performance draws attention to the ways blackness is tied to the bodies that are "bound to appear"[1] on its platform, and the ways those bodies are gendered. Within the schema of blackness, race, gender and sexuality are intractably entangled. This particular intersectionality contributes to a claim I pursue, which is that historical blackness is force that lends itself to reenactment and makes itself available as a model of antagonism for the gendered, the sexed, the classed, the differentiated. In this, blackness is the vanguard of negativity, the avant-garde of difference.

The second register I move through is the period of the sixties, during which the enactment of blackness as a liberatory tactic was strikingly evident. The excessive sixties I discuss, spanning from civil rights and anticolonial movements of the late 1950s to the official end of the American war in Vietnam in 1973, have been described as a period of dramatic social and political change. The sixties resist the homogenizing mode of "epochal memory" Joseph Roach warns against, through which historical coherence and continuity is manufactured.[2] As Frederic Jameson writes in "Periodizing the 60s," "the 'period' in question is understood not as some omnipresent and uniform shared style or way of thinking and acting, but rather as the sharing of a common objective situation, to which a whole range of varied responses and creative innovations is then possible."[3] While this historical situation can be thought of within "structural limits" including the parameters I describe, the sixties are characterized by a lack of organic unity among social and political forms. The transgressions of that time have shaped the very idea of transgression. When Barack Obama referred in a 2008 interview to the "excesses of the 1960s,"[4] he summarized a popular notion that the period's radicality and heterogeneity were unmanageable, disordered. Obama, whose own biography emerges from radical sixties combinations, constrains even his own narrative with this expression that the sixties were too much. That familiar limitation puts the period's political transformations into a fixed temporal space; just as the sixties are marked by excess, the closure of the sixties marks a recontainment of resistant possibilities. That boundaries of authority have since been reinstituted around those transgressions is part of the promise of the sixties. Mindful of this promise, my act of periodization seeks to measure what was transgressed in the first place. Recontainment, or the supposed failure of sixties politics, foregrounds the provisionality of this resistant power, and draws attention to the power of the provisional.

The third register I read maps race and time onto space, via a particular transnational route. The locations I consider, situated within the United States, West Africa, and Western Europe, are connected by pathways of colonial adventure and state conflict that were effectively retrod by black diasporic travelers and international leftist actors. By the sixties this route served not only to connect various political figures, intellectuals, and artists, but represented mobility in excess of the prohibitive and punishing regimes of nation-states and their colonial territories. Kristie McClure is among those who have described the ways racial, gender, sexual, and other differences construct political identities not limited to national citizenship.[5] Each nation-state organizes identificatory positions, but those who exceed its permissions may find ways to circulate beyond its boundaries, revealing the limitations of citizenship as a container for ways of being in the world. While the violent pressures of differentiation have mobilized much black movement, the black transnational network I explore is a place of imagination where different models of participation and agency have been rehearsed and performed, powerfully resisting governmental assertions of who belongs where.

Among the many notable confluences one might consider along this black transnational route, I pay particular attention to the relationship between black expressive and leftist revolutionary practices. While Marxist theory and communist structures had an international influence on the era's political movements, they usually lost their orthodoxies in transit. As the left traveled, it encountered differences that exceeded its Marxist capacities. Ernesto Laclau and Chantal Mouffe have described this difficulty:

> What is now in crisis is a whole conception of socialism which rests upon the ontological centrality of the working class, upon the role of Revolution, with a capital "r," as the founding moment in the transition from one type of society to another, and upon the illusory prospect of a perfectly homogenous collective will that will render pointless the moment of politics. The plural and multifarious character of contemporary social struggles has finally dissolved the last foundation for that political imaginary.[6]

The singularity of class revolution is shown to be illusory when plural and multifarious social struggles emerge. In the performances considered here, representations of race and gender often interfere with class's ordering influence. Frank Wilderson has argued that in the case of the United States, where capitalism and white supremacy form an inter-related matrix, Marxist analysis is fully inadequate.

[M]arxism assumes a subaltern structured by capital, not by white su-premacy. In this scenario, racism is read off the base, as it were, as being derivative of political economy. This is not an adequate subalternity from which to think the elaboration of antagonistic identity formation . . .[7]

While Wilderson deemphasizes economic politics as a methodology for organizing black resistance, Laclau and Mouffe theorize a discursive space that revises classical Marxism with a logic of *"complementary* and *contin-gent* operation,"[8] situated in a "post-Marxist terrain" where plural forms of resistance expand the leftist struggle.[9] In either view, this struggle is ambiv-alent; whether class analysis resists race and gender or expands to include race and gender, in neither case will class adequately stand for race or gen-der. Negotiating this entanglement of economic and social powers became a primary task of many anti-racist left-oriented projects that gained vis-ibility in the sixties. Around the black world, these projects moved toward local specificities that modified the idea of world revolution.

Reflecting this anti-unanimous contingency, blackness, the transfor-mative sixties, and the transnational circulation of these notions all con-tribute to the radical ambivalence of the works I discuss. Ghana's African Marxism, San Francisco's communal practices, the radical sensibility of West Germany's 68ers, and the revolutionary rhetoric of America's black power movement all drew liberally from communist ideologies, selec-tively appropriating useful notions and terms. But a class-based analysis would not sufficiently account for any of the other identificatory struc-tures that had come to bear on these political liberation movements. These works instrumentalized political aesthetics that were associated with leftist movements while bearing inconsistence with the doctrines of the left. Nor did they adhere to any other unifying ideologies. They were produced by prolific authors, but most all of these performance works were made collaboratively with a group and were not precisely original; they are adaptations, combinations, and revisions, and are decentered by the intertextuality of their forms. While connecting to problems of black representation, the artists and their collaborators exhibited a range of racial and sexual signs, diminishing the possibility of orienting their performances around racially or sexually unified identities. And these works emerged from multiplicitous modes of production; none of these artists specialized in so coherent a way as to be called any one thing, and this flexibility is a critical element of their works. This difficulty of naming is symptomatic of their critical excess; in each case, the normative script would not contain these characters. By embodying paradox, contradiction, and ambivalence—in relation to identity, political doctrine, authorship, and disciplinarity—these performances produced transformative energy for their reimaginative worlds.

In tracking performance through the three complicit registers I have outlined above, and in reading their complex heterogeneity, attention is returned to the importance of difference in constituting the subject, the citizen, the consumer, the agent. Foucauldian epistemological observations suggest that modernity, rather than instituting total conformity, actually mobilizes difference to rank and order a complicated totality. Difference is a necessary structuring element of capitalist societies. But this difference must be managed and regulated in order for the totality to assert its own dominance.[10] To take a prime example, Hortense Spillers is among those scholars who have interrogated freedom as a category organized in relation to enslavement, describing American slavery as "the invisible portion of freedom's meanings."[11] In slavery, Spillers identifies an alterity that disturbs the ontological sense of unity proposed by the notion of freedom, which only comes into being in relation to that which breaks its rule, the unfree. Toni Morrison has noted of Enlightenment ideologies: "in that construction of blackness and enslavement could be found not only the not-free but also, with the dramatic polarity created by skin color, the not-me."[12] Through such arguments, difference, between the free and the enslaved, or among the ranks of the free and the ranks of the enslaved, emerges as the underpinning of meaning. While its distinctions are typically naturalized, as in racializing discourses that affirm the imminence of hierarchy, the disordered visibility of difference, unmanaged into its proper space and time, antagonizes ordering power. In these performances, we see a destabilizing excess of difference, a radical heterogeneity made visible through actions and performed representations.

This is not simply a matter of visibility politics, of corrective representation, or of adding a black face to this or that image. I am describing a precarious engagement with the terms of representation, with the place of the image, as a way to stress the ties between visuality and power's organization. These artists' works challenge ideas of what can be seen, and agitate through forms that connect to the visual: live music performance, theater, film and television, public spectacle. These performances offer textual demands and provocations that pressure representation's tandem operation of language and image. In so doing, these performances represent a crisis of the sixties: the invisible heterogeneous elements of culture, including resistant sexual, racial, and political difference, burst out of their hidden ranks and orders and into spectacular visibility, instigating cultural experimentation and often triggering violent repression.

Vagrant Divas, or Imagination

In the mid-sixties, the American civil rights movement and the tremendous violence to which it responded were front-page news around the world. Claims from leftists outside of the United States on the energies of black American politics were used to mobilize renewed critiques of capitalism and colonialism. One such example comes from the Paris-based Situationist International, which in the article "The Decline and Fall of the Spectacle-Commodity Economy"[13] linked American civic unrest of 1965 with an international class struggle: "The issue is no longer the condition of the American blacks, but the condition of America, which merely happens to find its first expression among the blacks. This was not a *racial* conflict . . . Martin Luther King had to admit in Paris last October that the riots did not fall within the limits of his specialty: 'They were not race riots,' he said, 'they were class riots.'"[14] This article, which goes on to make linkage between the uprising in Watts, California, and the French colonial war in Algeria, notably deracinates what was widely considered a race riot in the service of an international Marxist project. "American blacks" and "America" are conflated into a single symbol of capitalism and its exploitation. Black bodies "merely happen" to be appropriated in order to draw universal relevance out of a local political conflict, a recolonization that's seemingly authorized by the preeminent black American political leader, Martin Luther King, Jr. Blackness serves here as a cipher for progressive ideology.

Despite the limited capacity of Marxist analysis to address the identificatory differences around which political solidarities arose in extra-European resistance movements of the sixties, these movements frequently turned to the international left and its Marxist sources as a reservoir of revolutionary possibility. Malcolm X, whose autobiography hinges narratively on the development of a transnational consciousness, writes of the education he gave himself while in prison, and how his understanding of history informed his view from 1965. He outlines the history of China's relationship with the gendered figure of "the white man" from the Boxer Rebellion forward, and continues from there to assess the relationship between race and international communism: "Red China after World War II closed its doors to the Western white world. . . . Some observers inside Red China have reported that the world never has known such a hate-white campaign as is now going on in this non-white country where, present birth-rates continuing, in fifty more years China will be half the earth's population. And it seems that some Chinese chickens will soon come home to roost, with China's recent successful nuclear tests."[15] Malcolm X's satisfaction at the possibility of non-whites holding nuclear weapons is framed by a sense of cosmic justice: "Let us face reality. We can see in the United Nations a new world order being shaped, along color lines—an alliance among the non-white nations. America's U.N. Ambassador Adlai Stevenson complained not long ago that in the United Nations 'a skin-game' was being played. He was right. He was facing reality. A 'skin-game' *is* being played. But Ambassador Stevenson sounded like Jesse James accusing the marshal of carrying a gun. Because who in the world's history ever has played a worse 'skin-game' than the white man?"[16] Malcolm X absorbed international leftist and anticolonialist attitudes into his political organization, finding in his militant anti-racist agenda an accommodation of both American specificity and a "new world order." This example pairs with the previous reference to the Situationist International to underscore the transnational dialogues engendered by black American politics, and the breadth of leftist politics in which these performances of the sixties were situated.

Of course, black political movements in the United States always have been invested with internationalist concepts, given the triangle trade that

Figure I.2. Dr. W.E.B. Du Bois addresses the World Congress of Partisans of Peace at the Salle Pleyel in Paris, April 22, 1949. (AP Photo)

delivered Africans to America and America to the world. Notably, in the early twentieth century, both Du Bois and Marcus Garvey launched black liberation movements that were linked to transnationality: DuBois through a notion of Pan-Africanism that matured under African decolonization projects of the sixties, and Garvey through a back-to-Africa separatism that had an ideological impact on radical thinkers of the civil rights era. In the wake of transatlantic slavery, nineteenth-century abolitionist causes circulated around that same sphere, as in Frederick Douglass's persuasive 1846 speech at Covent Garden in London. Indeed, the eighteenth-century foundation of transatlantic capitalism, with its reliance on the slave trade, carries the weight of black bodies and their representations, both of which were instrumental in building modern European nation-states. The recognition of the self through the identification of the other, as discussed above by Spillers and Morrison, has been intrinsic to European colonial projects, and is notably articulated through Said's *Orientalism*.[17] Blackness has figured prominently in that system of recognition. Scholars Paul Gilroy and Joseph Roach both illustrate the ways in which white colonizer and black colonized have constructed each other's cultural experience through the development of modernity. All of this is to say that the emergence of blackness as an international political trope in the sixties was nothing new: blackness is among European modernity's most prolific authors.

Du Bois's own circulation is an important route that demonstrates the transnational situation of black political thought in the twentieth century. The first African American to earn a Ph.D. from Harvard University, Du Bois also studied at Tennessee's Fisk University and the University of Berlin; the former setting placed him in the American South shortly after Reconstruction, the latter put him in intellectual contact with leading social scientists of the time and allowed him to travel throughout Europe. Du Bois notably brought an enlightened, positivist approach to the social sciences in the U.S., particularly in studying African Americans in relation to the larger society. A founder of the NAACP, Du Bois's work on the "color line"[18] in the early twentieth century was a tremendous influence on the civil rights activism of the fifties and sixties. Du Bois was also a leader of the Pan-Africanist movement, which by the fifties and sixties had fostered the first post-colonial political leaders of Africa. In Du Bois's writings, one can identify a synthesis of German political and aesthetic philosophies, the African American experience of racism, and an international consciousness related to class struggle. Adapting notions from a different struggle, Zionism and its diasporic sensibility provided an important template for the Pan-Africanist ideology Du Bois developed.[19] The transnational route he traveled, from the American North to the American South and back, and from Western Europe to the Soviet Union and communist China to West Africa, enabled a circulation of political ideas that inform each other, despite the diversity of historical situations under which they were articulated. These routes were commonly traveled by the sixties, bringing artists and intellectuals in touch with a worldwide leftist movement.

This international project, along with his disillusionment with the possibility of positivist scholarship putting an end to American racism, moved Du Bois toward an international Marxist political position, a position he declared while speaking in China. Shortly before the time of his death in Ghana in 1963, the anti-communist United States government had refused to renew his passport, prohibiting him from ever returning to his own country. His obituary in the *New York Times* described him as "controversial," citing his membership in the American Communist Party.[20] This leftward movement is striking, given Du Bois's history of resistance to Marxism, figuring in his writings across decades. His reticence, articulated in numerous essays that struggle with radicalism, such as "Socialism and the Negro Problem," published in 1913, "The Negro and Radical Thought," published in 1921, "The Negro and Communism," published in 1931, and "Marxism and the Negro Problem," published in 1933, all affirm Du Bois's mistrust of working-class American whites, whom he viewed as unlikely allies in the project of black liberation in the United States. Finally, by 1961, toward the end of his life, Du Bois concluded that "[c]apitalism cannot reform itself; it is doomed to self-destruction. No universal selfishness can bring social good to all."[21]

While Du Bois represents an industrious black thinker, suggestive of other black American and Caribbean intellectuals whose travels during and between the world wars built foundations for sixties liberation projects, performers were also contributors to this project, building a lineage of powerful traveling images that revised modern conceptions of blackness. Paul Robeson, famous for his portrayal of Othello, notably connected a black American theater tradition to a position of black communist internationalism. Robeson and Du Bois both fell out with the American state, as outlaws, reenacting the trope of black masculine criminality despite the virtuoso masculinism of their incredible compensatory performances. The black American performer Josephine Baker is an important link in this chain, enacting another form of exiled transnationalism, and further highlighting the gender instability that's embedded in racial difference.

Baker's 1920 debut in the *Revue Nègre* caused a stir and a sensation in Paris, performing a European fantasy of essential black energy through the frenetic modernity of jazz and extra-European dance. Resembling other primitivist avant-garde experiments of the time, the image of non-white exuberance in Baker's performance served as a salve against the staid Europeanness of classical conventions. Baker's difference was alluring, yet confounding, as one French critic's account suggests:

Is this a man? Is this a woman? Her lips are painted black, her skin is the color of banana, her hair, already short, is stuck to her head as if made of caviar, her voice is high-pitched, she shakes continually, and her body slithers like a snake. . . . The sounds of the orchestra seem to come from her. . . . Is she horrible? Is she ravishing? Is she black? Is she white? Nobody knows for sure. There is no time to know. She returns as she left, quick as a one-step dance, she is not a woman, she is not a dancer, she is something extravagant and passing, just like the music . . .[22]

In this interpretation, both gender and race are implicated in a general confusion instantiated by Baker's performance. She disrupts binaries, not only of man and woman, of black and white, but of peculiar signs associated with cultural oppositions, such as bananas and caviar. While the primordial fantasy Baker instigates in this critic casts her both as a slithering snake and a magical medium who can channel sound, the urgent speed of modernity is also present, which limits contemplative abilities, making distinctions difficult to ascertain. Though this critic insists Baker is unknowable, there were those who did "know" Baker, including her black American mother in St. Louis, Missouri, who, according to Baker's biographies, had had a relationship with a local Spaniard; Baker's supposedly unrecognizable body was a product of this miscegenation. Despite reasonable explanations, Baker is received in excess of rational necessity, as an "extravagance." Baker's energetic, topless performance in the *Revue Nègre* both challenged and excited European audiences by disrupting established categories, destabilizing in this viewer and others the entire apparatus by which race and gender are understood.

Baker's transgressive performance relied on both elaborate costume and nudity. This fungibility of presentation built a variety of gender and racial presentations onto her body. Her apparent bodily difference suggested all differences, invoking through costume the limitless possibilities that difference stirs in the imagination. Baker's well-known looks, evident in publicity photos, demonstrate this range of possibilities. These include her cross-dressing persona, Baker's well-known drag look, which she sported at the Casino de Paris in 1932. One publicity image shows Baker smiling and holding a cigarette while wearing a tuxedo, with a white tie and top hat. This formal masculine attire suggests class, authority, and ease, and stands in distinction to the famous banana-skirt costume Baker wore in 1926 at the Folies Bergère. Of that costume, a biographer suggests that "[m]any will claim to have invented it, but only Josephine would dare to strategically fashion herself a substitute phallus."[23] With breasts exposed, and her pelvis surrounded by these wild, elongated fruits, this costume spectacularizes a primitive power. Even while implying a feminine fertility and a fruity consumability, the bananas act as a string of phalluses, multiplying the performer's apparent potency. As discussed in chapter 1 in relation to the West African deity Esu-Elegbara, whose transformational powers can be represented by dual engorged phalli, the presence of the many members can be used to travesty the singular power that resides in the masculine. Whether in a tuxedo, or half-naked and surrounded by fruit, Baker's gender is performed as a contestation of reliable representations. This is also the case with Baker's blackface clown costume, which she wore at the Folies Bergère in 1927, which included giant checkered pants and a top hat. This costume reveals Baker's roots in the American black vaudeville circuit, where she began touring and performing at the age of fourteen. In this case, race is theatricalized through the convention of blackface makeup, just as gender is performed through costume. In all of these costumes, the surprise and the sensation of Baker's look plays racial expectations against gender expectations, radically innovating the possibility of a black, female body, in all of its significatory instability, standing in for numerous configurations of being.

In her study of Baker, Bennetta Jules-Rosette suggests a comparability of nudity and gendered costume in her performance.

Removing clothing and dressing as a male were sources of feminine empowerment that carried a shock value. In an apparent contradiction, nudity was also a mask that Baker donned as part of primal image. By 1930, Baker had already begun to move away from this image. In the 1932 production of La Joie de Paris, Josephine appeared as a bandleader dressed in a tuxedo and top hat. . . . In publicity displays, she frequently used photographs of herself in this sophisticated role, which, on the surface, contrasts starkly of the image of her as a banana-clad savage. In her final performance at the Théâtre Bobino in Paris, in 1975, the sixty-eight-year-old Baker, wearing a white beaded motorcycle outfit, complete with cap and gloves, roared onto the stage astride an old-fashioned Harley for her number on New York and Chicago. This gender-bending imagery influenced Baker's musical and stage persona throughout her life. Her practice of cross-dressing was continued by the female impersonators to whom she gave her clothes during the 1970s.[24]

The radicalizing theatricality of blackness in this European context was such that a body could work as a mask. While Jules-Rosette sees a progression from savage to sophisticate, it is in contrast and juxtaposition that essentialist meanings dissipate and new meanings form in contextual difference. This body and its array of costumes speak in a syntax of transformation that inspired both Sylvester, as will be shown in chapter 4, and the Parisian "female impersonators" referred to above. Nina Simone, subject of chapter 1, joked about Baker's costume in relation to her own money problems: "She started in bananas. I may end in bananas."[25] Expanding on Simone's image, at the end of her own life, Baker insisted on an androgynous "beaded motorcycle outfit" rather than attire that would reliably index her age or a biological sense of gender.

Like many of the performers discussed in this study, Baker's performance was not relegated to the stage, but shaped a way of life. This was a groundbreaking influence on generations of black performers. In a moving example, Baker made a rare trip to the United States to attend the 1963 march on Washington, D.C., the civil rights demonstration at which black American performers and political leaders, most notably Martin Luther King, Jr., but also Josephine Baker, spoke. "You know I have lived a long time and come a long way,"[26] she said. Standing in front of the Lincoln Memorial on the National Mall, the walls of which enshrine an engraved history of American slavery, Baker related her own experience with racist discrimination, the journey she embarked upon to reinvent herself apart from that racism, and her hope that members of a new generation might find a sense of self without having to leave the country. Baker described her evolution from an interest in her own freedom, eventually into a consciousness of the larger social question. "You know, friends," she explained, "that I do not lie to you when I tell you I have walked into the palaces of kings and queens and into the houses of presidents. And much more. But I could not walk into a hotel

Figure I.3. Josephine Baker at the march on Washington, August 28, 1963. (DALMAS/SIPA)

in America and get a cup of coffee, and that made me mad. And when I get mad, you know that I open my big mouth. And then look out, 'cause when Josephine opens her mouth, they hear it all over the world."[27] Baker's speech connected personal subjectivity to a sense of the world made possible through her own powers of expression, which she finally described in the third person.

Even then, Baker's utterances were punctuated by her costume. As described by her sister Marion Douglas, "Josephine was wearing her uniform with all her decorations. . . . She had on the Médaille de la Resistance with rosette, the Médaille de la France Libre, the Croix de Chevalier de la Légion d'Honneur, and the Croix de Guerre."[28] Displaying the honors that had been bestowed upon her for her work collaborating with the French Resistance during World War II, Baker's military bona fides complemented her legendary status. This former banana-clad savage, whose earliest childhood memories were of brutal racial violence in America, whose grandmother had "talked about the slave days,"[29] had fought against German Nazi domination on her way to this civil rights demonstration in the American capital. Of her many androgynous looks, this outfit perhaps best summed up Baker's transnational experience agitating against racial and gender expectations. The militancy of this costume illustrated a contested modernity that had delivered Baker, and those influenced by her, to the sixties.

Du Bois had died in Ghana the day before the march on Washington, D.C. On the summer afternoon in 2009 when I visited his grave in the capital, Accra, I was confronted by two African American performers of international magnitude. Upon entering the small gazebo that had been built to entomb Du Bois only feet away from the Pan-Africanist cultural center that was once his residence, I acknowledged a sense of emotion that I had come to associate with such pilgrimage sites. Strikingly, at this moment, I heard the familiar voice of Beyoncé singing a stirring ballad. The pop star's voice was emanating from a small audio device held by a teenaged boy who was sitting in the open passageway of the structure. The boy appeared to be local. He was repeatedly listening to one of Beyoncé's then current hit songs, "If I Were a Boy." The song narrates a heterosexual yet gender-crossing fantasy in which the singer brings a performative critique to the construction of masculinity:

> If I were a boy
> I think I could understand
> How it feels to love a girl
> I swear I'd be a better man[30]

Beyoncé's performance of divahood has served as a platform for an amplified voice, one that resonates both globally, in the field of commodities, and transnationally, as in the strange black identificatory conundrum happening among the boy, Du Bois, Beyoncé, and me in that Ghanaian gazebo. After sitting for a minute on a ceremonial stool, I left to explore the grounds, where I soon ran into Danny Glover, the African American movie star and activist. He was visiting the Center for a conference associated with PANAFEST. I had attended other festival events in the previous week that had troubled notions of originality and authenticity with reenactments of black American alienation. These included: a young Ghanaian theater ensemble's amateur play about the slave trade performed inside a sixteenth-century fortress, speeches from culture ministers promoting diasporic tourism to slave sites, a march to a memorial grave for former American slaves who had "returned" to Ghana, and a large reggae concert, where I had previously run into Danny Glover. On this second occasion, on a walkway near a golden bust of Du Bois, I approached the actor. "May I take your photograph, Mr. Glover?" I asked. Glover gave me a thumbs-up sign as I documented his presence with my mobile device. The blurry image, in its context, suggests the complicity of performance in producing a black transnational political discourse. This discourse conveys psychic content, as in the identifications between disempowered people and images of black expression that exceed negative constraints. The discourse is also a material consequence of the physical dissemination of these images and texts, facilitated by travelers. While the black transnational network is not a recognized political body capable of bestowing and defending official rights, it is a place of imagination where different models of being and belonging can be performed.

This notion of imagination can be creative and playful, as in many of the expressive choices made by the performers discussed here, but it is also a political mode. Arjun Appadurai has argued that works of the imagination create a collective platform from which to project notions of "resistance, irony, selectivity, and in general, *agency*."[31] This collective imagination can be directed more potently than the aimless fantasy, and is broadened by a community's access to circulating images and the experiences of migration. In the black transnational context, this imaginative space has been shaped by people with extraordinary access and privilege, such as Du Bois and Baker, but has informed a widely accessible terrain of imagination that can not be described exclusively in elite terms, as the proximity between me, the Ghanaian teenager, and Du Bois's remains suggests. Another such anecdote comes from the biography of Black Panther Party leader Elaine Brown, who remembers her working-class grandmother's own fond memory of Ghanaian president Kwame Nkrumah, recalling a time when he, as a college student at Lincoln University, had visited her home in Pittsburgh.[32] Nkrumah had played saxophone with a family friend. There is an understanding in this telling that African liberation and American inner-city difficulties are part of the same struggle. In this sense, imagination is a potent political tool for envisioning solidarities beyond those authorized by state control and international economic conditions. Also evident in the many examples found here is that performance links imagination to expressivity, producing real articulations of potential power.

Specific enactments of imagination follow as the subject of these chapters. Chapter 1 considers Nina Simone's performance strategies. Her combinatory textual approach, her transformational uses of persona, costume, and voice, and her expressive revision of political critique are mobilized into what I call "quadruple consciousness," multiplying Du Bois's famous formulation, making the alienations of marginality into a set of radical positions from which to perform. Chapter 2 considers plays by Efua Sutherland and Ama Ata Aidoo in the context of post-colonial Ghanaian liberation. The synthesizing tendency of the new state's ideology is resisted in the multiple positions and points of view brought together in these politically challenging performance texts. Simone, Sutherland, and Aidoo each trouble the masculinism of black liberation and leftist politics by critically engaging feminine signs and proto-feminist concepts that revise those revolutionary models.

Chapter 3 travels to West Germany and considers the performances of Afro-German actor Günther Kaufmann within the oeuvre of director Rainer Werner Fassbinder. Blackness is explored as a sign of Western modernity, informed by transnational images but specifically articulated here in a Bavarian context. The ambivalences of queer desire and camp serve to sexualize and destabilize notions of identity and the hierarchies those are meant to conform to. A complex of race, class, gender, and sexuality is enacted by Kaufmann in these works, radicalizing his character and the narratives in which he appears. The performative antics of San Francisco's Cockettes, a multi-racial troupe that exploded conventional notions of gender and sexuality with elaborate costumes and outlandish performances, are explored in chapter 4. The virtuosic performances of Sylvester, the group's most prominent member, extends the black diva image into radically destabilizing territory. The troupe's imaginative reinterpretations of American textual materials and political events rewrote hegemonic histories, and proposed modes of sexual liberation through anarchic, ambivalent representations of subjectivity. Their performances extended beyond theatrical contexts and into their daily lives, fostering a queer space where expressive acts of imagination provisionally transform everyday experience, contributing to what L. H. Stallings has observed in "transaesthetics" as "a reorganization of senses and the sensorium."[33] Their tactics resonate with a wider context of sixties movements that brought performative techniques to political resistance projects.

In each chapter that follows, decentered performances of racial and sexual difference suggest radical political outcomes, but these potential outcomes are complicated by the expressive power of imagination, which in itself exceeds the rational containment of the body into legible, manageable, individual subject-status. While such status had been conventionally denied to the marginalized, these performances of the sixties launch what would later be understood as a deconstructive critique of the center around which margins have been oriented. Through text, image, voice, and action, these performances made influential interventions into the field of representation, bolstering the enduring sense that the sixties were an era of remarkable transformation.

1

Nina Simone's Quadruple Consciousness

For some time there has been much talk about the Negro. A
little too much.
—Frantz Fanon

One time in New York I went to see an off-Broadway play
with Bill Dukes and Brock Peters—two fine black actors—in
the cast. I thought the roles they played were insulting to
black people, and I got up there on stage in the middle of
the show and told them so. I stopped the play in its tracks
to ask them why they were doing trash like that. One of
them said something about needing the money, but that was
no excuse. They apologised, and took me home in a cab. I
was half-crazy with anger that night, a woman on fire, and
that was how I felt most of the time as I watched my people
struggle for their rightful place in America.
—Nina Simone

Introducing Miss Nina Simone

While performing her anthem "Mississippi Goddam" in a 1964 concert,
Nina Simone quipped, "this is a show tune, but the show hasn't been
written for it yet." This statement typifies the singer and pianist's expressive approach, performing agency where it is a structural impossibility.
Simone's body of recorded music reveals an anti-racist agenda enacted
through performance. Simone used black American musical, textual,
and theatrical strategies, elaborating a history that has transformed the
locations of marginality and exclusion into improvised positions from
which to speak. This black American approach was consistent with the
breadth of Simone's non-exclusive musical culture; the artist situated
her own activist compositions among songs by Bertolt Brecht and Kurt

Weill, songs associated with black authors, standards of the American theater, a diversity of ethnically marked folk materials, popular hits, and works belonging to other genres and types. Her combinatory textual approach, along with her transformational uses of persona, costume, and voice, are mobilized into an expressive mode that I call quadruple consciousness. Drawn from a reading of the song "Four Women," this hyperbolic term multiplies W.E.B. Du Bois's famous double consciousness formulation, transforming the displacing alienations of marginality into a set of unreconciled positions from which to perform. Simone outperforms the oppositional structure of Du Bois's divided self, forecasting Brent Edwards's demand of double consciousness: "Just two, Dr. Du Bois, we are forced to ask today? Keep counting."[1] The precariousness of this position is its ambivalence: neither singular authority nor dialectical progress can be oriented around the shifting terms of quadruple consciousness. Rather, this ambivalence produces multiple positions, provisionally destabilizing the concrete terms around which race and gender have been punitively oriented. In the black expressive context, as in Simone's performance methodology, multiple positionality is a source of provisional power, and a way to act in excess of the permanent exclusion experienced in any one location. Rather then a dialectical synthesis achieving wholeness and agency for a divided subject, Simone's performance goes the other way, allowing multiplicity to transform the negativity of alienation into a productive force. This kind of productive ambivalence is evident throughout Simone's activist performances of the sixties.

This chapter contributes to an emerging field of Nina Simone studies, building on the work of performance scholars Fred Moten, Shane Vogel,[2] and others, who have sought to define the feminist and resistant terms of jazz and blues vocal traditions, and notably elaborated by Daphne A. Brooks's "Nina Simone's Triple Play," which pays particular attention to the radicality of Simone's combinatory approach. Brooks notes that "Simone's social activism was not only overtly incorporated into the content of her material, but, just as well, that it permeated the form of her musical heterogeneity that worked to free African Americans from cultural and representational stasis."[3] Investigating this heterogeneity, Brooks's study considers Simone's revisions of music by Bertolt Brecht and Kurt Weill in order to evaluate her relationship to that tradition of political performance. This chapter continues that investigation, seeking to further define the political dimension of Simone's theatricality.

Simone's quadruple consciousness, a dexterous deployment of authorship, presence, and voice that exceeded the prohibitions of race and gender while performing those terms, is a performance position that marshals paradoxical and simultaneous differences to present a provisional form of subjectivity. Quadruple consciousness playfully hyperbolizes double consciousness while rehearsing a movement beyond its confines, from positivist subject to divided subject, through negated subject and into multiplicitous subjectivity. Though exceeding a dialectical choreography, this position draws on a Marxian analysis suggested by her association with Lorraine Hansberry and other intellectuals, and alluded to by her investment in Brecht, while Simone's performance also relies upon the affect of black expressive forms. The contradiction between critical distance and authentic experience is assimilated into the performance of blackness. Within the field of representation, blackness is infinitely visible as an object, in the third person. It has been argued that blackness cannot constitute a full subject position from which to view and, as Frantz Fanon points out, ontological models like that of the knowing Cartesian subject fail to account for blackness, which can exist as a term only in relation to a prior term: as an object of inquiry, as the other who lends meaning to the self, as a slave to the master's dialectic. In this sense, any iteration of black subjectivity where a black subject is prohibited, whether grounded in intellectual criticality or emotional affect, is a constructed position, made provisionally available through combinations rather than an *a priori* unity. Consequently, there is no clear political distinction to be made here between an alienated and an embodied performance. In comparing this African American expressive strategy with a Brechtian program, the role of alienation must be reevaluated, not simply as a performance technique, but in relation to its location at the source of African American identity. Further, reapproaching Brecht from this provisional black and gendered position foregrounds the impurity of that dramatist's own supposed theatrical orthodoxy. As in Simone's performances, performative blackness, in all of its ambivalence, destabilizes the rational terms that constitute power, but also complicates the terms under which Du Bois, Brecht, and the enlightened left operate.

Protest Performances of the Black Intelligentsia

Simone credited her friends of the black intelligentsia for facilitating her political education in the sixties, offering a set of strategies for critical analysis of the cultural situation. Prominent among them were other socially engaged writers and dramatists: Langston Hughes, James Baldwin, and Lorraine Hansberry. Significantly, these figures were outspoken critics of American racism whose literary and dramatic works reflected this critique. Of further importance is that Simone's political tutors, like herself, brought to their works a sense of race complicated by gender difference, underscoring a sense that race and gender are always critically entangled. All three of these authors expressed what could now be called queer affinities. Simone's circle was deeply involved in civil rights activities and the development of black political consciousness, and brought the nuanced experience of race imbricated with gender and sexuality to their civil rights efforts. It was with Hughes that Simone made her first trip to Africa. Hansberry's unfinished play "To Be Young, Gifted and Black" became the source of Simone's anthem of the same name, later adopted as a theme song of the NAACP. It was with Hansberry that Simone attended organizing meetings in New York.

By the early sixties, politicized black artists like Hansberry and Simone were bringing the politics of race and gender together in their works, and thinking about both of those in a world context informed by class struggle. Of Hansberry, Simone wrote: "Although Lorraine was a girlfriend . . . we never talked about men or clothes or other such inconsequential things when we got together. It was always Marx, Lenin and revolution—real girls' talk. . . . Lorraine was most definitely an intellectual, and saw civil rights as only one part of the wider racial and class struggle. . . . Lorraine started off my political education, and through her I started thinking about myself as a black person in a country run by white people and a woman in a world run by men."[4] Because of her leftist activities, Hansberry had been under FBI surveillance since 1952, following her work on Paul Robeson's newspaper *Freedom*. The agency had an informant report on the content of her play *A Raisin in the Sun* before it opened, to be sure it was not overtly communist.[5] Informed by Hansberry's analysis, Simone's account of her own thinking reflects a critical self-awareness defined by broad terms of opposition and contextualizes a performance of resistant subjectivity politicized by race and gender.

Simone's original song "To Be Young, Gifted and Black" reflects the politicization of her music and performances, and the influence of Hansberry. Having incorporated the composition into her regular set, Simone performed the song from the piano while her band accompanied in a 1969 concert in a Morehouse College gymnasium in Atlanta, Georgia. The men in the band wore dashikis, while Simone wore an elegant black suit, made fashionably militant with high black boots and a large Afro hairstyle, and accessorized with silver jewelry, Cleopatra-style eye makeup, and a corsage. The song suited the college gymnasium setting, as its repetitive refrains and simple melody convey a direct, pedagogical quality removed from Simone's jazziest techniques. As one of the choruses explains:

> When you're feeling real low
> There's a great truth that you should know
> To be young, gifted and black, you've got your soul intact[6]

The song is an exercise in black pride, directed at motivating the coming generation, such as the excited group in attendance at Morehouse College, many of whom were young African American women wearing Afros themselves. With black studies courses and programs emerging around this time in American universities, this song asserts a politics of redefinition, updating a Du Boisian "talented tenth" sensibility with the more inclusive language of black positivity. That music star Aretha Franklin adapted the song for her successful 1972 album *Young, Gifted and Black* indicates the popular reach of this discursive effort.

Speaking directly to her audience, Simone ad libs a few words in this energetic performance, adding to the song's written lyrics. Rather than "when you're feeling real low," Simone elaborates, "when you're feeling depressed, alienated and low"[7] framing the notion of feeling with emotional and political dimension. Typical of Simone's performances, additional utterances lead to sections of mid-song oration, delivered here as the music continues to play.

Feeling good now? Yes, yes, yes. Langston Hughes is gone but he meant the same thing. And all you know about Billie, poor Billie, they killed her for the very same thing that you have a party on. You know? They killed her 'cause she smoked pot. Really. They killed her. And now of course Lorraine is gone. Enough, enough, enough, Nina. Feels so good. By the way this is a black orchid given to me last night—where were we?—Jersey City—by the black students council and I preserved it until tonight so you could see it.[8]

This interjection, typical of Simone's self-interruptions, specifies a historical context for the performance. Simone places herself in a tradition of transgressive black women singers when she invokes Billie Holiday, who had died in police custody a decade earlier. Simone's creative interpretation of Holiday's death suggests an act of black imagination, while indicating the stakes of the song, oriented around an urgent political need for new black leadership. Simone aligns herself with Hughes here, offering herself as a surrogate when she says he "meant the same thing." A similar sentiment is offered in a 1967 live recording of Simone's song *Backlash Blues*, an adaptation of a Hughes poem, in which she sings: "When Langston Hughes died—He told me many months before—Nina keep working until they open up that door."[9] Simone figures herself as a continuation of Hughes's political and artistic project. At the Morehouse event, Simone completes this story with Hansberry, who had died of cancer several years before. By the time of this 1969 concert, these deaths would have been framed in the imagination of this young, predominantly black audience by the assassinations of Martin Luther King, Jr., and Malcolm X. Simone's elegy meditates on life and death in Afro-America, but rather than discussing black leaders in the political sphere, she emphasizes artists as radical agents. The meaningful absences invoked in this spoken libation are finally met by the presence of the corsage, given to Simone by black students in the North and delivered here to the South in a symbolic act of solidarity. Simone's messenger/courier routine manages twin surrogations, establishing a continuity of her political project with her deceased mentors, while linking their project to the emerging black political movement of which "young, gifted, and black" students would be the custodians.

A similar investment in futurity is found in Hansberry's use of the phrase, which Simone adapted for her song. Hansberry wrote the term "young, gifted, and black" into an address to the winners of a United Negro College Fund writing contest. In her comments, Hansberry adds, "in the month of May in the year of 1964, I, for one, can think of no more dynamic combination that a person might be."[10] This episode appears toward the end of the published text of Hansberry's *To Be Young, Gifted and Black,* a posthumously assembled series of fragments in the late author's voice. The book, which was adapted as a play and presented at New York's Cherry Lane Theater in 1969, speaks from multiple perspectives about the problems of race, gender, and life's possibilities. The decentered text, which moves through scenes of plays, letters, short prose, and other notes provided by the author, resembles the multiplicity found in Simone's formal approach, one which assembles diverse materials, and allows for interjections and exclamations to circulate throughout her performances. The continuity of *To Be Young, Gifted and Black* is the discontinuity of Hansberry's experience. Hansberry was not only a friend and tutor to Simone, but this final work in her oeuvre formally resembles Simone's own complex enactment of multiple positions that exceeds prohibitions on a unified black subject. However, unlike the work of Baldwin, Hughes, or Hansberry, Simone's expressive mode was not just founded in her body, but deployed through her body as well.

Accordingly, Simone's criticality was not only configured in intellectual terms. Simone describes the physical dimension of her political awareness in her autobiography: "The bombing of the little girls in Alabama and the murder of Medgar Evers were like the final pieces of a jigsaw that made no sense until you had fitted the whole thing together. I suddenly realized what it was to be black in America in 1963, but it wasn't an intellectual connection of the type Lorraine had been repeating to me over and over—it came as a rush of fury, hatred, and determination. In church language, the Truth entered into me and I 'came through.'"[11] In her most politically direct works, it is through an embodiment of exclusion that Simone articulated a position from which to act. Simone, who became known commercially as "The High Priestess of Soul," empowered this position by channeling a transitory revolutionary spirit, as in the religious allusion above. Simone authorized the criticality of her political consciousness by performing a deeply invested physical presence.

This personal investment is evident in Simone's typically animated delivery of "Mississippi Goddam," which was composed shortly after the events described above. The 1964 album *Nina Simone in Concert*,[12] which documents a performance at Carnegie Hall in New York, contains the first of many live recordings of Simone's notable civil rights composition. Simone's provocative chorus indicates both a personal subjectivity and a national political context:

> Alabama's got me so upset
> Tennessee makes me lose my rest
> And everybody knows about Mississippi Goddam[13]

What "everybody knows" is what was then the state of race violence in the American South. Prominent cases from 1963 included the slaying of activist Medgar Evers in Jackson, Mississippi, and the bombing of the 16th Street Baptist Church in Birmingham, Alabama, which killed four young girls. In her autobiography, Simone cites these two widely publicized events as important influences on her activist intentions, claiming that like anyone "with half a brain," she had followed the civil rights movement, but that these murders contributed to a personal political awakening, of which "Mississippi Goddam" was an acknowledgement. Simone elaborated on her motivation in a television interview in September 1964: "First you get depressed, then you get mad. And when these kids got bombed, I just sat down and wrote this song. And it's a very moving, violent song 'cause that's how I feel about the whole thing."[14] For Simone, the experience of feeling was a contact point with the broader political context. Political specificity began to emerge in Simone's work through this engagement with personal subjectivity; the "me" who was so upset by Mississippi and Alabama was surely Simone herself.

Still, "Mississippi Goddam" produces noticeable intertextual gaps. Simone's genre-invoking quip about the song being a show tune is delivered with an ambiguous tone, and the song's mood is strangely ironic. While presenting a radical politic with lyrics like "This whole country is full of lies—You're all gonna die and die like flies,"[15] the song is delivered

Figure 1.1. Jazz singer Nina Simone in London on December 5, 1968. (AP Photo)

over a bouncy 2/4 piano beat in a quick and witty pitter-patter of lyrics, each "Goddam" accompanied by a major-chord crescendo. This upbeat vaudevillian quality belies the anger of the lyrical content and the earthy ferocity of Simone's performance. Her unique voice conveys sincerity, but also a hint of sarcasm. This ambiguity is tested after the first verse, when she asks the audience, "You thought I was kidding, didn't you?"[16] Her direct yet theatrical presentation distances while it makes familiar. While grounding her performance in a seemingly authentic expression of black subjectivity, the intertextuality of that performance creates gaps of intelligibility through which Simone projects evident criticality.

Affect Effects in Afro-American Acting

Simone's body of work draws from a wide variety of sources, ranging from her own compositions to folk songs from many traditions to pop music, show tunes, and European art music. These allusions reflect Simone's interest in intertextuality, and indicate a discourse on modernity not confined to sources that are demonstrably black in origin. Rather than instantiating a polemic of black authenticity, this intertextuality permits a reading of Simone's oeuvre through critical sources that frame rather than constitute the idea of race. Simone was trained in classical European piano music, an influence that is heard throughout her playing. More generally, Simone frequently chose European materials that played against her racialized persona, such as the Scottish Appalachian ballad "Black Is the Color of My True Love's Hair," which she popularized in the mid-sixties, suggesting an element of black pride not indigenous to the material. In cases such as this one, Simone converts European materials to suit her purposes, finding critical resonance within the intertextual gaps.

With this intertextual borrowing in mind, the distancing elements in Simone's performance technique bear comparison to Brecht's idea of gestic theater. Simone's adaptations of Brecht/Weill materials confirm that she was familiar with the German dramatist. Daphne Brooks affirms that Simone was reflecting on Brecht's "Moon over Alabama" when she composed "Mississippi Goddam." She likely had specific knowledge of Brecht's theoretical premises, having been tutored by her friends who were major dramatists themselves—Langston Hughes had already collaborated with Kurt Weill on *Street Scene* by the time of their association. Hughes had compared Simone to Brecht in a poetic newspaper column in 1960, before the two became friends, insisting that like the plays of Brecht, Behan, and Genet: "She is strange."[17] Following a 1964 fundraiser concert at Carnegie Hall, a Student Nonviolent Coordinating Committee officer wrote to Simone, furthering the comparison: "As Bertolt Brecht expressed the turmoil of Germany, so do your songs express the terrible ramifications of our oppression."[18] Brecht's ideas of political theater were certainly circulating around Simone. Her own leftist, critical performance mode supports the comparison, but also presents key differences from Brecht's model of alienated action.

In "On Gestic Music," Brecht writes: "The musician's attitude to his text, the spokesman's to his report, shows the extent of his political, and so of his human maturity. A man's stature is shown by what he mourns and in what way he mourns it. To raise mourning to a higher plane, to make it into an element of social progress: that is an artistic task."[19] Here as elsewhere, Brecht describes the importance of furthering social progress through art, and the ways in which an artist may achieve this, particularly through evident criticality. Using Lenin's death as an example, Brecht's allusion to mourning aptly addresses the murders that instigated "Mississippi Goddam." But Brecht suggests that evocative content is not enough. "Every artist knows that subject-matter in itself is in a sense somewhat banal, featureless, empty, and self-sufficient. It is only . . . social gest—criticism, craftiness, irony, propaganda, etc.—that breathes humanity into it."[20] This idea of "social gest" begins to describe Simone's evident attitude toward her subject matter. There are features of Simone's performances that resemble Brecht's *Verfremdungseffekt*, under which an actor indicates her critique of her character by presenting distance. But while "Mississippi Goddam" has a bouncy undercurrent that produces gaps of intelligibility when placed in the context of its brutal subject matter, Simone's own theatricality carries a unifying force. This force can be reduced to her performance of authentic black experience, an authenticity authorized by her body and emotional delivery, as well as her musical virtuosity. This is not to say that Simone realizes an essential racial authenticity, but rather, that she plays it exceedingly well. Bringing Brechtian tools to her own project, Simone combines her performance of authenticity with the gestic strategy, and negotiates both simultaneously.

This simultaneity of gestic and authentic is evident in Simone's version of Brecht and Weill's "Pirate Jenny," which she also performed at the Carnegie Hall concert. Drawn from the pair's most popularly successful piece, *The Threepenny Opera*, "Pirate Jenny" is sung from the point of view of a maid fantasizing about being a ship captain who pillages and punishes a town full of greedy consumers. Simone uses American socialist composer Marc Blitzstein's English translation. While a Brechtian staging of this song would call for an estranged delivery, as is demonstrated by Lotte Lenya's recorded performances, Simone brings a radical intensity to the song, lingering here and there with frightening whispers, dismissive grunts, and commanding exclamations. While these spoken moments resemble a Brechtian *Sprechstimme*, Simone's intensity exceeds that mode's metered parameters. Simone's sensibility veers further into cathartic drama than Brecht would likely accept, excavating a black dramatic strain within the oppositionality of epic theater.

In her study of Simone, Daphne Brooks identifies a Brechtian purism that associates emotional expressivity with bourgeois complacency. Brooks quotes German studies scholar Russell Berman as he describes Simone's post-Brechtian restaging as "at a distance from distanciation," and not Brechtian at all. Certainly Brecht's own writings assert that an emotionalized character bears an anti-critical coercive force on audiences through mimetic drama. Brooks argues that this criticism is beside her point, as Simone was uninterested in a faithful reconstruction of Brecht's German materials, and that these performances "emerge as reimagined executions of black feminist distanciation."[21] This argument suggests provocative questions about Brecht's regime, about the fixity of his proposed subject who is the agent of his own distanciation. Further, it prompts us to ask what can be made of an emotionalized black subjectivity where a fully recognized subject position is prohibited.

Brecht, who famously adapted, appropriated, and borrowed many of his narratives, drew extra-German influences into the formal structure of his theater works. This strategy is not so different from Simone's own, separating expression from originality, and in Marxist manner, insisting upon history as a context for theatricality. Brecht and Weill's score for *The Threepenny Opera* experiments with jazz music. Rooted in black American folk music, jazz has functioned broadly as a metaphor for modernity. The interest in this form suits the Brechtian concern with the popular as it relates to classed sensibilities, but also accompanies the urban criminality and sexuality of the play's plot. Lotte Lenya, wife of Weill and key collaborator on Brecht and Weill's works, sang "Pirate Jenny" in both the 1928 Berlin premiere of the opera and in the 1954 New York production, which used Blitzstein's translation. Lenya described the first reactions to the groundbreaking piece: "Well-known Berlin theater prophets, as soon as they left the dress-rehearsal, told all who cared to listen that Brecht and Weill intended to insult the audience with a wild mixture, neither opera or operetta, neither cabaret nor drama, but a bit of each with the whole thing bathed in an exotic jazz sauce."[22] Subverting convention, *The Threepenny Opera*'s jazziness was a departure from serious music of the time. This "exotic jazz-sauce" seasoned perfectly the gritty urban sexuality, commerce, and violence around which *The Threepenny Opera* revolves. While the established critics were initially taken aback, Lenya conveys that after the opening night, "Berlin was gripped by *Threepenny Opera* Fever."[23] The ease with which black urban vernaculars drifted into the German cultural imaginary further suggests that blackness had prepared this modernity.

Again in "Pirate Jenny," Simone relies on the authorizations of her body to inhabit the role, this time of a beleaguered servant who dreams vividly of revolution, not a far stretch of the imagination in sixties black America. While her performance conveys cues taken from Brecht, Weill, Blitzstein, and Lenya, Simone's embodiment places the work into her own history. In black diasporic contexts, origins, which have often been obscured by colonial history, are typically less important than presence. Simone is more present than estranged, even as she performs this bit of semi-opera from 1928 Berlin. She uses many but not all of Blitzstein's words, radically deconstructs Weill's strict martial rhythm, by far exceeds Lenya's most daring phrasing, and again, fills Brecht's intended gaps with her physical intelligibility. This, however, does nothing to diminish the criticality of her portrayal. It is in the drama and emotionality of it that the political critique resonates most stirringly. After she mutters the question "Kill them now or later?"[24] Simone pauses with such intensity as to suggest she is really quite seriously pondering the question.

Brecht's appropriation of "Chinese acting," which he cited as an inspiration for the *Verfremdungseffekt*, is well known. His practice of borrowing textual sources and influences suggests the impure orthodoxy of his program, but also helps to reveal another element of Simone's performance. Among those scholars who have pointed out Brecht's limited understanding of Chinese Opera, Haiping Yan has identified an aesthetic sense of "suppositionality"[25] connected to that theater form, a subjunctive mode that, through stylization, distinguishes itself from reality, and resembles what Brecht identifies in his essay "Alienation Effect in Chinese Acting," when he writes, "The artist's object is to appear strange and even surprising to the audience."[26] Yan continues, however, to describe a broad aesthetic goal within Chinese music drama as "moving the humans as moving heaven and earth."[27] Here, feeling is as important as thinking and ethics work in tandem with aesthetics. Citing a thirteenth-century opera, Yan describes a famous protagonist, Tao Ngo, who, like Simone's pirate, is rendered invisible by the ruling order, and who "cannot be."[28] Yan identifies a mode of a performance that "serves as a site where the 'cannot be' activates her potential by not only appropriating the terms of the staged ethics but broadening its scopes, transforming its boundaries, and gesturing beyond its limits."[29] Yan describes this gesture as both emotionally and intellectually engaging, as it extends from a form that is intended to be both moving and distinctly theatrical. As Walter Benjamin describes Brecht's theater, "It is less concerned with filling the public with feelings, even seditious ones, than in alienating it in an enduring manner, through thinking, from the conditions in which it lives."[30] Benjamin, extending Brecht's concepts, prioritizes thinking over feeling in critically engaged art production. As Yan asserts, the Chinese acting Brecht supposed he was observing does no such thing. All of this may be purely academic: the immediate popularity of *The Threepenny Opera* indicates that it may have instigated as many feelings as thoughts in its audience. It is also worth noting that Tao Ngo did not propose revolutionary action to its thirteenth-century audience. But this critique suggests that Simone's black dramatic portrayal of "Pirate Jenny," though emotionally expressive, is no less critical or politically effective than Lenya's alienation, nor is the Brechtian *Verfremdungseffekt* as tidily bound as its authors and defenders would perhaps imagine. Simone's performance draws on these sources and proposes that in the context of black embodiment, thinking and feeling are as inseparable as politics and aesthetics.

Brooks has described an "afro-alienation"[31] that marks African American performances, acts that have channeled "varying forms of alienation and dissonant identity politics," and have "stylized alternative forms of cultural expression that have cut against the grain of conventional social and political ideologies."[32] Significantly, Brooks compares this African American tactic with the Brechtian sense of alienation and finds liberatory potential inherent in the fragmentation of black subjectivity. Brooks relates the theatricality of blackness to critical performance techniques, including Brecht's (as reflected upon by feminist scholar Elin Diamond), that are able to articulate not the wholeness of black identity, but rather the constructedness of all identity. In this sense, the multiple turns one must make to enact a provisional black subject outline a critical intervention against the totalizing ideologies through which the notion of race has been formed in the first place. Theories that locate critical power in the multiplicity of black expressivity transform the negative alienation of double consciousness into a productive force.

Still, we must take Brecht at his word when he explains that emotional expression in performance is undesirable; it would be seen in his time and place to bolster a sense that the self's experience is inevitably construed by nature and uncomplicated by historical factors, a sense he attempted to undercut through the estranged performance of affect. In contrast, Simone's emotional expression, emerging from a prohibited provisionally configured self, is already fraught with alienation. It is in fact the confounding sense of alienation that conjures so much of the emotion; expression fills the gaps between irreconcilable senses of self. Rather than orchestrating an alienation effect to undercut emotional affect, Simone deploys an affect effect to assert herself in excess of her alienated possibilities. Simone deploys thinking and feeling as components of each other in a performance of political expressivity.

This point is illustrated succinctly in a later incident from a 1976 concert at the Montreux Jazz Festival. In her first encore, Simone begins to sing the well-known ballad "Feelings," a banal song about a victim of heartbreak who is "trying to forget . . . feelings of love." She stops herself mid-verse to declare, "I despise the conditions that created the situation that made it necessary to write a song like this," offering an impromptu Marxist critique of the historical conditions of emotional devastation. For Simone, feelings themselves are historical and material. From there she continues playing and singing, transforming and personalizing the song with her typical tempo shifts and vocal emphases, compelling her audience to quietly sing along with what, in her revision, has become the melody's haunting refrain. A bourgeois ballad of self-pity becomes a social action, framed by Simone's own politics of expressivity. This incident demonstrates the complicity of alienation and affect Simone brought to bear on the materials she used and the scenario of performance.

Quadruple Consciousness

The notion of quadruple consciousness draws its form from Simone's song "Four Women," which is sung along with the slow, repetitive blues groove of her piano and accompanying bass and percussion. "Four Women" offers a brief chronicle of different women characterized by stereotypical markers of African American femininity: Aunt Sara, Sweet Thing, Saffronia, and Peaches. For example, the second verse describes Saffronia:

> My skin is yellow
> My hair is long
> Between two worlds
> I do belong
> My father was rich and white
> He forced my mother late one night
> What do they call me
> My name is Saffronia[33]

Each woman is first identified by her coloration and then by the sexual and labor dynamics that frame her identity. Moving seamlessly from one to the next, Simone inhabits each of these roles with transitory but committed determination.

Of "Four Women," which Simone composed and recorded in 1966, she wrote in her co-authored biography:

> The women in the song are black, but their skin tone ranges from light to dark and their ideas of beauty and their own importance are deeply influenced by that. All the song did was to tell what entered the minds

of most black women in America when they thought about themselves: their complexions, their hair—straight, kinky, natural, which?—and what other women thought of them. Black women didn't know what the hell they wanted because they were defined by things they didn't control, and until they had the confidence to define themselves, they'd be stuck in the same mess forever—that was the point the song made. When "Four Women" was released in 1966, some black radio stations banned black DJs from playing it because they said it "insulted" black women. It didn't, and banning it was a stupid thing to do, but I wasn't surprised. The song told a truth that many people in the USA—especially black men—simply weren't ready to acknowledge at that time.[34]

"Four Women," complicates race consciousness with gender consciousness. The work was politically controversial. Significantly, Simone identifies external physical characteristics through which black women achieved self-consciousness: by their complexion, hair, and so on. The final woman in the quartet, Peaches, makes a political acknowledgement not found among the others: "I'm awfully bitter these days, because my parents were slaves." While bound to a historical situation, this figure is able to define herself, thus bringing the song to a close, as Simone reaches her distinctly unsubtle final crescendo, wailing ironically, "My name is Peaches." While Peaches does not control her historical situation and is dissonant with her own name, her act of self-definition transgresses the repetitive groove in which these women circulate.

In a 1969 concert in Berkeley, California, a recording of which was released as the album *Nina Simone Live*, Simone offers one of her typical live deconstructions of this controversial number with an elucidating meta-dialogue. As the groove plays, Simone intersperses into her story fourth-wall-destroying commentary. She observes that "Aunt Jemima is all in vogue everywhere," a sarcastic response to the fashion trend evident in the audience, the wearing of what Simone calls "head-rags."[35] After she launches the song with an extended and unusually textured version of Aunt Sara, Simone begins the second verse and then stops herself to address the audience again while the groove plays on: "I could tell you a story about my mama in the South when they called her Auntie. In these grocery stores. I only wish I had been there when they called her Auntie. No Mrs. Hey. You see I know Berkeley is on fire, I know that anyway. I say that in a positive way. But I kind of have to hold myself down here, the vibrations are so strong. But I'll tell you this, if I had been there when they had called my mama Auntie, I would have burned that whole goddamned place down."[36] While alienation is the subtext of her story, Simone's performance here is stirringly coherent. Stopping in mid-drift between two of her women, she plays herself at this moment. The final supposition that she would have burned down the stores of the grocers who insulted her mother is forced awkwardly from her mouth as if she is overcome with emotion, and is met by an immediate roar of support from the audience. Her interstitial assertion is both politically radical and emotionally believable. Here as elsewhere in Simone's performances, affect is oriented to produce a critical theatrical effect. As in "Four Women," the place of affect is not located in an individual consciousness, but emerges from the tensions between each of these women, the specific audience, and Simone's performing self.

An excessive hyperbole, quadruple consciousness describes Simone's mode of performance, which is intensely dramatic while politically challenging, blending numerous musical traditions, and channeling, as in the manner of a high priestess, an authentic black American experience. But quadruple consciousness also literally traces four turns in the discourse around the possibilities of black action. The first consciousness in this formulation is the Cartesian subject of the Western philosophical tradition who thinks and therefore is. Second is the historical experience of alienation of the person marked by blackness, which Du Bois identified and proposed as a term ideally reconcilable with the first through the dialectical process. Third is the radical negativity of that alienation which, despite Du Bois's hope, lingers unreconciled. This is what Fanon has described as a kind of "triple person" status, which is perpetually misrecognized within a field of representation.[37] Saidiya Hartman, for example, has explored this negativity within American law, which has tended to invent the black subject only as a negative subject, becoming intelligible as an outlaw, "on the side of culpability."[38] Simone's incantatory performance, however, transforms the experience of negation into a set of possibilities. Following the first three maneuvers—the movement through a sense of self, a sense of self-as-other, and the obliterating negativity that denies selfhood altogether—the transformation of that negativity is the fourth move in the quadruple consciousness quartet.

This idea is a common theme in critiques that assert a provisional agency within black expressivities. Many scholars have written about the importance of creative expression as a means of black American cultural continuity, particularly as a way to negotiate prohibitions on black authority. Writing about plantation slavery, Beverly Robinson described song, dance, and game-play as an unusual "area of creativity in which people could sustain their culture and express themselves with a certain amount of freedom, or at least without immediate repression."[39] Through such expressivities, notions of identity were provisionally articulated, just as prohibitions were carefully negotiated. Hortense Spillers, writing about Ralph Ellison's *Invisible Man*, points out the ways in which creative expression has produced a politics of black identity: "Invisible Man made 'blackness' a *process*, a *strategy*, of culture critique, rather than a condition of physiognomy and/or the embodiment of the *auto-bios-graphe*; we had come a considerable distance in layering 'blackness' as subject possibility. Under the 'laws' of this novel, the game of 'blackness' was no longer captive to the auspices of dominance, somewhere 'out there' beyond the veil, but came home, as it were, right between the ears, as the glittering weapon of an 'invisible' field of choice."[40] Rather than the "subject of dominance" instantiated by the legal regime, expressions like Ellison's novel, like Simone's protest songs, have produced a black subject possibility that is in itself a strategy of cultural critique. That possibility is formed not from biology or biography, but through layers of black representations. Spillers describes this as a synthetic position, arguing that "the culture, because it locates a synthesis, as well as a symptom of resistance, shows all the instabilities of definition and practice."[41] While Hartman's move negates black subjectivity within the legal category of human being, Spillers describes the ways that black expressivities can exceed legal categories altogether, at least representing the possibility of action. This is a fourth level of consciousness that Simone manipulates with her embodiment of four different women who each speak in the first person, an embodiment that is mediated by her performance of herself.

Du Bois and Fanon have both described a kind of hyper-visibility to which they are subjected as black men. Their masculine status places them in the field of representation—in public—where their differences are contextualized. When class and gender are inverted, this hyper-visibility may register as invisibility, as in the figure of Simone's Aunt Sara, whose pain is unrecognized in the familiar name she's given. Another relevant piece from Simone's set at this time was the song "Images," which she had adapted from Harlem Renaissance poet William Waring Cuny's poem "No Images." Invoking the voice of a woman who exists without context, Simone performed this song without instrumentation, as in a 1965 concert in Holland in which she also performed "Four Women," "Mississippi Goddam," and other activist songs. Singing elegant scales in a falsetto register, Simone delivers the poem's message:

> She does not know her beauty
> She thinks her brown body has no glory[42]

This woman, a domestic worker, is invisible. She will not even locate herself in an act of self-recognition because, as the poem's final line confirms, "dishwater bears no images."[43] Whereas recognition is fraught with too many destabilizing possibilities for Du Bois and Fanon, "Images" imagines the impossibility of identification for those who have no access to representation.

A subjunctive potentiality is finally invoked in the song "Images." Simone foregrounds this possibility by inverting the title of her song from Cuny's more negative "No Images." The heart of the poem, and the song, expresses what is not and could be:

> If she could dance naked under palm trees
> And see her reflection in the river
> Then she would know[44]

Self-consciousness becomes a possibility even for this marginalized woman worker, through the expressivity of dance, the reimagining of the body, and the provisional representation of an unstable reflection. A similar possibility is invoked by Hansberry in one of her collages included in the published text of *To Be Young, Gifted and Black*. A self-portrait line drawing of the author reading a newspaper stretches across an actual newspaper page from a classified section bearing advertisements for domestic help. At one level is the image of a contemplative black woman who reads; another level maintains the more conventional

Figure 1.2. Illustration by Lorraine Hansberry. Printed in *To Be Young, Gifted and Black*, adapted by Robert Nemiroff, Vintage Books, 1969.

modes of being that were available to black women at the time, construed only in commercial texts. This kind of expressivity on top of impossibility is the genius of quadruple consciousness. While Spillers describes this position as synthetic, it appears that such incongruities need not dissolve into each other, as in Simone's four distinct women, as in the simultaneous impossibility and subjunctive agency of "Images," and as in the incongruous black experiences depicted together in Hansberry's portrait. In these, the emphasis is on maintaining the contours of difference, rather than synthesizing impossible incongruities. Simone uses such evident differences to activate her texts' critical potential.

Transformation

Simone manages multiplicity in virtuoso manner. Her ability to weave together a whole performance and a full embodiment out of fractured sources bears a transformative quality that has been described as magical, articulating a supernatural explanation for the ability to exceed the conditions that limit black women's representation, attributing to magic the transgression of racist limitations that are understood as natural. Simone's compelling persona orients her many sources around her magnetic presence, a medium for all of the historical and identificatory possibilities she implicates within her performance. This transformative quality is met with her incantatory musical style, as in the driving repetitive rhythm and chantlike delivery of "Four Women," and her theatrical, excessive presentation, to create an image of a "high priestess." This is a gendered and raced archetype, a figure significantly more empowered than the compliant nun or the outlaw witch, through which Simone's transgressions—of authorship, of musical sensibilities, of political doctrine, of professional behavior, of inferior racial and gender status—are enabled. While conjuring an archetype through which agency can be enacted, Simone's commercial nickname, "The High Priestess of Soul," outlines the contours of her difference. The exotic otherness of a high priestess is appropriately excessive; its pagan connotation elides Simone's upbringing in the Baptist church. This image is of a feminine authority from another dimension, one where the prohibitions of Christianity and enlightened democracy are negated by a woman with power. That this realm is called "soul," both a genre of black performance and the spiritual

Figure 1.3. Nina Simone in concert, Holland, 1965. (Video still from *Nina Simone: Live in '65 & '68*, Reelin' in the Years Productions, 2008)

essence of Christian man, speaks to the conflation of marginal experience with universal principle that contradictorily defines blackness.

The idea of Simone as a "high priestess" is bolstered by her critical reception, beginning in the early sixties. This image draws from Simone's incantatory formal presentation, the sense of drama that characterizes her performances, and also her use of content, which channels various diverse materials into a present articulation. A 1963 *New York Times* review bearing the headline "Nina Simone Sings at Carnegie Hall" emphasizes this latter quality in its subhead: "Contralto and Pianist Offer a Diversified Program."[45] Simone appears here as eerily doubled; the subhead's conjugation implies two subjects, but the review makes clear that Simone herself is both the contralto and the pianist. There are significant differences between Simone's singing voice and her piano playing, and this distinction produces a multiplying effect that resembles what in this case is likely an inadvertent misprint. Even without making too much of a typo, the review clearly emphasizes a kind of diversity instantiated by Simone's singular presence. A close look at this review reveals the important contours to Simone's mode of performance identified above.

New York Times music critic John S. Wilson begins his first of many reviews of Simone's live performances by noting her dexterity with source materials. "In this age of musical specialists, Nina Simone is refreshingly different. In her program at Carnegie Hall last night Miss Simone ranged from Saint-Saens to Oscar Brown Jr., from what she described as 'a dirty folk song' (a sly tale of frustrated medieval seduction) to an African work song, from a Bessie Smith blues to a French pop tune and from Gershwin to a sentimental ballad of her own creation."[46] In the first instance, Simone's power is her apparent difference. Wilson has her transcending the historical situation with this difference. The list of materials Wilson provides offers several ranges that emphasize extremes of difference that Simone is able to draw together: authors from a Romantic French composer to an African American songwriter; folk materials invoking European sexuality on one hand and African labor on the other; and so on. Following the extremes of Bessie Smith and Gershwin, the list culminates in Simone's own creation, which is perceived as sentimental. Simone's own emotionality is the final stop on this musical tour, as she embodies these numerous texts with her physical articulation. This kind of listing of source materials is a hallmark of her *New York Times* reviews over the following decade, as writers continue to situate Simone's presence across a diverse field of authorship.

The review moves next from content to form, emphasizing Simone's "feline contralto," and her performance style, through which she "seemed totally absorbed in the mood of the moment." These terms bound Simone within a feminine position, first through the imagery of a catlike delivery. Wilson picks up this image again in a 1967 review, which he concludes: "She was all fire and ice, playing and singing with a feline sense of power."[47] Here, Simone is linked to a feminized creature while also grounded in contradiction, tropes associated with the non-rational nature of femininity. This position is empowered, however by another trope of femininity, that of intuitive emotionality. This idea, which culminates in Simone's shamanistic persona, is elaborated here through the emotional sense, or mood, associated with her performance. The idea of mood is a key one in subsequent reviews. Wilson himself describes

Simone in 1965 as a "brilliantly creative artist who has a great talent for evoking moods,"[48] and later that year as "a performer who works with moods."[49] Other reviewers, perhaps picking up Wilson's cues, continued this line of interpretation. Furthermore, as the sixties progress, this idea of mood becomes more explicitly magical. A 1966 review by Robert Sherman, in which the writer asserts that "Miss Simone is a moodsetter, rather than a singer of songs," bears the headline "Nina Simone Casts Her Moody Spells."[50] By 1971, Wilson's declarative subhead "Mood Still Powerful," accompanies the claim that "[i]n the past she has been a mood builder, a sort of musical sorceress who cast a hypnotic spell on her listener and, within that aura, skillfully worked whatever emotional stops she wanted to."[51] The idea of mood has finally connected to a notion of sorcery. Spells and auras have become part of Simone's materials, lending to the emotionality of the performance. Mike Jahn, writing in 1971, points out Simone's "spell-binding, jazz singing, hypnotic mood and many intricate shades of black."[52] In these reviews, we see Simone's persona as a high priestess emerging. Hers is a shamanic position that is not only gendered, but raced as well.

Simone validates this interpretation in her autobiography. She describes her performances as ritualistic experiences. She compares her work to both the effects of the black church in America and the dynamics of a bullfight she witnessed in Spain: "it was the same thing, the same sense of being transformed, of celebrating something deep. . . . That's what I learned about performing—that it was real, and I had the ability to make people *feel* on a deep level."[53] Simone links performance with real feeling, indicating a unifying authenticity through which her various materials cohere. But Simone continues to demystify her own sorcery:

> I got my reputation as a live performer, because I went out from the midsixties onwards determined to get every audience to enjoy my concerts the way I wanted them to, and if they resisted at first I had all the tricks to bewitch them with. I know it all sounds a little Californian and wired [*sic*], but it wasn't that at all: I had a technique and I used it. To cast the spell over the audience I would start with a song to create a certain mood which I carried into the next song and then on through the third, until I created a certain climax of feeling and by then they would be hypnotized.[54]

In this description, Simone outlines a performance technique through which she achieved her famous mood. While the feline sorcery described in the *New York Times* reviews carries metaphysical resonances consistent with an idea of unknowable black feminine power, Simone's own magical description barely conceals a science of performance, grounded in intention and achieved through a specific process. Simone combines the language of bewitchment with a rational technique. Judging from the critical reception, this technique achieved its intended effect of "hypnotizing" her audience.

The third element of Simone's performance that is frequently described in reviews, in addition to her intertextual dexterity and her shamanistic presence, is her theatricality, or as Wilson put it in that first 1963 review, her "strong sense of showmanship." That review continues: "Miss Simone has a highly developed sense of the dramatic, both the sneaky type that emerges from initial understatement and the direct type that comes from striking changes in costume and hair-do (or wig)."[55] This dramatic sense is attributed to the way she moves through her material, but also her physical presentation. Simone's clothes are frequently described in her reviews. Here is the diva position, a figure that originates in European opera, which complements the non-European high priestess. In Simone's oeuvre, anecdotes abound of her scolding her audiences, appearing late, and other divalike behaviors. Her various publicity stills and album covers depict an array of hairstyles, from the short natural, to an elaborate bouffant dripping with pearls, to hair hidden beneath a tower of African cloth. Simone's persona is completed with such elaborate displays, and again, she achieves power by elaborating on authorized feminine positions.

These reviews of Simone's concerts draw out three distinct elements of her mode of performance: her intertextual material, her shamanistic technique, and her theatrical presentation. Another of Wilson's reviews sums the three up together. Describing her performance for an audience of fifteen thousand at the 1966 Newport Jazz Festival, Wilson recaps previous claims under the subhead "Mixture Charms Audience": "She is, however, primarily a weaver of spells who draws her audience to her—even as vast an audience as this—by skillfully mixing the most tender love songs, fiercely forthright protest songs, songs of worldly knowledge and the blues. Seated at the piano in gold lamé evening pajamas . . . Miss

Simone sang in a voice that ranged from muttered murmur to a defiant shout."[56] In this description, spell weaving is evidenced by the promiscuous co-mingling of texts, theatrical performance, and costume. Rather than presenting these as three distinct elements, Wilson here indicates that the shamanistic position relies on their mixture. The "range" identified in her voice is both Simone's own mode of expression and a marker of the polyvocality that historically characterizes black American expressive forms.

Maybe I Can Fix Things Up So They'll Go

Simone's complex relationship to authorship, her embodiment of presence, and her theatrical construction of transformative costume and persona all shape her performances. A fourth important element of her performance mode is the technical combination of voice and piano, and the simultaneous differences she brings into contact through this combination. Her voice and playing, which move fluidly across gendered and racial signs and indicate a transnational set of sources as well as a diasporic location, and her transgressive use of politicized language, can be described as transvocal.

While recordings reveal significant range in Simone's singing voice, a gravely timbre and deep register can confuse the ears of the uninitiated listener, veiling the singer's gender with a vocal quality that can be quite androgynous. Though Simone songs often celebrate heteronormative sexuality, the slippery way her voice signifies her gender creates a kind of ambiguity that disturbs the standard subject/object relationship of the American song. A particularly tricky example comes in a rare duet: Simone performed the folk ballad "Black Is the Color of My True Love's Hair" in live concerts during 1968, having released a recording of the song on the 1966 album *Wild Is the Wind*. As noted above, Simone's interpretation mines a black-is-beautiful sensibility out of the Scottish Appalachian tune's lyric, suggesting a racialized historical dynamic to the simple tale of lovers who cannot be. In the recorded concerts of 1968, Simone splits the song in two, turning the vocals over to her male bandmate, guitarist Emile Lattimer, who sings a second iteration of the tune, a continuation of Simone's own. Eerily, Lattimer's voice sounds very similar to Simone's. They sing in the same octave, have a similar vocal quality, and Lattimer seems to be replicating Simone's signature phrasing. Listening to a sound recording of this concert performance, it is easy to confuse Lattimer with Simone herself. The live footage reveals two distinct performers. Lattimer appears as a male alter ego of Simone; a shift in pronouns resituates the song so that it comes from a desiring male perspective. The continuity between Simone's voice and Lattimer's enacts sexual ambiguity, if not a fully transgender performance, a stark example of the loose play between gender and signification that Simone performs.

In performance, Simone's voice is most often paired with her piano playing, a combination that further emphasizes the intertextuality of her work. Many of her live performances and recordings emerged into a marketplace through the jazz oeuvre, where the virtuoso soloist is another gendered position, most always male. In her performance, Simone performs doubly as the singer of diverse materials and the virtuoso soloist. What we might call Simone's transvocality is broadened by this doubling, as voice and piano speak complementary languages. In addition to the differences brought together in Simone's voice, her intertextual piano technique includes the pounding rhythms of church, improvisatory jazz chords and runs, baroque-style contrapuntal riffs, romantic arpeggios, and blues lines, deployed singly or in combinations. Simone learned to play the piano in churches in North Carolina where her mother was an itinerant preacher, and refined her practice through private and institutional classical training before entering an East Coast cocktail circuit. Her piano's voice, founded in the inverted church of the black mother, shaped by the rigors of male German composers and professionalized through the American songbook, is also transvocal. This transvocality draws on ideas of gender and extends those to consider the movement between instruments that are both human and not, underscoring the precarity of all of those conditions.

Examples of Simone's multiply expressive combination of voice and piano abound: one can be found in a 1962 filmed performance recorded in a studio in New York.[57] Simone, accompanied by a guitarist, bassist, and drummer, sings the standard "For All We Know," an existential love song previously recorded by many significant African American singers. The song questions the lovers' ability to know, or to rationalize experience through consciousness, challenging basic premises through which reality is understood. Simone's version comes four years after Billie Holiday recorded the song on her final album. The lyric's suggestion

Figure 1.4. Nina Simone in concert, England, 1968. (Video still from *Nina Simone: Live in '65 & '68*, Reelin' in the Years Productions, 2008)

that tomorrow might not arrive resonates with the story of Holiday, who innovated an original African American woman's voice, but who was physically defeated by the circumstances of which she was an object. Unlike popular singer Dinah Washington's orthodox interpretation of that same year, Simone radically deconstructs the song. Avoiding the swing of jazz altogether, Simone draws out the lyrics in extended whole notes lacking vibrato and without melisma. Contrapuntally, her piano playing consists of rigidly structured runs of eighth notes and sixteenth notes, performing the material in, as she described the arrangement elsewhere, "a hymn-Bach-like way."[58] The song loses its faithful coherence with black musical forms, pairing European classical piano technique with an incantatory vocal delivery. By estranging the material from its familiar context, Simone's unique voice is able to make an intensely immediate statement from an overplayed song.

Simone's musical deconstructions reenergize the most timeworn or banal lyrics with new interpretations or added personalized content. But as striking as Simone's specific uses of language in her live performances are the instances when words fail altogether. She seems to mispronounce words often, inventing her own non-standard emphases and intonations. As she makes up bridges, codas, and reprises for her songs, the piano and melody can move out of sync with the words that won't come quickly enough, necessitating unusual vocalizations. In these instances, language and meaning are fully estranged as Simone seems to be singing in tongues, or perhaps inventing her own Afro-Caribbean language. Relating to the vocal practice of jazz scatting, these aren't words, but sounds devised at the moment of articulation. Is it that meaning has broken down under the weight of the performer's intertextual materials, leaving only non-lingual utterances? Or is it that this transvocality bears too many contradictory meanings, a tower of Babel in excess of language? Is Simone saying nothing or everything?

Partly, we can follow Fred Moten's line of thinking when he inverts Hartman's scene of subjection into a scene of objection, probing the "dispossessive force"[59] that objects exert upon their subjects, and curiously, the sound that exertion makes. Moten smartly answers Marx with Frederick Douglass. In chapter 1 of *Capital*, Marx speculates about what commodities would say if they could speak. The voice he gives them is ambiguous. Douglass begins his life narrative with the story of his Aunt Hester's whipping and her terrible screams, depicting the speaking commodity Marx forgot, the slave. For Moten, Aunt Hester's scream joins the scene of the slave song as first beginnings of this object's resistance. Moten quotes Douglass at length, as he describes slaves singing together:

> . . . wild songs, revealing at once the highest joy and the deepest sadness. They would compose and sing as they went along, consulting neither time nor tune. The thought that came up, came out—if not in the word, in the sound;—and as frequently in the one as in the other. They would sometimes sing the most pathetic sentiment in the most rapturous tone, and the most rapturous sentiment in the most pathetic tone . . . they would sing as a chorus, to words which to many would seem unmeaning jargon, but which, nevertheless, were full of meaning to themselves.[60]

Simone's vocalizations and improvisations which are also estranging, resonate deeply in black music history. In Douglass's recounted memory, these provisional songs could express thought in sounds that were as often as not, not words. Where language was used, it cohered to the slave's contradictory subjectivity, as in the bitter irony of Simone's fourth woman angrily declaring her name over a major-chord crescendo. The slave song is a form that lends itself to the assimilation of contradiction. Like Hester's scream, its expression is an object of, and in excess of, the prohibition on the black subject.

Moten's analysis extends Aunt Hester's scream into the voice of Abbey Lincoln, a contemporary of Simone's whose non-verbal utterances punctuate her *Freedom Now Suite*, a 1962 collaboration with Max Roach and Oscar Brown, Jr. In this piece, vocalist Lincoln fills the movement called "Protest" with sung screams and moans, exceeding language's ability to express the pain and pleasure of her resistant position. This movement is a particularly telling gendered moment in the development of free jazz; Lincoln asserts a feminine possibility beyond that which is authored for her by the men who surround her. A performed version of this movement taped for German television in 1964 shows Lincoln standing in a set that resembles prison bars as she sings. Comparable to the context of Simone's non-verbal utterances, Lincoln's situation in "Protest" is perhaps less complicated, in that the contours of her object status are visibly and aurally delineated within this male-dominated project. Simone's performative position is contextualized by her self, or selves, as in the layers of being situated within her quadruple consciousness, and the multiple simultaneous expressions delivered through her transvocality. Though Lincoln's early recordings deliver a striking black subjectivity, her gender position is framed by the masculinism of jazz. Conversely, both categories—jazz and masculinity—lose their shape as a result of Simone's multiple positionality and intertextual strategy.

Lyrics written by Lincoln for Simone, in collaboration on a song called "Blues for Mama," move toward the ambivalence of Simone's position. The song, recorded by Simone in 1966, tells the story of a woman who has lost her man and is consequently the victim of gossip, or duplicitous language. As one verse explains:

> They say you love to fuss and fight
> And bring a good man down
> And don't know how to treat him

> They say you ain't behind him
> And just don't understand
> And think that you're a woman
> But actin' like a man
> Hey Lordy mama,
> What you gonna do now[61]

At issue is the mama, who is the object of the lyric, and her contradictory expressions. She is publicly blamed for her man's failures. By speaking in excess of her object position, she is accused of engaging in impermissible gender acts. Lincoln initiated this lyric, but it was first popularized by Simone through her 1966 recording. Lincoln, who was understood as a jazz vocalist, is able to articulate a feminist critique through Simone, whose ability to cross genres while acting autonomously in the moment of performance empowers her significantly. The final query voiced by both, "what you gonna do," asks this object-mama to act on her own, representing that possibility for black women.

Mahagonny Again

By the 1970s, Simone, like other of her contemporaries and predecessors, had left the United States, developing a transnational presence that followed routes developed by black artists, intellectuals, and divas throughout the twentieth century. Like Du Bois, Baker, Robeson, and many others before her, Simone was shaped by black American experience, but could not be contained by an American nation-state through which her blackness had been rendered legible but not intelligible. A combination of money problems and political frustration contributed to Simone's embarking on a lengthy exodus from the U.S. to Barbados to Liberia to Switzerland to France. The political promise of the civil rights era had been warped by the spectacular violence of assassinations and war. Hansberry and Hughes were deceased. Her friends Miriam Makeba and Stokely Carmichael, like Du Bois, had been driven by political persecution from the United States and had relocated to a newly independent West African state. The heyday of sixties activism had passed, and while she continued to critique American racism in her recordings and concerts, Simone had become an international figure. Long after she had left the United States in self-imposed exile, Simone again performed Brecht/Weill materials in a 1985 concert in London, released as the album *Live at Ronnie Scott's*. Playing again with Brecht's critical approach to theater, Simone interrupts her song "Mississippi Goddam" after a line that questions both the possibility of belonging and Christian faith. As her hands continue to bounce on the piano, she introduces Brecht and Weill's "Moon over Alabama" from their opera *The Rise and Fall of the City of Mahagonny*, set on a fictitious, Caribbean-inflected island. Her mid-song reintroduction draws a direct connection from her own song to that material: "As you know, this song was written by Nina Simone. It is very much like 1932, when Bert Brecht and Kurt Weill wrote 'Moon over Alabama.' The fact is they wrote several songs for *Mahagonny*. We don't have time to do them all for you now; what we're going to do is combine 'Mississippi Goddam' with 'Moon over Alabama.'"[62] After drawing this parallel between the two works, Simone immediately launches into "Show us the way to the next whiskey bar," combining her own composition about the realities of Southern violence with Brecht and Weill's fantasy world of capitalist greed. Though the civil rights era is by this time decidedly over, a fact made clear by her ending improvisation "everybody knows about Jesse Jackson, everybody knows about Ronald Reagan, everybody knows about Michael Jackson,"[63] Simone insists that her own activist material is tied to a broader critique of capital than a simple focus on Southern violence might suggest.

The Rise and Fall of the City of Mahagonny, as one English translation's introduction notes, "must offend and repel its audience if it is to succeed."[64] Riots greeted the first performances in 1930, and this antagonism fits well with the Brechtian idea of alienated performance. Weill's music, which is more stylistically challenging here than in the catchy numbers from *The Threepenny Opera*, goes further to combine black vernacular sounds with serious European art music, his combination of which is rarely melodically appeasing. In addition to "Moon over Alabama," Simone also uses the song "Mr. Smith" from *Mahagonny* for her Ronnie Scott's engagement. While Lenya's 1955 recording of "Mr. Smith" again demonstrates an alienation effect aided by a quick pace and a cool attitude, Simone lingers and dwells in this brief story of a black prostitute bargaining for cash, finding deeply emotional resonance and again resorting to a black authenticity that is only blithely alluded to in the original material. Simone draws out the tempo into a soulful meditation, adding a mournful piano accompaniment. When she sings a lyric that places sex work in a context of racial legacy, she emphasizes the word "dollar" with particular interest and disgust, as if it were the most daunting concept in the English language. Her emphasis illustrates the ways that an international critique of capitalism can be expressed through the transvocality of black American subjectivity.

Well beyond the era in which the "vibrations"[65] of activism could carry her away, Simone still delivers a performance that is both political and aesthetic, and quite moving, illustrating the enduring necessity of a political critique developed in the context of the civil rights movement, and the applicability of this critique to her present. Through her performance, Simone is able to reinvest the contemporary moment with activist energy from another time and place. The continuity of her performing body bridges the rupture between sixties activism and eighties capitalism. This distance is geographic as well as temporal; Simone lived in Europe by this time. Even as she sings to a London audience, via a German composer, about coming from Cuba, the resonances of black American experience fill out her performance. This experience exceeds the confines of the nation.[66]

Conclusion

In the opening of Simone's autobiography, she recalls the words of encouragement that her friend James Baldwin would repeat to her: "This is the world you have made for yourself Nina, now you have to live in it."[67] This bit of cleverness asserts that for a real Nina Simone to exist, she'd had to construct a world for herself that would accommodate this subjectivity, and even under that circumstance, living that possibility would be a tremendous difficulty. This anecdote can serve as a metaphor for the difficulty of agency. Even beyond the age of a black American president, when the legal frame has expanded enough to include that possibility, black identity remains provisional, and marked by ambivalence. Despite these limitations, Simone effectively marshaled the heterogeneity of black experience in her performances in order to create a radical theatrical position from which to act.

2

Efua Sutherland, Ama Ata Aidoo, the State, and the Stage

Africa is no historical part of the world.
—G.W.F. Hegel

In this way we speak of African civilization as "traditional"
in contrast to Western civilization, as if there could be African civilization, Western civilization in the singular, and as if
civilization were not, by nature, a permanent clash of contradictory cultural forms.
—Paulin Hountondji

Introduction

In the early sixties, Accra, Ghana, was the capital of a provisional "Afro-
topia,"[1] the center of a new nation-state pursuing a leftist black liberation
project. The plays that emerged at this time from Ghana's National Theater Movement theatricalized the experience of citizenship in this black
state. The state's president, Kwame Nkrumah, proposed an African citizenship forged in black unanimity, an African Personality that could
synthesize social differences. While this model depicted a form of black
solidarity, it also formalized an erasure of difference. Syntheses elide differences, and this case, while descriptive of traditional gender roles and
histories of matrilineage, the vision of a unified African subject does not
preserve differences such as those enabled by gendered subjectivities.
The plays of Efua Sutherland and Ama Ata Aidoo offer a different set
of possibilities. These works fulfilled the government's call for original
Ghanaian artistic production, while also staging the difficulties of assimilating a diversity of gender, class, and cultural situations into a singular
African identity. The political context in which these writers worked
was one which encouraged their expressions. However, the subjectivities they scripted, constructed from local and transnational notions of

black identity, announced a polyvocality that exceeded the cohesion of a proposed ideal citizen. Situated in a national and transnational black liberation context, Sutherland's plays *Edufa* and *Foriwa* and Aidoo's play *The Dilemma of a Ghost*, are African feminist performance texts that complicate the synthetic notion of African Personality.

Africa has served as a central site and symbol in the black transnational discourse described throughout these chapters, and represented in the imaginative performances discussed here. Commenting on her first trip to the continent in 1962, Nina Simone remembered, "I knew I had arrived somewhere important and that Africa mattered to me and would always matter."[2] Having traveled on a cultural mission with Langston Hughes, the singer Odetta, and a number of other black American artists to Lagos, Nigeria, the entourage represented a coalition among performers, writers, and intellectuals who shared an interest in black empowerment, and identified in African liberation efforts its possible elaboration. The notion of Africa as a homeland for non-African blacks has worked doubly as a romantic image and a political concept. At once an imagined origin, a site of traumatic subjugation, and a utopian destination, Africa has persistently symbolized both impossibility and invention in the diaspora. For many including Simone, the historic forced separation from Africa—in the form of transatlantic slavery—was a source of the alienated experience of black American life.

Also from the African perspective, reconciliation with diasporic blacks was an important element of post-colonial liberation projects, particularly according to the program of Nkrumah, Ghana's first prime minister and then first president. While the colonial histories that lead to the sixties had produced more immediate political problems than American slavery for Africans, slavery's forced displacements had created transnational avenues that could be retraced back to the continent. Among the artists who made this journey, Simone's travels to Nigeria and Liberia helped shape her worldview. Simone's friend Miriam Makeba, in exile from South Africa and fleeing the United States, settled at this time in Guinea, where she recorded liberation-themed music for the state's record company, singing in multiple languages of the African diasporic world. Major art festivals in Senegal and Cape Verde helped shape a transnational concept of black expressivity in the sixties. These countries' leaders had been influenced by events in Ghana, where a nexus of international visitors and local cultural initiative were instrumental in this process of post-colonial redefinition.

The image of this black transnationalism was mobilized in the 1963 Ghanaian state funeral for W.E.B. Du Bois, who had retired there. As in many black cultures, funerals are of great importance in the Akan tradition of Ghana, and Du Bois's affirmed the state's combinatory political mission by incorporating both local and Western forms of performative mourning. As Du Bois biographer David Levering Lewis reports, the proceeding included a laying in state where dignitaries and visitors could pay respects, a processional along the beach attended by thousands, and a first burial on the grounds of the former slave fortress that still serves as the seat of government. The details of the ceremony indicate the variety of cultural influences at play in Ghana at the time. African libations were poured and chants were recited, a Christian hymn was performed, red, gold and green liberation-colored chords were wrapped around the coffin as it rested beneath a Chinese lantern, Soviet limousines carried the bereaved throughout the processional as elite Ghanaian infantry executed the "distinctive ceremonial glide, the famous Slow March, learned from British drillmasters."[3] These foreign influences complemented the local emphasis on funerals, setting the stage for a post-colonial nation-state invested in its past and embedded in a mixed modernity. Following the ceremony, Nkrumah read Du Bois's final message, written years earlier, in a radio address:

> I have loved my work, I have loved people and my play, but always I have been uplifted by the thought that what I have done well will live long and justify my life. That what I have done ill or never finished can now be handed on to others for endless days to be finished perhaps better than I could have done. And that peace will be my applause.[4]

In this speech, Nkrumah adopts Du Bois's own first person "I," suggesting that it would be he who would finish the elder American's unfinished work. This act of surrogation, to borrow Joseph Roach's term, indicates the intergenerational depth of the present moment of liberation, as it was being enacted in this time and place. The imagery of play and applause suggest Du Bois was aware of the important cultural role he had performed as the innovator of Pan-Africanist thinking and in encouraging Nkrumah to succeed him as the movement's leader. This state performance marked the end of Du Bois's life, while presenting continuity between his life's work and the future of Africa.

Writer Efua Sutherland also played an important part in this funeral production, indicating her stature at the time. Sutherland tended to Shirley Graham Du Bois, the author's widow, and oversaw some of the customary details of the event, including the preparation of Du Bois's body.[5] These tasks conform to a conventional role reserved for women elders of the matrilineage within the Akan funeral structure.[6] As in her cultural advocacy and dramatic writing, Sutherland drew on the roles that women occupied in Akan life to act within this transnational circumstance.

African Personality and the State Art Mandate

After independence in 1957, the Ghanaian leadership sought to create new institutions that could counter a deleterious colonial legacy, and emphasized cultural projects in the effort to elaborate a specifically African formation of subjectivity. This subjectivity was devalued under the colonial authority, through policies that subjugated African cultural experiences to British knowledge, particularly through an education system that disparaged African traditions. The transformation of the British Gold Coast into an independent Ghana began a process of black autonomy that intervened against the European notion of history itself, one that had proposed a white subject as its universal agent. In renaming the Gold Coast after an ancient kingdom that shared some territory with the British colony, Nkrumah's African agency broke radically with the recent past and signaled a distant past worthy of recuperation in order to instantiate a progressive future. This renaming was a prominent symbol of the effort to create an African agency founded in African subjectivity. This subjectivity, or African Personality, managed many contradictions. A universal figure that is specifically raced, an agent of modernity whose authority precedes the influence of European methodologies, and an ideal citizen who locates an authentic situation among regional practices, a national liberation agenda, and a Pan-Africanist ideology, African Personality demonstrates an ambitious synthesis.

Figure 2.1. Britain's Duchess of Kent dances with Kwame Nkrumah, the first prime minister of Ghana, at a state ball in Accra on March 6, 1957, to celebrate Ghana's independence, proclaimed earlier that day. (AP Photo/Staff/Burroughs)

Though the Ghanaian nation-state was Nkrumah's instrument of liberation, his liberation philosophy transcended national boundaries. Nkrumah's movement was an exemplar. As Okwui Enwezor describes the historical scene:

> With the independence of Ghana, in 1957, a powerful psychological and ideological force put in place what would become the main political event of the 1960s: what Nkrumah, Ghana's first prime-minister, in a 1958 speech at the First All-African People's Conference in Accra, announced as Africa's decade of independence. In 1960, a loud cannon-shot was fired across the bough of the political spectrum, in Africa and around the world: not only did seventeen African countries gain independence that year, but the United Nations, upon admitting them en masse into the international body, declared that year to be the year of Africa. For the rest of the decade, independence celebrations and solemn ceremonies of the colonial hand-over of power were as commonplace as the zeal with which citizens of the new nations embraced their new reality.[7]

In the early sixties, independent Ghana stood in metonymic relation to a global anticolonial, anti-racist movement. While its mechanism of authority, the nation-state, was bound to Ghanaian territory, Ghana represented a promise of liberation that instigated a wave of independence. With Ghanaian independence came the idea and then the fact of broad African self-rule, followed by an international acknowledgement of African liberation. Within the decade and a half that had passed since the end of World War II, the notion of an end to European colonial domination of Africa had gone from a radical ideological position to a U.N.-sanctioned reality. Nkrumah played an instrumental role in this transformation of world order.

Leading a vanguard of liberation, Nkrumah proposed cultural initiatives that would combat the enduring effect of colonization. Valentin Y. Mudimbe has described this effect in terms of alienation:

> The alienation of colonialism entails both the objective fact of total dependence (economic, political, cultural, and religious) and the subjective process of the self-victimization of the dominated. The colonized internalizes the imposed racial stereotypes, particularly in attitudes toward

technology, culture, and language. Black personality and negritude appear as the only means of negating this thesis, and Fanon expounds the antithesis in terms of antiracist symbols. Negritude becomes the intellectual and emotional sign of opposition to the ideology of white superiority. At the same time, it asserts its authenticity which eventually expresses itself as a radical negation: rejection of racial humiliation, rebellion against the rationality of domination, and revolt against the whole colonialist system. This symbolic violence ultimately turns into nationalism and subsequently leads toward a political struggle for liberation.[8]

Mudimbe describes both objective and subjective processes as constitutive of this colonial alienation. The colonized is the object of the political fact of domination, but also internalizes this position through the subjective experience of domination. In a dialectical arrangement, Negritude and Black Personality, used here as synonyms, form an antithetical movement against the premise of European domination. The struggle for liberation results from what is imagined as an authentic African embodiment, but this image of real presence is paradoxically invoked as firstly a radical negation. The alienated situation of domination makes possible an empowered subjective position, articulated through intellect and emotion, beyond the object-status of the colonized. Importantly, African originality is imagined here as an aftereffect of the colony. It is only in the "symbolic violence" of the colony that this Black Personality emerges.

While citing Frantz Fanon's anti-racism, Mudimbe equates Black Personality with Negritude. Negritude is a concept commonly attributed to Martinican author Aimé Césaire, though Brent Hayes Edwards convincingly traces the term's origin to Jane Nardal in Paris.[9] It was most firmly codified in the African context by Senegal's first president, Nkrumah's ally, Léopold Sedar Senghor, who picked it up in Paris from his fellow transnational intellectuals. The idea of Negritude, which described an authentic African identity rooted in the very fact of blackness, influenced liberation ideologies in Francophone regions, though it was not met with universal approval by African intellectuals—Wole Soyinka, for instance, famously quipped, "A tiger does not speak of its Tigritude."[10] While an essential, biological Africanness is perhaps even more pronounced in the concept of Negritude than in the Anglophonic Pan-

Africanist tradition, Nkrumah's idea of African Personality certainly mobilizes essentialist strains that connect race, geographical origin, and shared political experience into a biologically grounded nationalist identity. African Personality and Negritude illustrate a politicized cultural effort that spanned the continent while also speaking to blacks across the diaspora. Its promise was to mine resources buried within black bodies and turn those materials into modern instruments of self-determination. This self-determined state was, through the image of a shared cultural source, presented as a scene of reconciliation and re-union for all Africans and all those of African descent. Negritude and African Personality were the means toward a black utopia. Importantly, according to their theorists, the cultural possibilities of African independence were grounded in an essentialist idea of an *a priori* Africanness. Its cultural authority was sustained by this biological premise, which countered a European essentialist notion of supremacy that authorized the latter's colonizing powers.

The Anglo-Christian education system, under which "African cosmology, religion, spirituality, medicine, music, dances and plastic arts were equated with the working of the devil,"[11] was one such institution that Nkrumah quickly sought to reorient. Upon assuming power, he quickly placed all levels of education under government control. At the University of Ghana, shortly before its independence from the University of London in 1961, Nkrumah effectively fired the entire academic staff and made new appointments subject to government discretion.[12] He opened the Institute of African Studies at the university to help institutionalize African culture. In his speech "The African Genius," Nkrumah identified the Institute's performing arts wing, the School of Music and Drama, as "the nucleus of the National Theater Movement."[13] These institutions' mandate was fourfold: First, they were to disseminate information on African arts through research; second, they were to help develop new artistic forms consistent with African traditions; third, they were to express "the ideas and aspirations of the people in post-independence Africa";[14] and fourth, they were to combat the insidious colonial legacy of cultural distortion and misrepresentation.

Nkrumah, who throughout his presidency kept the comic actor Ajax Bukana as a court jester, asserted a sustained interest in performance. According to Kwabena Nketia: "It is because of this interest that he in-

stituted the National Theatre Movement shortly after independence. . . .
[It was] his experience of some of the best African American modes of
expression which he used as his yard stick. As he points out: 'What other
countries have taken three-hundred years or more to achieve, a once
dependent territory must try to achieve in a generation.'"[15] Nkrumah's
Pan-Africanist experiences exposed him to black American theater,
which was among his inspirations in supporting a theater movement.
Lorraine Hansberry's 1958 play *A Raisin In The Sun* was a prominent
example of black American drama that was known to Ghana's intellectuals in the early years of independence, having been performed in 1963 in
Accra's Ghana Playhouse.[16] In the American context, Hansberry's play
provided a critical black subjectivity to New York theater, using a conventional realist idiom to challenge racist premises. In the post-colonial
situation of Ghana, a similar move was being choreographed, using
black American expressivity as a template for action.

Among the new liberatory institutions proposed by Nkrumah was
the National Theater Movement. In his 1958 autobiography, Nkrumah
offers some perspective on theater. He writes of his time at Teacher's
Training College in Accra: "During my third year at Achimota. I became interested in amateur dramatics and played the title role in a
house play called Kofi goes Abroad—a study of the student who went
to England to study medicine and the difficulties he encountered with
the witch doctors. He proved to the people that his scientific knowledge
could outwit superstition and witchcraft."[17] Nkrumah learned early in
his education about the pedagogical uses of theater. It's instructive that
he includes this moment in his autobiography. This scene depicts Nkrumah as the leading actor performing Kofi, an industrious Ghanaian
who had studied abroad—a character type of which Nkrumah would
later become the ultimate example. In this scene, Nkrumah/Kofi uses
knowledge acquired in Europe to "outwit superstition," setting up a dialectical conflict in which Nkrumah/Kofi is the agent who synthesizes
European knowledge and African practice. In Nkrumah's memory, theater was a place where ideology could be performed in a dress rehearsal
for political reality.

Within this cultural effort, the writer Efua Sutherland emerged as the
leader of the fledgling National Theater Movement. Sutherland's works
were in direct dialogue with the emergent Ghanaian nation-state. Kwa-

bena Nketia, who was the first director of the African Studies Institute at the University of Ghana, remembers the cultural scene at the time:

> There were also my close friends who were associates of Nkrumah, such as . . . Efua Sutherland, of blessed memory, with whom I worked very closely and who briefed Nkrumah from time to time on the status of the Arts or offered suggestions. . . . As a perceptive writer and philosopher in her own right, Efua Sutherland was someone Nkrumah listened to sometimes with rapt attention. She could advise or even criticize him where others might hesitate. I remember her telling me about an action on which she strongly disagreed with Nkrumah and pressed him to reverse it. But this was too much for him to accept so he left her abruptly after telling her to her face that even his own mother would not dare to talk to him in that manner. This did not slam the door on the Arts, for Nkrumah had a soft spot for creative people of Efua's intellectual calibre . . .[18]

This passage indicates Sutherland's particular role in the new artistic production. She was an actor on the stage of state, an advisor with unusual access to Nkrumah himself. Respected by her colleagues, Sutherland's work combined cultural advocacy with creative expression. Far from proposing an autonomous artistic position, her work was embedded in the political and historical situation of independent Ghana.

Sutherland's plays must be read in the context of her broad project of cultural advocacy. After having studied in Accra and Cambridge, Sutherland went to work in Ghana to create and promote African writing, building an enduring legacy as a playwright, director, teacher, specialist in children's theater, author, advisor to Nkrumah (and later President Jerry Rawlings), and general facilitator of Ghanaian culture. Sutherland's daughter, Esi Sutherland-Addy, and Anne V. Adams write as co-editors of the volume *The Legacy of Efua Sutherland*: "Like many intellectuals and cultural activists of the 'independence generation,' Efua Sutherland saw herself as an African with responsibilities that included the representation and validation of indigenous thought, values, and knowledge; the fashioning of new institutions, and systems of thought."[19] The responsibility of the independence generation was to substantiate an indigenous African cultural inheritance, but this indigenous Africa is problematized by the colonial influence under which

Africans of this generation achieved maturity. Despite the call to present locally grounded concepts and aesthetics, Sutherland herself expressed the task of fulfilling this responsibility as a journey:

> I'm on a journey of discovery. I'm discovering my own people. I didn't grow up in rural Ghana—I grew up in Cape Coast with a Christian family. It's a fine family, but there are certain hidden areas of Ghanaian life— important areas of Ghanaian life, that I just wasn't in touch with; in the past four or five years I've made a very concentrated effort to make that untrue. And I feel I know my people now.[20]

Sutherland's comments underscore the alienation of colonialism as described by Mudimbe. Despite being Ghanaian, she expressed the sense that, at age forty-four, she had finally come to understand "important" things about Ghanaian life, meaning elements of the culture that are furthest from the colonial inheritance. The local and the indigenous played a crucial role in shaping her artistic purpose.

The Ghana Drama Studio, founded by Sutherland, produced original African dramas, including Sutherland's own plays *Edufa* and *Foriwa*. It was with the Drama Studio Players that Sutherland also developed her third drama, *The Marriage of Anansewa*, after the end of Nkrumah's regime. Known as the mother of Ghana's National Theater Movement, a designation that credits a traditional feminine figure with the origin of a radically innovative institution, Sutherland created performance works that resonate with the notion of African Personality, in that they were original Ghanaian products made from the various sources of African modernity. However, her plays present the perilous complexity of this modern character as it is problematized by gender, class, and cultural identity. Sutherland's artistic voice was initiated by the independence movement itself. Speaking of her decision to write serious plays, she claimed it was "the outcome of my starting the Ghana Writers Society . . . after independence . . . September 1957. I started that all of a sudden because I felt that a newly independent country needed a force of creative writers."[21] The Ghana Writers Society was only the first of many organizations that Sutherland founded to support Ghanaian artistic production after independence, and these organizations were embarked upon with some level of government support, and were identified with

Ghanaian national projects. *Edufa*, which premiered in November 1962, was presented within this frame of original cultural products engaged with the priorities of the independence government.

The Modern Locations of *Edufa* and *Foriwa*

While aligned with the national cultural initiative, *Edufa* also takes much from the colonial legacy. Written in English, *Edufa* adapts Euripides's *Alcestis*, borrowing from the structure of Euripidean tragedy while modernizing its ethical dilemma. *Alcestis* represents the conflict of the royal Athenian house of King Admetos; *Edufa* is situated in the house of a wealthy African entrepreneur who owns a mining company. Borrowing the plot of the Greek play, Edufa's usually happy household has been cast into uncertainty due to the illness of his beautiful wife, Ampoma, who, like King Admetos's wife, Alcestis, appears near the beginning of the play, speaking in broken, seemingly deluded riddles brought on by grave illness. Both Alcestis and Ampoma repeatedly fall to the floor in exhaustion. Both dutiful wives reveal that they are dying, and ask their husbands to honor their memory and to protect their children.

While in Euripides's version Alcestis expires early and is resurrected in the end, Ampoma's irreversible decline is the central thrust of Sutherland's play. Through Edufa's conversations and confrontations with various family members, an unexpected friend, and a chorus of townswomen, it is revealed that Ampoma inadvertently vowed to die in the place of her husband. Edufa's death had been foretold by a diviner, but his selfishness prompted him to seek refuge from his fate, passing the curse onto his wife. A remorseful Edufa and the rest of the household perform numerous remedies to avert the death of Ampoma; it even appears that she will recover after the women of the town offer a household blessing. This chorus of townswomen keep watch on the proceedings, a formal device that alludes to both a tragic chorus and local notions of collectivity. Sutherland's adaptation draws other parallels: between Athenian oracular tradition and the African practice of divination, as well as the conventions of libations, polytheistic reverence, and respect for taboo. By creating these African parallels with the Greek classical tradition, Sutherland inverts the English colonial ideology that devalued African traditions. By mirroring African practices with Athenian ones, she maneuvers African traditions into a position of classical inheritance, mimicking the choreography by which the English had positioned ancient Athens as a source of Western civilization.

Okwui Enwezor has pointed out the difficulties of asserting an African modernity in relationship to the colonial inheritance that artists like Sutherland sought to reevaluate: "Like the cracking of the slave ship, the relationship of African Modernity to Europe's construction of the universal subject is both a critique and a modification, a rip in the body of the colonial text . . . the internal cohesion of mid-century African aesthetics is first a discourse of an awareness of otherness, and second a process of regeneration that draws upon the particularity of an African perspective."[22] Enwezor's comment underscores the paradoxes of the utopian liberation project: in the wake of colonialism African cultures had been shaped by the experience of European domination, a process that decentered notions of cultural authenticity. *Edufa* itself, while asserting African Personality, does so within an "awareness of otherness," or alienation, particularly in its adaptation of a classical source claimed by the English as a part of their own origin myth. In this choice, Sutherland placed her African content within a theatrical convention that had shaped the Western notion of the universal subject, elaborating on the European concepts of dramatic action and cathartic instruction.

As independence movements swept the continent, many of Sutherland's African contemporaries were conducting experiments with Western structures and African content. Notable among these is Nigerian playwright Wole Soyinka, who wrote numerous plays in English that employed European dramatic conventions while narrating an ethical alignment with a Yoruba worldview. This approach received criticism from other African writers and critics, including Ngugi Wa Thiong'o, who has argued that African literature should only be written in African languages, and the Bolekaja critics, who described Soyinka and others as "writers whose works employed African imagery and situation in order to domesticate it within a European modernist literary formalism. They read this as a loss in self-confidence, and a compromise of the radical call for a total break with colonialism."[23] This latter view constructed an anti-European Africanness in an attempt to replace the Western universal subject with an original African substitute. In contrast to writers who sought to combat colonial history by bypassing its structural effects, Sutherland's plays are formally comparable to Soyinka's. Her plays suggest that the complexity of creating historically African work in a post-colonial context is resolved through materialist combinations of diverse cultural elements rather than an ideal of African purity. Distinguishing Sutherland from Soyinka is the prominent woman-centered orientation of her critique, one of the important differences Sutherland brings into this cultural combination.

This process of post-colonial combination has been read as a form of synthesis, through which opposing materials synthesize into a new form, as in the Hegelian dialectical model. But at the end of *Edufa*, as in other plays of the period, differences remain in place, and the African personalities that populate the drama must find a way to negotiate the irresolvable contradictions that mark their reality. Rather than achieving a total synthesis, through which differences melt away into a newly configured unity, the unconquered multiplicities of these works suggest that the synthetic model is insufficient. While forms are indeed being brought together in combination, the end result is not a unified totality, but a collection of differences that exist simultaneously. *Edufa* is an example of original African cultural production that speaks through radical ambivalences rather than syntheses.

With *Edufa*, Sutherland offers a Ghanaian modernity in which colonial elements remain. Far from eschewing colonial materials, the choice of *Alcestis* as the source for adaptation points directly to the English education Ghanaians received in the colonial Gold Coast. Regarding this education, historian Kwame Botwe-Asamoah describes a system that "instilled an affinity towards all things European. It was also a type that trained the African to assist the colonial administrators at the lowest ranks and to staff privately owned European companies. In effect, the education system was characterized by the absurdities in the transportation of Eurocentric education into Africa."[24] This system served the twin purpose of promoting European ideologies and supporting the economic program of the colonial administration. Despite the deleterious effects of this education, it formed the foundation of Sutherland's theatrical works. Of her introduction to Athenian tragedy, Sutherland recalled:

> I was interested in theater . . . because of my background at school and at
> college. . . . I went to schools in Cape Coast and Asante-Mampong. They

were run by nuns. They were actually very good about introducing us to literature. . . . I performed a lot when I was at school and college. . . . Also in Cape Coast where I grew up there was a secondary school, and they used to put on in Cape Coast an annual Greek tragedy, as a school performance . . . the staff and students. My uncle went to that school, which was probably why I got to attend those plays where he performed. And I remember seeing Robert Gardner . . . yes, as Creon in Antigone, when I was a child, as a young girl. Antigone, Agamemnon . . . I loved it . . . I understood what was going on . . . I read a lot of the Greek tragedies. And when I was teaching at training college, Asante-Mampong, I produced some of these plays myself. I produced the *Medea*. I produced *Antigone*, I produced the *Alcestis* . . . I tried to write some plays myself. Christmas plays and things like that. But I was playing at the time.[25]

In this education system lie the roots of some of the National Theater Movement's productive contradictions. As Sutherland herself described it elsewhere, prior to the European presence, Africans "did not stand on a platform to sing songs and say things, and dance to entertain static audiences ranged on chairs before them,"[26] nor were the concepts of drama or theater part of pre-colonial West African performance, which was based in storytelling, dance, and masquerades.[27] Theater was brought to Ghana by the nuns and bureaucrats who ran the school system. Despite her dedicated efforts to invest in African Personality, Sutherland "loved" the Greek tragedies she was introduced to in school, and some of her earliest artistic projects were to remake these non-African products. So, in *Edufa*, Sutherland planted her African content in ground she had discovered through the tutelage of the colonists. Nonetheless, such a Western inheritance was fundamental and basic to the consciousness of an African educated in the Gold Coast by the English. In this distorted sense, Greek tragedy could be figured as a productive element of African modernity.

The adaptation of a Greek text claimed as English patrimony provided Sutherland with the opportunity to make critical contrasts for the African situation. A key difference between *Edufa* and *Alcestis* speaks to the post-colonial context of *Edufa* and elaborates Sutherland's gender politics: in *Alcestis*, Hercules rescues the deceased spouse from Hades, rewarding her for her goodness and beauty. In *Edufa*, there is no *deus ex machina* that saves Ampoma, nor will Africa be rescued from the intrusion of masculine selfishness. In the modern Ghanaian version, consequences are severe and irreversible. Here, the capitalist economics of modernity, which were critiqued by the African Marxist politicians of the independence era, are shown as dangerous for the African social situation. Furthermore, Sutherland ties this critique of capital to critical gender politics. In *Edufa*, the modern African man's greed bears disastrous ramifications, particularly for women. Tellingly, the Greek plays that Sutherland cites as inspirations, *Medea, Antigone,* and *Alcestis*, all deal with a woman's struggle against a fate shaped by patriarchal forces. This particular conflict is echoed not only in *Edufa*, but in Sutherland's other original plays as well. Throughout *Edufa*, it is Edufa's female relatives, Seguwa and Abena, as well as the chorus of women from the town, who seem to have the best interests of the community in mind. Seguwa in particular tempers Edufa's emotional reactions with rational advice, and the rest do their best to help Ampoma overcome her illness. When Ampoma finally dies, it is Seguwa who places the blame squarely with Edufa. The women of the family and of the town form the ethical standard against which Edufa's actions are ultimately judged. Had Edufa taken any of the women seriously, disaster may have been averted. Sutherland's critique reveals an emergent African feminism. While the terminology for such a position is contested—Ama Ata Aidoo is one who has embraced the term "feminism," while others in Africa have resisted feminism as a concept grounded in Euro-American structures[28]—it is evident that Sutherland's plays, which predate feminism, womanism, and other such organized political formations, bring a consciousness of women's relations to power. The critique of patriarchy suggested by *Edufa* is relevant to traditional and colonial histories, but is of specific importance in the context of a new nation-state reevaluating its cultural and political norms.

Edufa's African feminist critique is consistent with local priorities. In *Edufa*, the narrative suggests that a successful modern African man has strayed too far from the traditional collective values of his community as he has pursued wealth and reputation. This sentiment is expressed by Kankam, Edufa's father (played by playwright Joe de Graft in the play's first production), who harshly admonishes his son for jeopardizing his wife's life in the pursuit of "emancipated"[29] modern life. It is Kankam who defends the faith in divination, thereby revealing the source of the play's conflict. His admonition of his son resembles that of Pheres in *Alcestis*. But while King Admetos has followed his father's path to a royal position, it is Edufa's break from tradition, made manifest in his pursuit of the modern trappings of wealth and status, that fuels Kankam's anger. When Edufa violates taboo by questioning his father's sanity, Kankam reacts with disbelief, exclaiming: "My *ntoro* within you shivers with the shock of it!"[30] The father uses a traditionally gendered notion to admonish his son by referring to the animating spirit passed from father to son in the Akan belief system. Kankam's recriminations place the diminishment of Edufa's traditional values at the source of the disastrous circumstance.

In *Edufa*, the traditionalist stance is complemented by a Pan-Africanist position. In addition to his father, Edufa is also challenged by his friend Senchi, a comic character who resembles the ridiculous Hercules of *Alcestis*. Senchi is a traveling musician who carries a worn leather case. Rather than tradition, what Senchi seems to value most are his flirtations with the women of the town. He sings to himself as he enters the scene: "and the wanderer . . . the wanderer . . . the wanderer comes home." [31] Senchi signals the diasporic and internationalist sensibilities that were fundamental to the independence moment. He quickly addresses Edufa's contested identity when he first arrives at his old friend's house:

> Say, have you changed your religion again? What are you practicing now? Catholicism, spiritualism, neo-theosophy or what? Last time I passed through here, you were an intellectual atheist, or something in that category. I wouldn't be surprised to see you turned Buddhist monk next time.[32]

Senchi playfully prods his friend, questioning his African authenticity. Though his social position is very different from Kankam's, his critique of Edufa is similar. Both the irreverent traveler and the wise elder recognize that Edufa's ambition has made him dishonest. Senchi depicts what Haiping Yan has called a kind of "modern vagrancy," a figure "moving across the fermenting horizons and organizing boundaries of 'intertwined modern world histories,'"[33] whose transgressive practice

Figure 2.2. *Edufa* by Efua Sutherland, Longman Drumbeat, 1967.

of border crossing can reshape the limits of national consciousness. In *Edufa*, the local traditionalist asserts an ethical mandate that is supported by the irreverence of the vagrant Pan-Africanist. Sutherland presents both of these subjective positions as valuable, giving voice to two critiques of African modernity that never resolve into each other. *Edufa* offers no successful synthesis of these voices. Though Kankam and Senchi speak for two critical perspectives, neither is able to save Ampoma.

Sutherland may have been cast as the traditional "mother" of the National Theater Movement, but like Senchi, she had traveled, and had met illustrious travelers. Her own experiences were shaped by the internationalism of the Pan-Africanist politics that shaped Ghanaian independence. African independence movements were affected by the influence of European, black American, Caribbean, and Chinese sources, all contributing to the era's international discourse of liberation politics. Her husband, William Sutherland, was a black American, who was engaged in transnational political organizing. Sutherland had met many international visitors in Accra, which, at the time of independence, was a Mecca for leaders of black leftist liberation efforts. As a prelude to forming the Ghana Writers Society, Sutherland cited a trip she took in 1957 to the Tashkent Afro-Asian Writers Conference in Soviet Uzbekistan, where she realized the importance of producing African literary works.[34] That this lesson was learned abroad at a communist writers conference is compatible with the African Marxist philosophy that Nkrumah was pursuing at home in Ghana. Ghana was founded in the Pan-African struggle, aided by the support of Trinidadian intellectual George Padmore. At the 1945 Pan-African Congress in Manchester, Nkrumah had effectively succeeded W.E.B. Du Bois as the leader of the movement. Du Bois spent his final years in Accra working on an Encyclopedia Africana. Shirley Graham Du Bois later ran the state's television network. Accra was a meeting point for Third World leftists and African diasporic activists. Malcolm X, in his autobiography penned with Alex Haley, describes admiringly his 1964 trip to Ghana, where he was feted by Maya Angelou and the Chinese ambassador. He declares that "nowhere is the black continent's wealth and the natural beauty of its people richer than in Ghana, which is so very proudly the fountainhead of Pan-Africanism,"[35] and that "[i]n Ghana—or in all of black Africa—my highest single honor was an audience at the Castle with Osagyefo Dr. Kwame Nkrumah."[36] Ghana and Nkrumah represented a realizable radical black potential, reenergizing political movements around the world.

In *Lose Your Mother*, a critical memoir outlining Ghana's role in American slavery, Saidiya Hartman describes the movement of blacks to Ghana in those years.

> The architects and laborers of the Pan-Africanist dream had arrived in these first waves. They were comrades in the Black International. It was an age of possibility, when it seemed that as soon as tomorrow that the legacy of slavery and colonialism would be overthrown. Richard Wright had visited the Gold Coast in 1953 and written a powerful account of the struggle for independence. In 1957, Martin Luther King, Jr., Ralph Bunche, Adam Clayton Powell, Jr., A. Philip Randolph, and Horace Mann (at the request of Nkrumah and against the expressed wishes of the U.S. State Department) had traveled to Ghana for the celebration of its independence. King, upon seeing the Black Star replace the Union Jack as the flag of the nation and listening to the audience of half a million people shout, "Freedom! Freedom!" began to weep.[37]

This list of black American visitors, which includes both statesmen (Bunche, Powell) and leftist activists (Randolph, Mann), attests to the mix of black perspectives coming together in Accra at the time. Sutherland was among the Ghanaians who met with traveling visitors. She describes the independence event from her own perspective:

> And then independence itself. I was terribly excited about independence. I had been excited about it for two or three years . . . and then it actually happened. At the day it happened there were a lot of people at that time, including Martin Luther King; he and Coretta King came. I actually was with them on the night of the transition. We went to the midnight parliament, the first parliament they put together. Then we came out. . . . And, I remember very clearly in the streets outside with Nkrumah and all those people saying "Ghana is free forever." . . . We watched the Ghana flag go up and the British flag come down. . . . Very, very exciting times . . . I'm not surprised that that moved . . . with that inspiration and that excite-

ment and he [Martin Luther King], he was moved too. . . . Actually I heard him say, "Free at last,"' that night . . . in that street, that early morning . . . he echoed the "free at last" statement . . . at that moment . . .[38]

These anecdotes underscore Ghana's important place in a black world network, and that Sutherland was herself an actor in Ghana's Pan-Africanist movement.[39]

The transnational entanglements of Sutherland's cultural projects reached into the sphere of development, as evidenced by a trail of funding from the Rockefeller Foundation in New York, which sought to support a decolonized Africa through training and grants in the arts and sciences. "The Foundation is proceeding on the assumptions that this advanced training should be home based," states the organization's 1961 annual report. "Strong local universities must be the main reliance for educating the numbers and varieties of leaders required."[40] The Foundation saw a crisis in the lack of leadership indigenous to new African states. Sutherland was among the national beneficiaries of its assumptions. The Foundation's 1962 report shows $10,000 given to the Arts Council of Ghana, Accra, of which Sutherland was a founding member, for "development of the Ghana Drama Studio, under the direction of Mrs. Efua Sutherland."[41] Three smaller grants were awarded that year to the University of Ghana for Institute programs including the Ghana Writers Society founded by Sutherland and for "expenses for visiting professors in the department of physics."[42] She had received a similar grant in 1961. In 1964, another $10,000 from the foundation went to "research in literature and drama by Mrs. Efua Sutherland, Institute of African Studies."[43] These grants show a different form of transnational circulation that shaped Sutherland's plays. While agencies of aid and development have come to reproduce colonial dynamics in Africa, this support shows Ghana's prominent place in the emerging post-colonial world.

In Sutherland's plays, the broadness of black modernity intensifies the specificity of locality. In *Edufa*, it is the chorus of local women from the town who, echoing the Athenian chorus, offer a collective ethic by which to understand the action. But when Ampoma is mortally punished for her husband's carelessness, the action defies reasonable understanding. Together, they mourn:

> We do not know how,
> We do not understand,
> But she is dead.[44]

Like the astonishing rescue of Alcestis from Hades, *Edufa* produces a result that is equally confounding to its local spectators. *Edufa* proposes African Personalities that do not resolve in synthesis. The chorus cannot understand Edufa's fate. In the end, these African Personalities may remain partially illegible to one other.

Sutherland's play *Foriwa*, also first produced in 1962, elaborates the dialogue between locality and the wider discourses that penetrate it. *Foriwa* adapts Sutherland's short story "A New Life at Kyerefaso," about a stranger who brings positive changes, re-presenting its themes with more dramatic complexity. Unlike the mythic structure of Greek tragedy deployed in *Edufa*, *Foriwa* relies on a three-act format with elements that resemble those of Western realism in many ways: in its natural approach to dialogue, its narrative arch, and its textured group of characters from a range of class strata, whose stories revolve around a central family's conflict. It also departs from realism in important ways, maintaining the direct address of traditional storytelling and emphasizing a communal, rather than individual, ethical sensibility.

Recalling realist plays including Hansberry's, the state-published version of *Foriwa* includes directions that suggest an interest in truthful representation. It begins with a detailed, page-long description of the stage layout, by which a small group of buildings create an accurate depiction of the town of Kyerefaso. However, this veracious description concludes with the possibility of its own negation: "This play was intended to be performed in the open air in a street in any of many small Ghanaian towns. The details of the multiple set described above are drawn from such a setting. . . . An alternative method would be to present the play on a stark stage with abstractions of this multiple set, using simple props and rostra."[45] The preferred setting would make the dramatic representation accessible to people in various small towns, rather than just theatergoers in the capital. What is described as a set is actually a real world, reimagined by Sutherland, where actors would portray a semi-realistic fiction. Regardless of this intended setting, the original production was done on the outdoor courtyard stage at the center of the Drama Studio in Accra, which would constitute what Sutherland describes as an "alternative method."[46] Sutherland sets her play in a town that is really the town of Kyerefaso, but is also any town in Ghana, while it could permissibly be a town made only of "abstractions." Though using formal conventions of realism, as she used formal conventions of tragedy in *Edufa*, Sutherland deploys this realism as a theatrical genre, not as a *de facto* truth-telling position. As the set description indicates, the commitment to realism is ambivalent.

The play's narrative follows two intertwined threads of story. In the run-up to an important festival, the town's Queen Mother is having trouble coming to terms with the self-interests, prejudices, and habitual bickering of her townspeople. The Queen Mother commiserates with her city-educated daughter, Foriwa, who has returned to town but is refusing to marry any of the many suitors who have pursued her. Meanwhile, Labaran, an itinerant stranger who speaks directly to the audience from where he has been squatting near the Queen Mother's home, surreptitiously plans a revitalization of the town by building a library and organizing a collective agricultural project. These characters' lives are intertwined via property interests and a budding romance. The play's conflict is the tension between efforts to change the social structure and the resistance to that change. Notions of tradition and innovation are placed in a difficult balance.

In his long opening monologue, Labaran lays the logic of nation-state over the provincialism of Kyerefaso.

> I am not Kyerefaso born. Three months is all I've lived here, and many still call me stranger. . . . Who is stranger, anywhere, in these times, in whose veins the blood of this land flows? O, let us wake; wake in the time that is given us.[47]

Marshaling Nkrumahism, this protagonist invokes African Personality in the face of his foreignness. This line of reasoning relies on an essentialist notion of "blood of this land," in conjunction with a historical situation produced of "these times," proposing the co-adaptability of these two analyses. Labaran's perspective is eventually vindicated when the town reluctantly aligns with his agenda. However, in this first alienated instance of oratory, replete with a literary "O," Labaran's speech is punctuated with a stage direction: "*There is a splash to his right where someone is emptying a chamber pot.*" With this bit of low comedy, Sutherland presents the optimism of the utopian moment alongside the bodily realities that produce skepticism and indifference. While his rhetoric offers to transcend various exclusions, Labaran can't escape the splashing waste of the street. Labaran's own reaction is also ambivalent: "*He makes a sour face, laughing it off.*" Labaran is undaunted by these contradictions, and even sees within them expressive possibilities. After relaying how he made a public spectacle of himself by cleaning a vile rubbish heap in his best suit, his speech concludes with the observation:

> Many of the townsmen who had been troubled about my seeming aim-less presence here, gave me up for mad after that. Fine! If mad men knew their strength they would band together and save the world. Everybody listens to them, permitting them full expression. What freedom![48]

Finding liberatory possibilities within madness, a particularly potent taboo in Akan culture, the industrious hero promises to challenge conventional thinking in Kyerefaso to bring about positive changes for the town.

The Queen Mother's daugher, Foriwa, brings an education and untraditional attitude toward marriage with her upon her return to Kyerefaso. Matching Labaran's industriousness with her spirit of commitment, the pair represent the progressive possibility engendered in Ghanaian independence. Though she and Labaran join forces by the end of the play, no marriage has been announced. Foriwa and Labaran have their first substantive meeting as she inspects the books he has acquired for the village. While looking through the stacks, the two laugh at the colonial texts with which they were educated.

> FORIWA: . . . I see you didn't forget the old stalwarts, the Oxford English Readers for Africa.
> LABARAN: [*with humour*] We were all dieted on it, weren't we?[49]

They go on to glance appreciatively through an old picture book depicting a child's life in colonial India. While the pair is dedicated to empowering the locality with better educational resources, colonial experience cannot be extracted from these resources.

The Queen Mother welcomes this new generation's enthusiasm. From the start, she has expressed frustration with the town's decline. Occupying a ceremonial role, the Queen Mother, who early in the play refers to the Kyerefaso street as "this decrepitude," embodies the disconnect between a traditionalist image of African life and the lived experience of African modernity. While the Queen Mother's chief critic, town elder Sintim, commonly invokes traditional values in his outbursts, the Queen Mother uses her traditional role to propose change. The Queen Mother figures an African feminism not incoherent with the idea of African Personality. She holds a traditional position and uses it to speak out for local progressive causes. There is a tradition to her feminism; Ghana is 40 percent Akan, a cultural group that has been customarily matrilineal. This matrilineal system has obvious differences from the patriarchal English authority, which generally disempowered women throughout the colonial era.[50] In the post-independence moment of *Foriwa*, the Queen Mother faces sexist resistance from both the traditional and modern discourses within her social sphere. Particularly aggressive is the blustering Sintim, who at one point declares, "Wise ones, when you restricted a woman with taboos, you damned well knew what you were doing."[51] But it is the Queen Mother who masterfully and independently calls upon her townspeople to honor their ancestors by building toward the future. Near the play's climax, as everyone is assembled for a festival to honor the legendary town fathers, the Queen Mother departs scandalously from her ceremonial script and takes the opportunity to make a political speech:

> Sitting here, seeing Kyerefaso die, I am no longer able to bear the mockery of the fine, brave, words of this ceremony of our festival. Our fathers earned the right to utter them by their deeds. They found us the land, protected it, gave us a system of living. Praise to them. Yes. But is this the way to praise them? Watching their walls crumbling around us? Failing to build upon their foundations? Letting weeds choke the paths they made? Unwilling to open new paths ourselves, because it demands of us thought, and goodwill, and action? No, we have turned Kyerefaso into a

death bed from which our young people run away to seek elsewhere, the promise of life we've failed to give them here.[52]

Though her ceremonial role should have restricted her speech, the Queen Mother defies convention and uses her position to redirect traditionalist energies. Through her analysis, the implication is made that the founders of local traditions would endorse the leftist program proposed by Labaran. The Queen Mother mixes discourses in Kyerefaso, countering sexist attacks by citing progressive politics based in the old-fashioned values.

While a political argument is won by the Queen Mother—by the end Sintim has agreed to go along with the collective will and acquiesces to the library, the collective farm, and the stranger—the Ghanaian village is depicted in *Foriwa* as the scene of disagreement. This is not the urban space of Accra, where the diasporic meet the Western educated. This is the village street, where an idea of African social structures can be publicly performed. Yet, within this African space, consensus is only tentatively reached, after much acrimony. If the seemingly homogenous space of village life can barely come to terms with itself, what are the possibilities of post-colonial synthesis on the national level? Modernity and tradition prove too unstable to be relied upon in binary terms of thesis and antithesis. Kyerefaso's discord is most pronounced in the run-up to the festival, destabilizing the notion of the traditional as a fixed set of practices unanimously understood by authentic practitioners. The prevailing claim of *Foriwa* is that cultural practices should be renewed and adapted to accommodate the shifting worlds of their participants.

The ambivalent figure of tradition can be quite problematic in the African context, as Paulin Hountondji has pointed out. As in Nkrumah's own writing, the idea of tradition is often conjured to locate aspects of African culture that extend a genealogical lineage into the Africa that preceded colonization. As Hountondji argues:

the adjective "traditional," in the phrase "traditional African civilization," must be banished once and for all because it favors a pernicious misconception. In practice the phrase is used to mean "pre-colonial African civilization," but again only in the sense of a purely conventional historical division. But when, instead of this neutral phrase, we use the more vivid phrase "traditional African civilization," we add a value connotation, and pre-colonial civilization as a whole is being contrasted with so-called "modern" civilization (that is to say, colonial and post-colonial civilization, with the connotation "highly Westernized"), as if they were two essentially distinct systems of value. The pre-colonial history of Africa is condensed into a single synchronic picture, whose points exist simultaneously and are uniformly opposed to the points in a different synchronic chart, symmetrical with the first, the two beings distinguished in terms of what is taken to be the only important division in the history of the continent, the moment of colonization.[53]

Hountondji is highly critical of the simplifying misconception of tradition. It is used to reduce diverse interactions of cultures, languages, and ideologies into a "synchronic picture," which emphasizes colonization as the focal transformative event in African history. Hountondji argues African cultures are not stable condensations frozen in time, nor are the pre-colonial, colonial, and post-colonial eras discontinuous with each other. The term "traditional" can be used to recuperate a unified totality that never existed. It also acts to render African originality incompatible with "Westernized" modernity. In the African context, tradition and modernity tend to reduce multiple historical differences into a fallacious binary.

Hountondji is equally critical of the broader ideological synthesis described by Nkrumahism. In his 1964 book *Consciencism*, Nkrumah proposes that neologism to describe a movement that would resolve Du Bois's double consciousness and counter the primacy of the conscious Western subject. Echoing other early writings, Nkrumah imagines a subject who could assimilate centuries of European and Arab influences into an African Personality, a character that resonates with an authentic African past. While tidily prescribing this ideological synthesis, Nkrumah locates within it African communalist tendencies that should cohere with modern socialism. Hountondji, an admirer of Nkrumah, nonetheless satirizes this unlikely premise, calling it a "unanimst illusion."[54] "Better still, it so happens that the ideological synthesis can be presented as socialist. And to the extent that it is collective and that all Africans, without exception, are expected to commit themselves to this new system in order to recover their authentic cultural personality, they will automatically be socialists and will all reject, out of conviction, the exploitation of man by man. Africa will have permanently recaptured its fine village unanimity and will thus offer the world the unique spectacle of a society without conflict, division or dissonance."[55] Hountondji points to an irresolution echoed by Kwame Anthony Appiah, who writes in his *In My Father's House*: "I grew up knowing that I lived in Asante and that the Asantehene was our king. I also grew up singing enthusiastically the Ghanaian national anthem—'Lift High the Flag of Ghana'— and knowing that Nkrumah was, first, our prime minister, then, our president. It did not occur to me as a child that the 'we,' of which this 'our' was the adjective, was fluid, ambiguous, obscure."[56] Appiah's childhood memory suggests the inconsistencies Nkrumah's program sought to synthesize. Appiah describes an ambiguous common identity that Hountondji identifies as an unlikely ground for socialist unanimity. In hyperbolizing Nkrumah's writing, Hountondji's point is that this synthesis of socialism and African collectivity is too simple, that its promise to recover a lost authenticity is far-fetched, and that this image of the unanimous village is already an illusion.

This unanimous village is certainly not Kyerefaso, where authentic tradition is the source of bitter dispute. The unanimist illusion is dispelled from Labaran's opening monologue. However, Sutherland does not fully foreclose on a future resolution, far-fetched as it may seem, coming closer to the possibility of synthesis in *Foriwa* than she does in *Edufa*. As a few modest social changes fall into place and an agreement is reached, the Queen Mother announces the play's final line, "There will be a festival tomorrow,"[57] forecasting a future engaged with a traditional past. But this promise is never actualized within the play; it resides in the characters' imagination, in a hope for collectivist possibility.

Even when a provisional unanimous position can be forged out of a promise of communality, this position is destabilized by an African Personality that is promiscuously inclusive. This figure of modern black citizenship accommodates the locality of the village, the transnationality of a Kofi who has gone abroad, and the exotic foreignness of diasporic blacks. The latter are for the most part the descendants of slaves who were traded away by West African chiefs, a fact that marks their participation in black unanimity with an historic act of expulsion. Ghana's long history with transatlantic slavery makes it a paradoxical focal point of modern black experience: what was once a primary point of exodus from the African continent—a "door of no return" for exported slaves—had emerged in the independence era as a site of black reconciliation.

Specters in the Fortress and *The Dilemma of a Ghost*

Ama Ata Aidoo's *The Dilemma of a Ghost* addressed the taboo subject of slavery directly. The play was first presented in 1964 on the University of Ghana, Legon campus, where Aidoo was an English major. This was Aidoo's first play, preceding also her other well-known works in fiction and poetry, and establishing a lucid yet lyrical literary voice that has been both supportive of Ghana and critical of nationalist rhetoric, while always maintaining a focus on women's relationships to the apparatus of modern power. A poetic posthumous tribute she wrote to Efua Sutherland, in which she remembers the ways in which Sutherland was simultaneously revered and diminished by the familiar feminine title "Auntie," is an example of the gender critique Aidoo has consistently contributed to Ghanaian literature.[58] Aidoo was younger than Sutherland and less connected to the government, a situation that lent itself to what appears to be a more direct critique of state power within her body of writing. While later works have become common subjects in studies of post-colonial literature, even Aidoo's first play imagines a Ghana contextualized by a legacy of uneven international exchanges.

Elaborating on a storytelling tradition constituting a "dilemma genre,"[59] the play begins with a single prelude that depicts two different places. An opening monologue delivered by the Bird of the Wayside sets the scene of the Odumna clan's household, which has used much of its wealth "in the making of One Scholar."[60] It is soon revealed that this scholar is the son of the clan, Ato, who has recently completed his studies in America. The Bird of the Wayside speaks partially in verse and through poetic images, recalling Akan storytelling traditions as well as the expository addresses that sometimes begin Athenian tragedies. This character's name suggests the birds found in the Christian Bible, which figure in the parable of the sower. A tale told multiply in the New Testament—the books of Matthew, Mark, and Luke all contain versions of this story—the parable describes a sower whose misplaced seeds have been consumed by the birds of the wayside. The story's message is that while the word of God is delivered in many ways, it is best received in fertile ground. Meanings misplaced along the wayside is sure to be lost in miscommunication. Aidoo, who was originally given the first name Christine despite having been raised in a Fanti royal household, received a Christian education in her youth in Cape Coast. While referring to a marginal creature of Christian mythology through which meaning is displaced, this bird also resembles Sankofa, a common Adinkra symbol or Akan pictogram, that is usually depicted as a bird facing forward but looking backward. The philosophical notion behind Sankofa includes the idea of bringing useful elements of the past into the future, a simultaneous consciousness of both tradition and progress. Aidoo's Bird of the Wayside looks toward the past and the future, suggesting a chain of events that have led to the present of the play, and foretelling the play's dilemma that it has perceived from its paradoxical position.

The prelude enacts the play's dilemma spatially: in one instance the Bird is speaking of the nearby village, in the next Ato and his new black American wife Eulalie are on their American university campus, discussing their post-graduation move to Africa. Eulalie is clearly uninformed and nervous about Africa, but imagines a cultural reconciliation that would have been common in the transnational imaginations of black Americans who really made such a move. Speaking to Ato, whom she affectionately calls "Native Boy," she speculates, "Ato, can't your Ma be sort of my Ma too?" Ato's affirmative assurances are not convincing, nor should they be, as the play's conflict will center around the difficulty of assimilating Ato's family, Ato's own transnational experience, and Eulalie's black American perspective into a harmonious blend. From the first moments of the pair's return to Africa, discord prevails.

In an interview with British director Michael Walling on the occasion of Ghana's fiftieth anniversary, Aidoo recalls wanting to write a play about a cross-cultural relationship, and thinking that a story about a Ghanaian and a white person was "so easy . . . not challenging enough." Such a play would also recall Joe de Graft's *Through a Film Darkly*, which dramatizes an English woman's effect on her African husband's community. De Graft's play had been produced at the Ghana Drama Studio in 1962. *Through a Film Darkly* portrays a stark difference that results in a traumatic violent outcome; a man kills himself remembering an off-stage English woman who scorned him. *The Dilemma of a Ghost* deals with a less distinct set of differences. Nor does Aidoo's play reach such a hysterical climax. *The Dilemma of a Ghost* is concerned with subtlety. Aidoo explains her process:

> AIDOO: What seemed to me really worth exploring was a relationship between an African and somebody form the diaspora.
>
> WALLING: And that's the way you get the slavery into the piece . . . and it's interesting, both of your plays are about slavery and this is very important in your reason for writing . . .
>
> AIDOO: Yes. Yes. . . . In fact, I only realized later, much later, by reading critics, you know all of these post-colonial critics, yes, African and non-African alike who pointed out as a matter of fact I am one African writer who had, you know, kinda concentrated on these issues. . . . Not many do. As usual, my response is, you know me, fools rush in where angels fear to . . . what I'm saying is these are very sensitive issues. . . . So that's where the dilemma came from, from the fact that people were here from the African exile, the global Africans, the fact that I thought that this presented quite a challenge.[61]

According to Aidoo, she chose to represent a relationship between an African and "somebody from the diaspora" because it was relevant to the local situation, it was challenging to represent, and it provided an additional challenge for being such a sensitive issue. Aidoo's account renders her young self unafraid to test the inclusiveness of African Personality.

In the play's first act, Ato arrives at his ancestral home and gathers his many relatives, revealing to them that he will not marry according to his family's arrangements, but has already married in America. He is "embarrassed"[62] saying his wife's foreign name to his family, who immediately translate Eulalie to Hurere, a more pronounceable word, and question this woman's roots. Upon hearing the wife is American, Ato's mother, grandmother, uncles, aunts, and sister assume she must be white. They are disturbed at the prospect; one aunt suggests people will laugh at them for not knowing "the ways of the white people."[63] Ato assures them: "I say my wife is as black as we all are." This news is met with "*Sighs of relaxation*."[64] The family can't relax for long, for the news that Eulalie is a descendant of slaves is an even worse state of affairs.

The cover displays the following text:

CHRISTINA AMA ATA AIDOO

$1.25

AFRICAN/AMERICAN LIBRARY

THE DILEMMA OF A GHOST

The Black American Dream confronts its African Heritage
in a classically wrought, contemporary drama.

125 ST

Figure 2.3. *Dilemma of a Ghost* by Ama Ata Aidoo, Collier Books, 1971, African/
American Series. (Image courtesy of Josh McPhee)

ATO: Please, I beg you all, listen. Eulalie's ancestors were of our ancestors. But . . . as you know, the white people came and took some away
in ships to be slaves . . .

NANA: And so, my grand-child, all you want to tell us is that your
wife is a slave? [*At this point even the men get up with shock
from their seats. All the women break into violent weeping.* ESI
KOM *is beside herself in grief. She walks around in all attitudes of
mourning.*]

ATO: [*Wildly*] But she is not a slave. It was her grandfathers and grand-
mothers who were slaves.

NANA: Ato, do not talk with the foolishness of your generation.[65]

Ato's mother, Esi Kom, mourns as if her son were dead. Ato's grandmother calls it modern foolishness to think a descendant of slaves is not
also a slave. Images of family roots, the fruits of wombs, and sewn seeds
vegetate much of this play; throughout, tradition and reproduction are
joined in the village imagination. That this ancient family line would
end in slavery is a tragedy to all of Ato's convened relatives.

Beyond Ato's family, the talk in the town is generally disapproving.
Like the chorus in *Edufa*, two women of the town offer analyses of the
unfolding events of *The Dilemma of a Ghost*, imbuing this mechanism
of Greek theater with an African communal ethical sensibility. This sensibility reveals itself in Aidoo's play as "a pair of women, your neighbors,
chattering their lives away."[66] These observations are the result of local
gossip rather than any unanimous perspective. Sandra Richards reminds
us that this dilemma genre "aims for the messiness of community pa-
laver or talk that may stop without validating any position."[67] These
messy observations begin scene 2 as the pair of women review the turn
of events, regretting that Ato had not married an educated local girl, as
had been arranged.

2nd W: And that is the sad part of it, my sister.
He has not taken this girl
Whom we all know and like,
But has gone for this
Black-white woman.
A stranger and a slave—[68]

From the village perspective, Eulalie is a paradoxical figure; she is both black and white, foreign and all too familiar. Eulalie's subsequent run-ins with the family create cultural misunderstandings that produce further grounds for disapproval. But before Eulalie has met any of these Africans, her status as a slave has preceded her. Slavery is the ghost that haunts this play. The difficulty of modern black identity is its dilemma. Aidoo, who treats slavery again in her later play *Foriwa*, disrupts the unifying mythos of Pan-Africanism by exposing this most sensitive of subjects. Aidoo presses against this sensitivity in the time and place of a utopian experiment in black reconciliation taking place in the nation's capital. As accounts including Hartman's illustrate, black Americans at the time did not find it easy to assimilate into Ghanaian culture; it is common today for Ghanaians to call local black Americans *obruni*, a Twi term that is both derisive and indifferent, meaning both foreigner and white. While the ideology of liberation includes a transnational solidarity among blacks of the diaspora, cultural differences among blacks have made this a practical difficulty in the local context.

The ghost of slavery appears in the play through an appropriated children's song. Aidoo has cited this song, one she remembers from her childhood in the coastal town of Takoradi, as the first inspiration for the play. In the play, the song is sung by children in the street, it recurs to Ato in a dream of his own childhood, and is heard again at the end.

> One early morning,
> When the moon was up
> Shining as the sun,
> I went to Elmina Junction
> And there and there,
> I saw a wretched ghost
> Going up and down
> Singing to himself
> "Shall I go
> To Cape Coast,
> Or to Elmina
> I don't know,
> I can't tell.

> I don't know,
> I can't tell."[69]

The song describes a point between two neighboring towns on Ghana's southern coast, Cape Coast and a smaller fishing town to its west, Elmina. More than just proximity, these towns share a history dominated by the huge slave fortresses that each abuts. Among the oldest existing European structures south of the equator, each had been used by a series of imperial occupants until landing in the hands of the British; finally, after independence, they were inherited by the Ghanaian state. Another castle fortress in Accra has been the seat of the government since the mid-nineteenth century. These giant white structures hover over their towns like ghosts. While their architecture attests to a brutal history of exporting Africans, the castles at Cape Coast and Elmina are also, ironically, tourist sites that attract blacks from around the world. As such, visitors enter dank holding pens, gaze beyond narrow doors-of-no-return through which emaciated salves were sent to waiting ships, sit atop rusty cannons, and visit the gift shop (at the time of my visit in 2009, Barack Obama's book *Dreams of My Father* was prominently displayed). Today, these castles provide tourism revenue for Ghana, much of which comes from diasporic blacks.

As Sandra Richards has explored, this prominent display of slave history contradicts Ghanaian sensibilities. In her study of tourism at these sites, Richards notes, "Slavery is not integral to how most Ghanaians define themselves. To attract tourists, Ghanaians must remember a history they learned to forget. . . . Until relatively recently, slavery was not a subject taught in Ghanaian school or transmitted orally in informal settings."[70] Richards describes Aidoo as among the few "artists and other cultural workers [who] have broken this taboo," citing both *The Dilemma of a Ghost* and *Anowa*. In the former play, Aidoo's children's song reveals slavery as the fortress in the room, weighing heavily on the memories of diasporic blacks and pressing against the forgetfulness of Ghanaians. Ato's family will more readily identify with ancestral elites who profited from slavery than with a contemporary black American whose ancestors were slaves.

Nor is Eulalie prepared to assimilate to the Fanti culture of her in-laws. Her many episodes of misunderstanding contribute to the alienation between her and Ato's family. Primary among these is the controversy around the couple's decision not to have children immediately. But other obstacles include Eulalie's dietary differences, her frequent drinking and smoking (which grow more frequent as her alienation becomes more acute), her use of expensive modern machines like a refrigerator, her lack of deference to her husband, and all the signs of her Westernness. Even without the pressures of conforming to a traditionalist role, Eulalie has many misperceptions of her own to overcome.

> EULALIE: Can't you hear?
> ATO: Ah, what is it?
> EULALIE: Can't you hear the drums?
> ATO: [*Cocks his ears*] Oh, those!
> EULALIE: Aren't you afraid? I am.
> ATO: Don't be absurd, darling. [*Holds her close*] But I thought that one thing which attracted you about Africa was that there is a lot of drumming here.
> EULALIE: [*Relaxes and thinks*] Y–e–s. But, you know, I didn't guess they'll be sort of like this.
> ATO: You thought they would sound like jazz?
> EULALIE: Sure. Or rather like, you know, sort of Spanish mambo.[71]

Eulalie is from Harlem, and speaks through Aidoo's awkward interpretation of a black American vernacular dialect. In Eulalie's limited experience, Ghana may as well be Spain; both are exotic to a Harlemite. Strikingly, though the dialogue is in English, Eulalie and her in-laws can't actually understand each other. In all matters of communication, they depend on Ato as an intermediary.

Eulalie's black American consciousness is a kind of Du Boisian double consciousness. In an experimental section of act 2, Eulalie has an internal dialogue with her own deceased mother—her mother's ghost—while she sips a Coca-Cola. Here she reveals a family tradition of self-awareness as racial other. She recalls looking in the mirror and rejecting dreams of looking like "them Hollywood tarts."[72] Eulalie cites her Native Boy as proof that she has been able to overcome the black self-hate facilitated by American racism. This meets with her mother's approval. Such expressions of racial uplift accompany Eulalie's anti-traditional modernity. Her displacement—as a black American in America, as a young woman whose own mother has died, as a black American in Africa—contributes to an empowering mobility of rootlessness that she brings to this Ghanaian scene. This progressiveness is tied to Eulalie's feminism, which has manifested in her reproductive self-determination. Eulalie is a kind of avant-garde: her internal dialogue—her double consciousness—constitutes the most formally unusual part of the play. Aidoo's stage direction indicates that Eulalie sits on stage while her and her mother's voices are heard in disembodied form. The note in the text also offers an alternate and simpler possibility, one in which Eulalie speaks in soliloquy and her mother's voice is heard from offstage. While the second option is less technical, they both demonstrate an untraditional theatrics.

In the end, Ato, the intermediary figure, has failed to bridge the differences that have framed him. He cannot facilitate cohesion between his African family and his American wife, nor can he maintain their permanent opposition. The family's anger at Eulalie stands in for their anger at Ato, whose masculine transnationalism has disparaged his mother's African traditions and marginalized his American wife. Eulalie, who becomes increasingly drunk, finally erupts:

> EULALIE: . . . Ain't I poorer here as I would ave been in New York City? [*In pathetic imitation of* Ato] "Eulalie, my people say it is not good for a woman to take alcohol. Eulalie, my people say they are not pleased to see you smoke . . . Eulalie, my people say . . . My people . . . My people . . ." Damned rotten coward of a Moses. [Ato *winces*.] I have been drinking in spite of what your people say. [*She sits on the terrace facing the audience.*] Who married me, you or your goddam people?[73]

Eulalie's act of mimicry mocks village unanimity, as she unleashes impious insults at Ato. Her final stage direction places her in a confrontational relationship with the audience, as she addresses the very people she curses in her speech. Ato's ambivalent attitudes throughout the play have resulted in a cultural crisis. At the end of this episode, Ato strikes Eulalie. Shortly thereafter, one of the women mistakes Ato for a ghost in the dark. Ato, the One Scholar, forms an eerie double for the ghost of slavery that haunts the play. His diasporic circulation is the transnational experience that has emerged in wake of international slavery. But as an inversion of a negativity, his situation between modernity and tradition produces an absence rather than a synthesis. The conflict between his family and his wife has left the former poorer and the other the victim of violence. In the play's final scene, the women make a first attempt at direct communication, bypassing Ato altogether. His mother makes an admission: "[M]y son. You have not dealt with us well. And you have not dealt with your wife well in all of this."[74] Finally, deciding that Eulalie's mother's ghost must be watching all of this, Esi Kom begins to adopt her own transnational consciousness and welcomes Eulalie into her house. In the end, it will be women who suffer the most negative consequences of African modernity, and women must learn to speak across difference.

Aidoo's feminism is a prominent element of her literary voice, as her short stories and novels have also demonstrated. Many commentators have discussed the significance of Aidoo's character Sissie, the protagonist of her short novel of 1966, *Our Sister Killjoy or Reflections from a Black-eyed Squint*. Originally written the same year Nkrumah was deposed in a coup d'état, but not published until 1977, the novel follows Sissie as she travels abroad to Germany and England. In England, she provides a gendered consciousness to a meeting of male Ghanaian expatriates. As Elizabeth Willey has pointed out:

> Like Nkrumah, Sissie argues for the necessity of incorporating and subjugating parts of Western culture to serve the need of the African Personality. The African Personality is furthermore described as the only possible basis for a strong Ghana. However, Aidoo's narrative does not have a simple relationship to the legacy of nationalism in Ghana. Sissie shows her suspicion of the rhetoric of masculinity that accompanies nationalist programs by reminding the reader that power in many contexts has been coded as masculine control over women and that this dynamic has not been challenged by nationalist thinking in Ghana. The point comes through most strongly when she links the image of the slave castle's along Ghana's coast with the feudal castle looming over the German countryside.[75]

While it is the scene in England in which she attempts to reconcile African Personality with a gendered perspective, her experience in Germany speaks to differences that aren't easily resolved. Her close friendship with a young Bavarian woman results in an awkward lesbian encounter, one that illustrates uncomfortably the differences gender and sexuality introduce into subjectivity. The German woman's life as a young small-town wife and mother reveals to Sissie the difficulties of white women's experiences, just as Sissie's racial difference instigates libera-tory possibilities in the mind of the Bavarian. Their limited connection depicts a transnational feminist relationship, one that is left unresolved when Sissie travels away. The relationship enables a transgressive imagi-nation in Sissie, as she wonders to herself what it would be like to be a man and what a romantic relationship with Maria might be like. Maria later acts upon this mutual fantasy, as she tries to kiss Sissie. Though Sissie is finally disapproving of the Bavarian's provisional lesbianism, a move that tends to frame her sexuality as a Western vice, its representa-tion in this context reveals an anti-normative African encounter unusual in literature of the continent. That Sissie can neither conform to this woman's German sexuality nor to the self-interested transnationalism of her male compatriots in England reveals differences on all sides of this protagonist's experience. While exploring the possibility of communi-cation across difference, these relationships also illustrate how difficult cultural differences can be to overcome. Beginning with *The Dilemma of a Ghost*, these themes have formed the foundation of Aidoo's literary work.

Conclusion

Edufa and *Foriwa* by Efua Sutherland and *The Dilemma of a Ghost* by Ama Ata Aidoo elaborate a critical, rather than utopian, vision of Afri-can subjectivity. In these works, local content, European forms, and transnational political perspectives are suspended in a field of relations, never fully resolving into each other. Differences remain and produce enduring conflicts. By staging black subjectivities in conflict, these plays demonstrate that modernity and tradition are themselves notions fraught with contradiction, and produce ambivalences that exceed the boundaries of the nation-state. Ghanaian statehood created the space for this critical position, instigating a theater that spoke against the colonial era's prohibitions. These combinations of differences, set in tension between ideas of progress and continuity, form a provisional position from which to speak, a position which resists the masculinist state of synthesis in which difference is obliterated. The discomfort of difference is always present within these dramas and this discomfort must continually be encountered in the experience of black transnationalism.

3

The Radical Ambivalence of Günther Kaufmann

Then, and more especially, immigration, which divides the
workers into two groups: the native-born and the foreigners,
and the latter turn into (1) the Irish, (2) the Germans, (3) the
many small groups, each of which understands only itself:
Czechs, Poles, Italians, Scandinavians, etc. And then the Ne-
groes. To form a single party out of these requires quite unusually powerful incentives. Often there is a sudden violent
élan, but the bourgeois need only wait passively and the dis-
similar elements of the working class fall apart again.
—Friedrich Engels

But what she also came to know was that someone somewhere would always see in any kind of difference, an excuse
to be mean.
—Ama Ata Aidoo

Ich bin doch auch ein Mensch.
—Marieluise Fleißer

Introduction

Rainer Werner Fassbinder's body of work was constructed through a
transgressive practice of mixing: of performance forms, labor modes,
literary sources, and messages. Fassbinder himself mixed sexually and
emotionally with the members of his troupe, enlisting their energies into
a perpetual mix of life and work. Fassbinder's promiscuous mixing contributes to his work's radical ambivalence. His plays and films reflected
a Bavarian situation informed by an international counterculture movement, national traditions inclusive of both fascism and leftist theater, and
the experience of West Germany in the throes of its post-war "economic

miracle." These sources formed a basis for adaptation, a set of materials critically reassembled in order to agitate against bourgeois sensibilities. While Fassbinder deployed leftist strategies, texts, and tropes, the often campy works just as often indicate the limitations of Marxist analysis or radical action against the state. This radical ambivalence is animated by the scenario of difference that is at the heart of each of Fassbinder's narratives; his characters reside at a nexus of gender, sexuality, and race that distorts the dynamic of class oppression. At the same time, they mobilize a highly critical politics of difference that denounces West Germany's post-Nazi order. Their differences theatricalize oppression and radicalize the work.

Within Fassbinder's oeuvre, the black Bavarian actor Günther Kaufmann serves as a particularly visible site of the collapsing of race, class, gender, and sexuality into a radicalized character. In a series of Fassbinder's early films and television productions, Kaufmann consistently problematizes the representation of national identity with his German blackness, contributing bodily to those works' ambivalence. Kaufmann plays an important role in the development of a politicized performance mode deployed by Fassbinder. The practice of political theater sets the primal scene for Kaufmann's relationship with the director; the pair met in 1969 while acting in a television version of Brecht's *Baal* directed by Volker Schlöndorff. Following that encounter, Kaufmann became a common feature of Fassbinder's work. He performed finally in Fassbinder's last film, *Querelle*, based on Jean Genet's novel, in 1982. In this performance, Kaufmann portrays an African barkeep who penetrates the male protagonist during a scene of aggressive anal sex. Like he does in *Querelle*, Kaufmann typically serves to radicalize each situation with his raced, sexualized body, enacting an insistent imbrication of these culturally inscribed categories.

Kaufmann introduces blackness into Fassbinder's field of representation, offering a polyvalent sign that helps destabilize a presumed fixity of German cultural identity. As with Sissie, Ama Ata Aidoo's protagonist discussed in the previous chapter, the hyper-visibility of blackness in the German context both confirms and distorts ontological racial ideas around which modern identities have been oriented. As in the other national contexts discussed here, black representation marshals the energies of difference. That difference is politicized both in relation to

local histories of racial subjugation, and also the transnational distribu-
tion of blackness as a countercultural force, which by the late sixties had
achieved global symbolic significance as a mode that had facilitated real
revolutionary actions. As each chapter in this study has explored, European contexts have been important laboratories for the intellectual and
imaginative experiments of diasporic blacks. The German philosophical
tradition was a direct influence on W.E.B. Du Bois, who studied in Berlin before embarking on his sociological studies of black American life.
Trinidadian George Padmore published a newspaper in Cologne before
going on serve in the Soviet Politburo and later helping to found independent Ghana. Much later, black artists and writers including Audre
Lorde, Adrian Piper, and Vaginal Davis have worked from Berlin, reflecting that city's status as a transnational meeting point. The image
of American runner Jesse Owens standing on a platform above athletes
offering a Nazi salute at the 1936 Olympics offers a potent symbol of
the ways blackness has antagonized modern ideologies. This history
of imagination and resistance is a feature of the blackness Kaufmann
brings to his German context, even as it was constrained by the German
racism with which Fassbinder was concerned. In his film and television
work, Kaufmann's racialized body is an agent of radical ambivalence, a
critical position that meets authority with unresolved multiplicity.

The potential of radical ambivalence is its ability to renegotiate the
terms of resistance to powers that are equipped to assimilate opposition.
Its multi-directionality provides a critical flexibility that capably meets
the varied, sometimes contradictory ideologies, legal structures, and
economic positions that support the form of global capitalism that invested in West Germany after World War II, an economic success story
mainly shaped by U.S. subvention and intervention through the Mar-
shall Plan. Fassbinder's practice of radical ambivalence dispersed the site
of opposition; it refused to affirm a binary understanding of power and
its lack, locating rather a field of power and complicity that shaped the
layered forms of oppression that pressed against differences. While effectively resistant to the norms of the West German state, Fassbinder's
radicality can also be disappointingly ambiguous. In Fassbinder's work,
many critics have found it difficult to locate a solution-oriented politics
in what Kaja Silverman has called "Fassbinder's radical refusal to affirm,
his repudiation of positivity in any shape or form."[1] As in his uses of the

actor Günther Kaufmann, who never performs an unproblematic image of black positivity, Fassbinder's ambivalence highlights the indifferences, cruel ironies, and failures that dominate the most marginal participants in his social world. The work's "refusal to affirm" resists the positivity of growth imagined in the post-war economic ideology, one that not only transformed West Germany into a capitalist power, but divided East from West in a global Cold War strategy. This global force's negative effects act upon individual, personal situations in Fassbinder's work. His own response to this negativity has been to point to its unsatisfying political function: "People often criticize my films for being pessimistic. There are certainly plenty of reasons for being pessimistic, but I don't see my films that way. . . . I never try to reproduce reality in a film. My goal is to reveal such mechanisms in a way that makes people realize the necessity of changing their own reality."[2] Fassbinder portrays oppressive mechanisms, but leaves the possibility of political solutions to the viewer's imagination. This non-programmatic approach, indicating a leftist critique without proposing efficacious action, is what Richard Dyer has called Fassbinder's "left-wing melancholy":

> [T]his is admittedly an imprecise term, referring broadly to a view of life that recognizes the exploitativeness of capitalist society but is unable to see any means by which a fundamental change in the society can take place. This melancholy is left-wing—and not just a general despair at the human condition—because it sees the specifically (historically determinant) capitalist source and character of misery in contemporary society and observes how the weight of oppression lies on the working class. In its "melancholy," however, it does not see the working class as the agent of historical change—instead it stresses the working class as the victim of capitalist society and/or as hopelessly complicit in its own oppression. The sexual-political version of this substitutes or adds, for the working class, women and gays.[3]

And, as Dyer neglects to mention, the racial-political version of this process adds black characters and foreign guest workers to the complex of class, gender, and sexuality identified above. While Dyer laments the hopelessness of Fassbinder's portrayals, this critical overlaying of

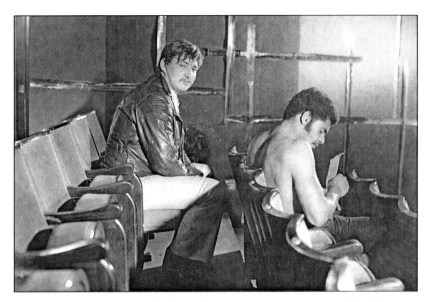

Figure 3.1. Rainer Werner Fassbinder and Günther Kaufmann, cinema, Munich, 1971, photo by Michael Friedel.

different, incommensurate historical structures, this ambivalent view of oppression, may be the fundamental change Fassbinder proposes in his plays and films.

The political program is verified in Fassbinder's formal approach, as the critic Peter Iden wrote of Fassbinder's early work with the antiteater company:

> What's striking in the mass of films is also evident in the theater work to date: an overflowing talent, prolific to the point of self injury, confused, but energetically switching material, style and aesthetic position. . . . [As] far as Fassbinder's theatre work is concerned, one confronts an "oeuvre" that refuses to be pinned down and defined as an entity, but rather presents itself as a series of disparate statements. Hasty, stark productions, often put together in minimal time under great pressure. Quixotic stories about plays and their performances, inadequate preparation and inconsequential realization to match . . . anyone who talks about Fassbinder and the theatre has to take these aspects into account too.[4]

The critics of Fassbinder's politics are met by the critics of his aesthetic. Here, a dispersed production apparatus, relying on collaboration, adaptation, and an "energetic switching," portrays a kind of formal ambivalence that also refuses positivity. While the disparateness of Fassbinder's oeuvre produces problems of formal and political legibility, it is this constant management of multiple differences that is Fassbinder's most radical innovation. Rather than arriving at any singular, centered version of art or life, Fassbinder's plays and films reflect a history mobilized by differences.

Theater and antiteater

Though Kaufmann was the first black actor to figure prominently in Fassbinder's work, the staging of ethnic difference precedes his appearance. *Katzelmacher*, which premiered at Munich's Büchner Theater in April 1968, was the first play Fassbinder wrote for his antiteater company, conveying the founding and consistent role that ethnic difference played among his primary considerations. *Katzelmacher* stages the anxieties that surface among a group of provincial characters when a Greek *Gastarbeiter*, Jorgos, arrives to work in their small Bavarian town. In a series of slow, petty exchanges among different groupings, the young men and women of the town's lumpenproletariat reenact the sexist, racist, and classist power struggles that keep them in perpetual stasis. Their xenophobia is amplified in the play's title, a derogatory term the group uses as a nickname for Jorgos, the implication of which is that he is a foreigner who has sex with cats, whose nonstandard ethnicity implicates aberrant sexuality. The men respond violently to his presence, threatening to "cut off his balls." The men also threaten regular violence against the women. The women perpetrate insidious gossip and are each either sexually pursuing Jorgos or making false sexual allegations against him. Everyone is confounded by his foreignness, which he himself emphasizes by pretending not to understand much of what is said. A bourgeois woman employs Jorgos in her business and later comes on to him, spurring further resentment. Short, economical scenes reminiscent of the style of the playwright Marieluise Fleißer, to whom the published script is dedicated, convey a series of interactions in which power differentials produce negative results.

While broad patterns of oppression are visible in all of the play's relationships, the characters' own apparent complicity in their oppression
makes a tangled mess of the ethical questions. In a twist near the play's
end, after the young men have finally attacked the *Gastarbeiter*, Jorgos
claims he is unwilling to work with incoming Turkish workers and says
he will move to another town. Jorgos, the victim of ethnic violence, appears to harbor ethnic prejudices. The women perpetuate the violent
attitudes of the men, while it is a woman who safeguards capitalist production in the town, fixing its multi-tiered class structure. The faceted
nature of this structure facilitates its own perpetuation: There is no distinct binary of worker and exploiter that would produce revolutionary
action according to a Marxist model. Ethnicity, gender, sexuality, and a
polyvalent notion of class all apply different pressures to this local situation. *Katzelmacher* begins a critical engagement in Fassbinder's work
with imagining the negative possibilities that manifest under these
pressures.

The play's narrative responds to what was a striking demographic
shift in Germany, the influx of workers from southern Europe, North Africa, and Turkey. Writing about *Katzelmacher*, Fassbinder scholar David
Barnett notes: "Gastarbeiter were brought into West Germany in great
numbers in the sixties as a response to a shortage of manual labourers.
By 1972, there were 3.5 million resident foreigners, or roughly 5 per cent
of the population. Fassbinder was the first dramatist to approach the
topic and he did so in a style which was typically ambivalent: the statuses
of perpetrator and victim, which are central roles in the play, do not
yield to negative and positive values, respectively."[5] Barnett identifies
the play's unusual attention to this striking social reality. West Germany,
aligned with the economics of the U.S., its former occupier, had joined a
Euro-American capitalist system, producing significant national wealth
in the generation following the war. Its move toward globalism enlisted
the transnational flow of labor. The guest workers produced not only
commodities, but also demographic changes in a state with a racial history that was troubled, to say the least. In responding to this, Barnett
reads ambivalence in Fassbinder's "style," conflating, appropriately, a political question with an aesthetic one. In *Katzelmacher*, the untidy relations among various sorts of workers demonstrates the complexity their
differences bring to the problem of exploitation. This play elaborates the

group's signature "style," which uses an alienating theatrical presentation to both engage and estrange an underlying social commitment.

The social inquiry of *Katzelmacher* indicates the political context that shaped the early development of antiteater productions. *Katzelmacher* emerged from Munich's Action-Theater, as Fassbinder's loyal faction of that company was beginning to form the antiteater group. The Action-Theater, and later the antiteater, were part of a politicized environment in which practices of theater and resistance were informing each other. While ideas of resistance informed the entire group's effort, it was actually an anti-Fassbinder faction that was more politically radical. The theater's co-founder Horst Söhnlein—perhaps anticipating the ambivalence of Fassbinder's politics—was dissatisfied with the more theatrically professional turn the company had taken under his influence. In an incident shortly before the premiere of *Katzelmacher* in 1968, Söhnlein destroyed the theater's equipment and parted with the group as he set out to burn down a department store in Frankfurt. Andreas Baader was a collaborator in this department store incident, which proved to be a test run for the Baader-Meinhoff group,[6] the well-known radicals. David Barnett argues that theatrical tactics contributed to the Baader-Meinhoff's arsenal, particularly evident in their anti-normative "performances" while on trial.[7] Theater and politics were in dialogue in Munich, but these politics produced ambivalent responses from Fassbinder himself; he later expressed a mix of admiration and dismissive pity for the Baader-Meinhoff. Ironically, around this time, Fassbinder took his first starring movie role in a military training film, *Schuldig oder nicht schuldig (Guilty or Not Guilty)*, in which he plays a soldier charged with violent insubordination.[8] Söhnlein's suspicions were justified; while exploring leftist performance strategies with the theater company, Fassbinder, as Barnett points out, was secretly collaborating with state power, a contradiction characteristic of Fassbinder's work.

Another collaborator in the Frankfurt department store action was Thorwald Proll, who had shortly before appeared as an actor in *The Connection* at the Forum Theater in Berlin, a play popularized by the Living Theatre, an American company whose co-founder Judith Malina was herself German. The Living Theatre's anarchic theater was an important influence on the antiteater as well. Fassbinder first joined the Action-Theater as an actor in 1967, after having seen the group's radical reinterpretation of *Antigone*, a reaction to the Living Theatre's version of the same story. The American experimental theater troupe had been based in Europe since 1963, had prominently aligned with the student resistance in Paris in 1968, and was well received by German audiences thereafter. The earlier production of *Antigone* evoked what Fassbinder would later describe as "something like a trance between the actors and the audience, something like a collective desire for revolutionary uto-pia."[9] Directed by Peer Raben, a close Fassbinder associate, the produc-tion was anti-individualistic, dispersing its text among various chorus members, which even included some "local hippies."[10] Raben's produc-tion critiqued both the bourgeois theater's penchant for "the centrality of the individual" and the broader issue of state violence, with the war in Vietnam looming as an obvious backdrop.[11] Complementing the Living Theatre's countercultural model, the hippie zeitgeist, with its focus on collectivity and its anarchic approach to revolutionary politics, formed an influential milieu. But even in this early production, structured lan-guage seems to have sublimated some of the hippie liberation; Barnett describes *Antigone* as having merged the Living Theatre's Artaudian physicality and a more textual approach that incorporated elements of Bertolt Brecht's version of the myth.[12] While the radicality of the Living Theatre served as an inspiration for this theater, a textual criticality as-sociated with Brecht comes to temper transcendent fantasies, an imposi-tion which is in full effect by the time of *Katzelmacher*.

Further reflecting the Living Theatre's influence, the antiteater staged Fassbinder's original play *Pre-Paradise Sorry Now* in 1969, which both engaged with and critiqued that group's revolutionary ethos. Fassbinder adapted the true-crime story of the English Moors Murders, set around a famous pair of child killers, as a context within which to question the utopian possibilities raised by the Living Theatre's *Paradise Now*. The documentation of *Paradise Now*, compiled by Malina and the troupe's other co-founder, Julian Beck, makes the claim that "[t]he play is a voy-age from the many to the one and from the one to the many . . . the voy-age is a vertical ascent toward Permanent Revolution. The Revolution of which the play speaks is the Beautiful Non-Violent Anarchist Revolu-tion."[13] The Living Theatre combined spiritual and political models of transcendence, offering performance that leads to a utopian end. Fass-binder critiques this position, as Denis Calandra points out, in the very title of his play: "Fassbinder's choice of an English title for *Pre-Paradise Sorry Now* places it firmly in its era. It was anti-Living Theater, the direct reference being to the American group's Paradise Now. Though Action Theater and antiteater seemed to share, theoretically at least, the ethos of collective creation and a vague yearning for anarchic freedom, Fassbinder's play clearly mocks the idea of ever achieving paradise, now *or* later."[14] Though Fassbinder seemed to appreciate the utopian longings apparent in the *Antigone* production, *Pre-Paradise Sorry Now* is ambivalent about the notion of transcendence via radicalized consciousness. The title makes clear that the certainty of the present precludes such fantasies for the future.

The international influence represented in the Living Theatre was met by a reliance on a local Bavarian sensibility in the early antiteater productions, a sensibility that marked Fassbinder's own difference. This local element is evident in the Bavarian settings and personalities of *Katzelmacher*. Though that play was performed, paradoxically, in proper German, many antiteater productions used Bavarian German, something that playwright Marieluise Fleißer described as not a dialect but "a set of South-German verbal attitudes."[15] Indeed, years later, upon hearing of Fassbinder's death, filmmaker Werner Herzog said that Fassbinder "wasn't a German at all but a wild Bavarian."[16] This Bavarianness is mobilized ethnically in many of Fassbinder's works, performing as a kind of subculture to the dominant West German society. Attendant tropes of Catholicism, the prevailing Bavarian religion, are imaged across many of the plays and films, particularly in rituals of suffering and sacrifice. Fassbinder described having been drawn to this set of religious images despite having not been raised in the Catholic Church—he claimed to be more influenced by the ideas of Rudolf Steiner, having attended a Steiner school as a child.[17] Even Steiner's ideas, a set of experimental theories about sound, rhythm, and space that Sue-Ellen Case has described as a "performative system that enacted an observant, intersubjective relationship to the social and to the environmental,"[18] could be seen as contributing to a mixed framework of radicality for Fassbinder's theater.

Forecasting difficult roles such as those Kaufmann would play, the early antiteater elaborated a political aesthetic, manifest in critical performance techniques and a countercultural situation. As Fassbinder's own portrayal of Jorgos in the company's 1969 film version of *Katzel-*

macher indicates, these politics were not only imagined by Fassbinder, but also enacted. Both the film and play begin to express his ambivalent mode, critical to the point of pessimism, estranged to the point of total detachment. They each maintain an economy of language reminiscent of both Fleißer, the subject of renewed interest during the "Fleißer-boom"[19] instigated by Fassbinder and his contemporaries, and the *Volksstück* (folk piece) tradition she innovated; *Katzelmacher* itself was understood as a *Volksstück* by some critics. In directing *Katzelmacher* for theater and film, Fassbinder pursued a slow, deliberate pace, a central technique throughout his works. He later describes this slow pace as producing "a kind of alienation. I approach the subject of a scene like this; when the scene lasts a long time, when it's drawn out, then the audience can really see what is happening between the characters involved."[20] This tactic, which in Fassbinder's films is framed by estranging compositions and long intervals between edits, allows for a critical distance between the presentation of the scenario and the moral understanding of the events, a distance that resembles the critical estrangements of Brecht's Epic Theater.

A Brechtian influence is evident in the anti-psychological performance technique used in *Katzelmacher* and other early antiteater productions. This technique took cues from Brecht's distancing methods, featuring in actors "attitudes, not characterizations."[21] The actress Hanna Schygulla, whom Fassbinder brought into the company in 1967, described working with Fassbinder when they were in acting school together. She recalled a version of John Gay's text that Brecht had adapted for his *Threepenny Opera*, remembering: "We acted together quite well, he as Mackie Messer and I as Polly in a Fassbinder version of *The Beggars' Opera* in Bavarian."[22] Schygulla describes the pair acting with "an entire alphabet of gestures (*Gesten*)."[23] From the start, elements of Brecht's Epic Theater are evident, including the centrality of adaptation and a gestic acting technique.

These methods came to form an acting orthodoxy in Fassbinder's work. Actress Ingrid Caven, who performed in early stage productions including *Katzelmacher*, later described the group's acting methods: "Rainer loved Brecht and Chinese tradition. . . . That approach was basically what brought me to my profession. Trying to appear 'natural' in front of a camera would have seemed simply grotesque."[24] This film technique, relying on Brechtian stage acting rather than the interiorizing of realism, was developed in the early antiteater, where actors including Caven and Schygulla were Fassbinder's collaborators. Of course, Brecht's own theory of "Chinese acting" indicated an estranged mode defamiliarized by racial difference; it would be "grotesque" for a German woman to act Chinese in any naturalistic way. Caven's association of Brecht with "Chinese tradition" indicates the politicizing valence a racial notion has exerted on German leftist theater. Like other experimental European dramatists of the early twentieth century, Brecht sought radicalizing anti-normativity in an extra-European source. As discussed in chapter 1, Brecht's *Verfremdungseffekt* makes an association between racial difference and the estrangement from veracious European feelings, an important element of his epic tradition adapted by Fassbinder and the antiteater.

The *Ingolstadt* Example

Brecht was an influence on the playwright Marieluise Fleißer as well, according to her own account.[25] The connections and tensions between Brecht's theater and Fleißer's are relevant to a consideration of the antiteater, and the way Günther Kaufmann's own difference would eventually appear. Both Brecht and Fleißer are considered significant parts of the pre-war German legacy taken up by artists of Fassbinder's post-war generation, and provide templates for critical theater adapted in *Katzelmacher* and other works. The differences between their two dramaturgical approaches are evidenced in Fassbinder's adaptations of Fleißer's *Pioneers in Ingolstadt*, first in 1968 as the play *Ingolstadt, for Example*, and then in 1970 as the television film *Pioneers in Ingolstadt* in which Kaufmann plays a prominent role. Fleißer wrote the original version of the play in 1926, and it was rewritten under Brecht's direction for a production at his Schiffbauerdamm Theater in 1929, starring Peter Lorre. It was the second Brecht production, after the writer's own *Threepenny Opera* adaptation, to appear at this theater. In the appendix of "Short Description of a New Technique of Acting," he describes it as one of the plays in which the development of his famous alienation effect took place.[26] Many scholars have noted the difficulties Fleißer experienced under Brecht's tutelage. Particularly, Brecht insisted upon changes to *Pioneers in Ingolstadt* in order to diminish the play's emotional foundation. He also insisted upon salacious sex scenes, which produced a terrible scandal after the play's Berlin premiere. Carmel Finnan describes the "anti-feminist"[27] strain in the discourse of the time, which not only subordinated Fleißer to men like Brecht, but made her the target of vitriolic conservative attacks that implicated her gender in the perceived moral depravity of *Pioneers in Ingolstadt*. While the controversy served Brecht's purposes, it was damaging to Fleißer's career and to her personally. In his own turn to Fleißer, Fassbinder replicates some aspects of Brecht's exploitative relationship with the author; Fleißer, for example, threatened to sue the Action-Theater for staging her play without her permission.[28] But Fassbinder's interest brought renewed attention to Fleißer's dramaturgy. In claiming her influence, Fassbinder was able to adapt one of her crucial contributions: a critical exploration of gender.

Pioneers in Ingolstadt follows the arrival of uniformed military engineers in a small Bavarian town, where they are commissioned with building a bridge. This town is Ingolstadt, Fleißer's own provincial home, which is also the pastoral setting of a historic military base. Two young working-class women, Berta and Alma, pursue the visiting soldiers, one seeking love, the other seeking advantage. The difference between the bourgeois fantasy of love and the exploitative economics of sexual relations come into stark relief as the women follow different paths. Exploitation plays out through class and gender dynamics, showing the ways that sexual desire infiltrates power relationships, and patriarchal structures compound women's experiences of class. These complications were eccentric to Brecht's masculinist Epic Theater, which asserts the primacy of capital in matters of oppression. Sue-Ellen Case has described the tension between Brecht and Fleißer that played out over *Pioneers in Ingolstadt*: "Not only did Brecht himself police Fleißer's text for a political dramaturgy that better fitted that traditional sense of public history and economy . . . but, theoretically, his strategies themselves are unfit to reveal the metonymic slippage of desire and its itineration through oppressive and liberatory mechanisms."[29] While Brecht's Epic Theater is "unfit" to reveal the personal politics of sexualities that interface with the larger social structures that contain individual experience, Fleißer's focus on these matters opens up a possible analysis of the gendered specificity that inhabits the broad economic history.

In evaluating the criticality fostered by both Brecht and Fleißer, Case explores their difference further: "Fleißer's plays are thus critical and 'distanced,' but not in the Brechtian sense. Whereas Brecht's distancing is mediated through an empirical presentation of material conditions, Fleißer's works through a critical representation of emotional relationships between men and women."[30] Though the mediating elements of Brecht's Epic Theater are diminished by Fleißer's emotionalism, Case argues for a different criticality inherent to Fleißer's approach, founded in gender. In *Ingolstadt*, Berta's emotional attachment to the soldier Korl is a function of both her desire to escape her job and her own sexual imagination, both of which are shaped by patriarchal economic forces. Their confluence thwarts Berta's ability to escape either. Dialogue in the play moves quickly from the price of wood to methods of sexual conquest. The distinction between historical and emotional dimensions is not clearly articulated.

Fleißer, who policed her own dramaturgy less strictly than Brecht, attributed this overlaying of critical lenses to her gender. Noting her mixture of epic and dramatic impulses, including her ability to situate emotion into the critical context, Fleißer herself claimed that "[a] woman does not have a deep relationship to a finely balanced structure."[31] Relying on some of the essentialist discourse that was so vehemently used against her, Fleißer suggests that her gendered perspective introduces a different politics that destabilizes a structure like historical materialism. Margaret Herzfeld-Sander elaborates: "Instead of Brecht's demand for a theater suited for the 'scientific age,' avoiding emotional identification and stressing an epic distance to eliminate 'unsavory intoxication,' [Fleißer] created a discourse focused on the internal, private passions and confusions of her characters in a narrow, provincial environment."[32] By the late sixties, when Fassbinder and his contemporaries were developing new methods, Brecht's historicism proved less equipped than Fleißer's emotional criticality to adequately address the evolving complexities of life at the margins of bourgeois society. Fleißer's "internal, private passions" allowed for subjectivity, bringing personal identity into the frame of social analysis.

Despite Fassbinder's "emotionalism," *Ingolstadt, for Example* pursued an alienated staging scheme. A photograph shows actors Irm Hermann, Kurt Raab (who is described by one writer as a "Peter Lorre imita-

THE RADICAL AMBIVALENCE OF GÜNTHER KAUFMANN | 109

tion"),[33] and a third performer arranged on a minimal set in an arbitrary triangular arrangement. Hermann wears lingerie and leather boots and poses suggestively with a riding crop, Raab stares listlessly into the distance while wearing what appear to be typical street clothes of the time, the third actor has her back turned to the camera while reading a text that she holds in her hands. Rather than the large group scene pictured in Brecht's production, and called for by Fleißer's text, Fassbinder isolates small interpersonal arrangements, typical of his constrained style. The action appears denaturalized and highly artificial. While drawing on the political possibilities engendered by Fleißer's critical emotionalism, Fassbinder resists allowing these to be read naturally, disallowing emotion to represent an authentic way of being.

The movie version of *Pioneers in Ingolstadt* provides a more convincing *mise-en-scène* by virtue of its real Bavarian locations. However, Fassbinder's slow pace and the theatricality of the mixed-period costumes provide the viewer with distance from the reality of the story. What is perhaps most denaturalizing about the film is the appearance of Günther Kaufmann as one of the military engineers. The black actor plays a friend of Karl, Berta's love interest, played by Harry Bär. Kaufmann's character, Max, most resembles Münsterer in Fleißer's script, a supporting character who pursues Berta after Korl has dumped her. While the script only implies of Münsterer's origins that he is from Münster, Max complicates this character-who-is-not-from-here with a maximum of racial difference. With this imposition, Fassbinder radically decenters the situation, creates further social alienations, and instigates other difficult sexual complications. Brecht emphasized class and Fleißer problematized that analysis with gender; Fassbinder further disorders the "finely balanced structure" by introducing a black man into the mix of *Ingolstadt*.

Despite Kaufmann's visibility, the other characters do not remark upon Max's racial difference. This suggests that though Kaufmann is black, maybe Max is not. Kaufmann could be simply playing the part, as any other German actor would, without regard to his race. This could explain why no one finds it awkward that Max, like the other soldiers, wears a uniform that includes a swastika. The film's non-military costumes present a theatrical anachronism throughout, mixing hip sixties dresses in thirties patterns with Bavarian provincial attire, conjuring, along with the uniforms, a time that is at once pre-, mid-, and post-war. This device makes the historical moment unspecific, while allowing Germany's fascist history to resonate into the present. It's also possible in this anachronistic context that Max is indeed understood as black, that his race is a part of the historical conflation of post-war capitalism with National Socialist life. Berta obviously prefers Karl to Max; his blackness helps explain his subordinate position. It is also remotely plausible that Max would be treated normally as a normal black Nazi; Tina Campt's illuminating study *Other Germans* documents a black German man who had served both in the Hitler Youth and in the German army during the invasion of the Soviet Union.[34] While black Germans were sterilized and marginalized in Nazi Germany, they also were in many instances, unlike German Jews, permitted to exist in some carefully restricted ways. A number of Afro-Germans in fact acted in colonial fantasy films in the 1940s. As one actress described it: "We earned good money, had fun, and didn't have too many qualms about it. At most it occurred to us once in a while that they could knock us mulattoes off while making a movie, all at one time. But where would they have gotten other Africans?"[35] This peculiar occupation precedes Kaufmann's own as a black German actor. Blackness has elsewhere in German history served ambivalent filmic purposes. His appearance in *Pioneers in Ingolstadt* invokes a German racial history that is already more complex than what purist ideologies could ever accommodate. Far from fitting comfortably into the *Ingolstadt* milieu, Kaufmann's presence in a Nazi military unit raises a number of difficult questions about race in Germany. By leaving his racial status unacknowledged, Fassbinder answers these questions with provocative silence.

Kaufmann's character finally becomes the most radical class agitator in town, fulfilling the extreme possibilities his marginal situation silently brings to the imagination. In a drawn out scene of abuse, Max leads a group of soldiers who beat a young entitled man, the son of Berta's employer, who is both aggressively snobbish and pathetically inadequate. Having drunkenly encountered the man on a dark street, Max smiles broadly as he and the others shove, punch, and kick him over three slow minutes, while the young man cries. Two scenes later, Kaufmann rows in a river with two other soldiers as their commanding officer stands at the front of their small boat. This officer has humiliated his subordinates

Figure 3.2. Harry Bär and Günther Kaufmann in a still from *Pioneers in Ingolstadt*, R. W. Fassbinder, 1971.

throughout the film. When they've reached a scenic spot, Max pushes the officer over. As he splashes around in the water crying for help, Max is seen in a picturesque long shot stomping on the man's head with his booted foot until he disappears beneath the water. In both of these cases, exploiters are vanquished by Max's violent act. In a town where not much else has happened, Max's dramatic actions spectacularize an idea of violent resistance. While Kaufmann's blackness is not explicitly addressed in *Pioneers in Ingolstadt*, it is Max, the black soldier, who is enlisted to perform the most radical possibilities.

These instances illuminate what turns out to be Fassbinder's consistent instrumentalization of Kaufmann as a radical agent, but also reveal something of Kaufmann's own acting mode as he is called upon to perform these transgressive acts. As is the case throughout Kaufmann's appearances, he commits resistant violence with glee, a broad smile across his distinctly handsome face, offering an unproblematic satisfaction with his sudden *élan*. While it is impossible to know where exactly

Fassbinder's direction ends and Kaufmann's intention begins, his is a performance technique that confidently assimilates the difficult social ruptures his differences facilitate. His outbursts of violence, sexy and satisfied, appear as a relief to the bleak repression that characterizes the rest of Fassbinder's world, and suggest that Kaufmann himself is enjoying the imaginary revolt.

Gods of the Plague and Afro-German Blood

Beginning in the 1969 film *Gods of the Plague*, Kaufmann performs the most radical acts. This film is the first in which the actor appears, driving in from the margins in a Volkswagen, as Franz, played by Harry Bär, and Margarethe, played by the filmmaker Margarethe von Trotta, walk down a Munich sidewalk. They have just bought a poster depicting Bavaria's King Ludwig II in an antique store. Franz had urged Margarethe to spend her money on his whim. The shopkeeper, who sits dramatically posed between two decorative black male nude figures, stares unmoving as she blithely comments, "a handsome man," referring ambiguously to Ludwig, Bär, or both. Bär agrees. An economic transaction ensues. Apparently angry that she had spent her money, Margarethe walks quickly down the street, nervously stroking the rolled up poster, the image of a mythic local patrimony, as Franz catches up with her. King Ludwig, Bavaria's last monarch, was known for outrageous excesses and for homosexual interests. His image signifies Munich's locality, an aristocratic class fantasy, and a queerness embedded in the provincial imagination. This is the context in which Franz and Günther first find each other.

Throughout the film up until this point, Bär's character, who was released from Munich's city jail in the first scene, has been going around town looking for someone called "the Gorilla." Ending this quest, Kaufmann drives past the camera, then drives back into the frame, then out again, and finally leaps in again. He and Franz greet each other affectionately; the pair smile with a tenderness rarely seen in Fassbinder films as they hug, tussle, and nuzzle their faces into each other's necks. He is the elusive Gorilla, Franz's criminal associate, who has exceeded the margins of this representation from his first appearance, driving in and out of the edge of the frame. Once his blackness is recognized, his nickname, which had preceded him, completes an uncomfortable racial association. Earlier, in a bathroom roulette parlor where Bär has mentioned the Gorilla, a sassy gay man asks, in American English, "Does he have a big cock?"[36] Before he is ever seen, this unanswered question anticipates Kaufmann's racial identity with a sexual stereotype, while also predicting his availability to a desiring male sexuality. Even before he appears, Günther's racial identity is invested with sexual energy. Later on, Margarethe asks Günther why he's called "the Gorilla." He quickly replies, "Because I'm big and strong and everyone has to have a name." In an understatement characteristic of Fassbinder's repressed language, Kaufmann's character sublimates the implicit violence of the name, while confirming its racist logic. His answer admits that his body authorizes the name, and it's his obligatorily.

Setting up the failed robbery at the climax of *Gods of the Plague*, Franz and Günther get a supermarket manager to let them inside his store after hours. Franz, who knows this clerk "from the old days," appears to have exploited the man's special fondness for him in order to create the possibility of a holdup. As the two follow the manager around the store, he takes his attention from Franz for only a moment to question Günther. "Where do you come here from?" the manager asks suspiciously. "From Bavaria," Günther replies with a mixture of amusement and pride. The manager responds incredulously, "What?" [37] The manager, who is soon after shot dead, finds Günther's identity dubious. His body doesn't seem to authorize his social script: it permits a racializing nickname but also originates in Bavaria. Biographer Robert Katz attributes Fassbinder with having "often" said in the presence of Kaufmann, that "Günther . . . thinks Bavarian, feels Bavarian, and speaks Bavarian. And that's why he gets a shock every morning when he looks in the mirror."[38] As if emphasizing this thought, the camera passes a mirror just as Günther has declared himself Bavarian, momentarily showing a reflection of Franz's face. Mirrors are used frequently in *Gods of the Plague* and throughout all of Fassbinder's films, alienating the actors from the camera, reducing their identities to spectacular surfaces, and redirecting the power of the gaze. In this flash of Franz's more plausibly German face, his differences emphasize Günther's embodied paradox, disrupting the assumed unity of thinking, feeling, speaking, and being.

The supermarket manager's reaction to Günther suggests he is a somewhat surprising figure. Katz plays into the manager's incredulity when he describes Kaufmann as "one of the rarest birds on the planet, a black Bavarian,"[39] suggesting a homology between blackness and foreignness. But it is possible that Günther is completely legible to this manager, and the manager taunts him nonetheless. Fassbinder's ambivalent characters can rarely be taken fully at their word. This petty manager's fondness for Harry could motivate him to play up Günther's foreignness, to alienate him from the exchange. When in fact, Günther's racial situation is produced from a local set of circumstances. Kaufmann himself came from a generation of so-called *Mischlingskinder*, whose German mothers had "mixed" with black American occupying soldiers in the post-war period. Such a family situation might not be unknown to a supermarket manager, as these children were subject to disproportionate study and publicity in the post-war years.[40] Although Günther may not be as mysterious as the manager suggests, he plays up the idea that Günther is an anomaly in order to extract value from his marginalization.

Kaufmann's apparent difference introduces German historical problems. Black soldiers who occupied parts of the country after both the first and second world wars had a notable paternal impact on German populations. Following the former war, French African occupying soldiers contributed to a generation of mixed-race children later described by Hitler as "Rhineland bastards."[41] After the fall of the Third Reich, black American soldiers, including Kaufmann's own father, defied the U.S. military's segregation laws in their liaisons with German women.[42] In each of these situations, German women and foreign black men share the production of a mixed embodiment. These paradoxical German children produced challenges for West German administrative authorities who perceived them as foreign. Many of these *Mischlingskinder* were adopted away to the presumed racial affinity of black families in the United States, or to Denmark, where the difficult cultural complexity was imagined to be overcome by a total alienating disruption. Kaufmann's generation of black Germans had circulated significantly through institutional channels and helped shape the bureaucratic and representational contours of German racial identity, in transnational relation, in the post-Nazi state.

The term *Mischlingskind*, which refers to hybridity, had been redirected to name these children, having been appropriated in the previous era to describe the children of Jews and Aryans. This intense marker of difference indicates the cultural importance placed on these Germans' partial blackness. The term is by no means politically neutral, as Germany's 1936 Nuremberg laws demonstrate: "Aside from persons of alien blood, *half-castes* [*Mischlinge*] born of relations between persons of German and alien hereditary factors are neither German-blooded or of related blood [*artverwandtes Blut*]. The legal treatment of half-castes is based on the recognition that they are the same neither as those of German nor as those of alien blood."[43] Within the Nazi racial bureaucracy, the policing of difference was pursued down to the fractional possibilities of heredity. The fallacious legal category of "blood" organized the logic, making a fine distinction between German blood and German hereditary factors. The era's bloodshed materialized socially the biological essence of race figured in this metonymic conception. This idea of politicized blood authorized the legal administration of life itself, from the Jewish genocide to forced reproduction among Aryan women and the forced sterilization of ethnic minorities and the disabled, to other atrocities. But blood's fluidity problematizes legal categories, demanding the baroque system delineated in the Nuremberg laws. Designed to anticipate various possibilities of Jewish heredity among Germans, this distinction of neither/nor in the segment quoted above reveals, through its own ambivalence, the difficulty racism faces when confronted by impurity. If these so-called *Mischlinge* can never be "the same" as Germans or Jews, then they are, in all contexts, perpetually different. Nazi policy makers defined this difference by referring to its permanent negativity, a neither/nor of being. After the war, this term, which had been previously oriented toward the insidiousness of invisible Jewish heredity, shifted toward the spectacular impossibility of German blackness. While the legal results of this terminology had changed, its cultural baggage had not been fully unpacked.

Kaufmann's presence in *Gods of the Plague* performs his ambivalent position in the culture, reflecting both the racist logic embedded in the German tradition, and a transnational radicality signaled by his German blackness. His embodied conflict is dramatized in his protracted death scene: after a shootout in the supermarket, Günther staggers down a Munich street, shirtless and wounded, his impossible, criminal blood on display. He is able to commit one final revenge murder, of a young woman, as he declares to the camera, "Life is very precious, even right

Figure 3.3. Günther Kaufmann and Margarethe von Trotta in a still from *Gods of the Plague*, R. W. Fassbinder, 1970.

now." His English words invoke a distant fantasy. In English, he is able to finally place value on his life, even as it paradoxically ends in a dramatic bloodbath. Particularly, this transnationality circulates around an imagined America, where both black radicals and gangster movies originate, overlapping here in the persistent image of black criminal violence. In both paternal and generic senses, Kaufmann's death scene invokes a transgressive lineage invoked by a black transnational imagination.

While Kaufmann indicates a political imagination in *Gods of the Plague*, he is also mobilized in a psychosexual network of desire. Likely reflecting Fassbinder's own amorous interest in Kaufmann, the most virulent exercise of directorial power in an otherwise modestly produced film appears in a lengthy helicopter shot surveying Günther's movements in the Bavarian countryside. Even when clothed, Günther's body is on display. In a conspiratorial visit made to a farmhouse, Günther dives into a pile of hay, rolls around affectionately with a sheep, and vigorously play-fights with Franz and another male friend, while his extremely tight pants are split in the crotch. The torn pants reveal white underwear when the camera catches Kaufmann from behind, which it capably does. Apart from his sexualized death scene, in which the shirt-less Günther, wet with blood, uses his final energy to clutch a gun and fire, Günther's semi–sex scene with Franz and Margarethe reveals his entire naked body from behind, placing his beautifully lit ass in the center of the frame.

This scene is treated specifically by Kaja Silverman in her chapter "Fassbinder and Lacan: A Reconsideration of Gaze, Look and Image." Noting the huge image of a woman's face that decorates the wall above Margarethe's bed, Silverman describes the scene:

> At a key moment in the film, Günther . . . , Franz, and Margarethe form an intimate grouping in Margarethe's bedroom prior to having sex, and talk about traveling to Greece. "We don't need money," says Franz, and Günther adds: "Because we're in love." As Günther utters these words, he embraces the poster above the bed, his body held in a spread-eagle position against the female face. This telling gesture suggests that it is not just Margarethe who views herself through that idealizing portrait, but Günther and Franz as well—that *it* is the cause and support of love, the terrain across which the two men meet.[44]

Silverman argues convincingly that the men occupy the image of the woman, diverting their male desire through her empty representation, using her face as a cipher for their own homosexuality, an act that diverts the usual directionality of male desire. In this instance, Günther's "telling" ass stops the look of Franz, the look of the camera, and the look of the viewer all at once, before they can complete their gaze at the empty sign of the feminine face behind Margarethe's own face. The scene's sexual fantasy overlays a fantasy of class liberation, in which the ass coincides with "love," not "money." Redirected desire is imagined as revolutionary.

Throughout her argument, Silverman looks for Fassbinder's non-standard phallus, identifying the way the director subverts male visuality by displacing its rule. Silverman identifies the potential that these marginal characters bring to the project of decentering power, writing that "Fassbinder's male characters acquire the capacity to become something other than what the male subject has classically been—to slip out from under the phallic sign, away from the paternal structure."[45] In search for this "something other," Silverman's Lacanian analysis encourages a closer look at the ass in the middle of the screen. The ass here is certainly more than just an anus, though the anus is promised by the ass, and doubles presence with absence, at once a Freudian gift-giver, a gift given in anxiety as Lacan points out, signaling the anxiety in the Freudian tradition around the anus as the focus of a misdirected sexual aim—while this presence also masquerades as lack in the anal sexual act. This lack plays hide and seek with the supposed fear of castration it supposedly represents. In queer male anal sex, the penis is doubled: one disappears into the anus, another remains, visible. Multiple penises already disrupt the singularity of phallic rule, much in the way mirrors, deflected looks, and unreturned stares disrupt the gaze in Fassbinder's cinematography. This is not a suggestion that anal sex between men is essentially liberatory or anti-patriarchal, when certainly phallocentric fantasies are capably enacted through that practice; my aim here is rather to complicate the reading of the sign of the phallus in its relationship to anality.

And even so, this doubly phallic anus that travesties lack is not the entirety of this ass. Sue-Ellen Case challenges the phallic preoccupation in her study of Fassbinder, suggesting it is a "heterosexist reading of queer discourse,"[46] which reduces Fassbinder's "same-sex desiring cinematic apparatus"[47] to the binary norms of man and woman. Case points to the image of Querelle's ass as a radical presence that distorts the binary operation of phallus and lack, orienting a multivalent desire through this queer apparatus. Case's intervention produces a way to read Günther's ass as "something other," as a particularly queer form of presence. But Querelle's alluring ass is costumed in tight white sailor pants, while Günther's ass is dark and bare. What do we make of blackness in this presentation, of the black ass that Günther offers to Franz's look, Fassbinder's camera, and our scopic pleasure? Case's multivalent ass-sign does not attempt to account for the negativity blackness produces in filmic representation. Throughout her chapter, Silverman recognizes race, class, and so on as categories of difference that complicate male subjectivity in Fassbinder's films, but cannot work blackness as a particular analytic framework into the problem of sexual difference, even reductively referring to race as "skin pigmentation"[48] in a particular moment of resignation.

This reduction points us to an alluring figure in Lacan's own description of the unapprehensible other for which the subject finds itself looking, the idea of the stain. "Coloration . . . is simply a way of defending oneself against light,"[49] Lacan posits. Though while coloration might serve a process of adaptation, "in mimicry we are dealing with something quite different."[50] Lacan points to a small crustacean that mimics its surrounding organisms. "It becomes the stain, it becomes a picture, it is inscribed in the picture. This strictly speaking, is the origin of mimicry."[51] Lacan's attention to color leads to mimicry, a self-conscious form of appearing, which feminist theorists such as Silverman, Elin Diamond, Mary Kelly, and Luce Irigaray have explored as a way to potentially act against a mimetic phallogocentrism, an act that Silverman describes as "one of those rare junctures within the Lacanian oeuvre where it becomes possible to impute to the subject some kind of agency."[52] This unspecified agency functions on behalf of the knowing mimic in the field of the gaze who plays with the screens upon which a repertoire of images constitute and differentiate subjects. Silverman, and elsewhere Laura Mulvey, point at this gaze-play in Fassbinder's cinema as a critical intervention against the dominant order of looking, which uncritically allies itself with a gaze of patriarchal power. Lacan's attention to color further invokes Silverman's "skin-pigmentation," as it acts upon the cinematic gaze in this instance of mimicry, where, under Fassbinder's system, incommensurate differences collude, where the embodied black man's ass overlays the vacant white woman's face as a complex site of identification. Their paired unapprehensible otherness makes distinct, rather than coherent, the differences that the white male gaze organizes into the project of phallic sameness, or in other words, the subject.

Approaching the ass from another angle, Jennifer Nash's essay "Black Anality" places this image in a historical field of signs not bound to psychoanalytic critique, though still concerned with sexual difference. Nash considers black female sexuality, which has been bound in representation to the buttocks, as in the iconic example of Saartjie Baartman, whose buttocks represented black sexuality's deviance and availability for its Victorian audience. As Kaufmann plays both the feminine position of looked-at-ness, and the black condition of compulsory visibility, it is instructive to follow Nash's movement from the buttocks back to the anus, and what she calls its anal ideologies, which include the notion of waste. Here we find the ass hosting another collusion of deviant sexualities, as in Leo Bresani's essay "Is the Rectum a Grave?," which shows how the distorted public representation of the AIDS crisis was framed by the presumed filth of anal sex. Kaufmann's aberrance is presented in the buttocks as an image of black male sexuality. Though earlier in the film, speculation surrounds the size of Günther's penis, activating a stereotype of such sexuality, it is in Günther's large black ass that the phallus is inverted as convoluted mimicry and its aberrant excess. Figuring doubly as a black hole of identification and an abundance of historical material, Kaufmann's ass exceeds the boundaries of normative representations, challenging the critical methodologies that have separated gender, sexuality, race and class into distinct operations. Neither Lacan nor Marx offers a suitable formula. Franz, who stares admiringly, seems to recognize in Günther's black ass a potentially revolutionary, undertheorized site of limitless possibilities.

Ambivalence and Camp

Following *Gods of the Plague*, Kaufmann plays a prominent role in five of the seven productions for film and television made by the antiteater company in 1970, including *Pioneers in Ingolstadt*. His absence from the remaining two projects is conspicuous: in *The American Soldier*, though Kaufmann sings Raben's ballad "So Much Tenderness" on the soundtrack, the leading role Fassbinder had written for him was later taken away; *Beware a Holy Whore* parodies the making of the film *Whity*, in which Kaufmann had starred. A consideration of these works highlights Kaufmann as a consistently important sign with which Fassbinder developed his visual language.

Fassbinder's biographers have noted the director's amorous commitment to Kaufmann during this time. Several accounts allude to a sexual relationship between the two. While many of his colleagues produced tell-all books after Fassbinder's death, Kaufmann himself was a rare troupe member who consistently declined to talk about the director, shedding little light on the nature of their relationship, contributing to its mystery. Gossip and scandal inform the written record that framed

Fassbinder's persona during his life and concretized that persona after his death. Kaufmann, a tall, muscular, attractive, married black man, glamorizes this tale. Within the drama of the Fassbinder social sphere, Kaufmann is a hyperbolic figure. He is introduced by biographer Robert Katz as one of Fassbinder's "great loves" who "will wreck four Lamborghinis."[53] Destroyed sports cars are mentioned by several commentators as indicative of Fassbinder's lavish affection and Kaufmann's erratic excesses. As in the films, Kaufmann's role in Fassbinder lore is as a provocative agent. The suggestion of queer sex with this "Bavarian Negro" further radicalizes the Fassbinder narrative. These biographical notes, while not always reliable, are important nonetheless because they suggest what is reflected in the work. Productions of the antiteater, in which the characters are often named for the actors who played them, restage these personal relationships. As Fassbinder later claimed of his first films, including those made in the intense Kaufmann period of 1969–70: "The films give a concrete expression of my situation at the time. When you see them all, it's clear they were made by a person of great sensitivity, aggression and fear. But even so I don't think the first nine films are right. They are too elitist and too private, just made for myself and a few friends."[54] The director, who described his early films as "exact reconstructions of the atmosphere prevailing among people of that sort at that time in Munich,"[55] indicates that they capably express aspects of the identity of the artists behind the work. The movies mark a period before the maturation of his more melodramatic style, influenced by the popular Hollywood pictures of Douglas Sirk and Raoul Walsh. The early films, rather, interpret a subjective experience so specifically that Fassbinder refers to them as too "private," self-consciously problematizing that distinction as a case of elitism. Here, as in so much of Fassbinder's output, personal and political dimensions indicate each other.

These personalized politics also inform the way race plays out in the life and work of Fassbinder. In the case of Kaufmann, his racial representation figures in interplay with a recognizable status as desired object. In *Gods of the Plague* and *Whity* particularly, Kaufmann is figured as an object of desire: presented in adoring close-ups, in lingering views of his body, in an extravagant aerial shot following his movements, but also in several punishing scenes of humiliation and violence. As in a memorable scene from *Whity* in which Kaufmann's character seems to enjoy being whipped by his white master, the scenarios racialize Kaufmann, spectacularizing his difference, while he is also sexualized, indicating a constant cross-current between the discourses of race and desire. This confluence is more subtly evident elsewhere in the director's body of work, particularly in the acclaimed 1974 film *Ali: Fear Eats the Soul*, which dramatizes the difficult marriage between an aging German housekeeper and a North African *Gastarbeiter*, played by Fassbinder's lover El Hedi Ben Salam. While Ali's indignities are not nearly as pronounced as Whity's, in both of these cases, the racialized object of sexual attention is also an object of racist abuse.

While these actors' performances critically frame racial oppression, it is still enacted against them, nonetheless. In the films, the persistent abuses against racialized characters could be conceivably construed as a form of racism itself, just as the centrality of abused women in Fassbinder's works has instigated claims of misogyny by some critics. The latter claims Fassbinder denied. But the linkage between the two is of central importance to the analysis of the works' radical ambivalence. In the late seventies, Fassbinder described a television project that was abandoned under pressure from network authorities over concerns that the original German source material would lead to anti-Semitic representations. Defending his right to portray Jews negatively, Fassbinder declares:

> Actually I find it anti-semitic to say about Jews—and other minorities— that just because they are minorities they are blameless. To believe that is dangerous and fascist. The best way to describe the majority's view of a minority is to show the kinds of failure and cruel pressures an individual member of that minority may be forced to accept.
> *But isn't that exactly the objection made about some of your "women's films"?*
> It's precisely the same.[56]

Fassbinder's logic is creative: it is not immediately obvious that describing a black Bavarian, for example, as blameless could be construed as anti-Semitic. More obvious is the possibility that presenting Jewish complicity in the Third Reich would be a controversial choice for the Westdeutsche Rundfunk television network. Putting those problems aside, or holding them in ambivalent balance as it were, Fassbinder helpfully describes the oppressive racial abuses in his work as critical entanglements with the situation of oppression. The "cruel pressures" that frequently act against such minorities are specifically deployed by Fassbinder to "show" what racism looks like. While Fassbinder begins here with ethnicity and race, the interviewer's question about "women's films" prompts the response: "It's precisely the same." Fassbinder willingly and deliberately conflates all of these systems, revealing the complicity of desire with gender, race, and class to form a complex system of oppression under which its objects are compelled to participate.

In a more precise analysis than Fassbinder's own, Laura Mulvey notes the director's mode of equivalences in a consideration of *Ali: Fear Eats the Soul*, arguing that "[t]he lower antinomy in the polarizations—man/woman, indigenous worker/immigrant worker—creates an unexpected parallel between the two terms, underlining the closeness of indigenous woman/immigrant man."[57] The domestic worker and the immigrant worker share their occupation of Mulvey's "lower antinomy," a binary relation beholden to a psychoanalytic framework that, like Silverman's, opposes power to its lack. Though Mulvey is surprised at these parallels, they are indeed a commonplace in Fassbinder's work. The multiple situations that oppose power are visible throughout the plays and films, where a view prevails that women, Jews, workers, the unemployed, *Gastarbeiter*, and black Bavarians, though interpersonally divided, all share their difference in the context of West German capitalism. That this hegemony authorizes the same abuses against so many modes of difference is the actual inconsistency, the fallacy inherent in dominant binary models, to which Fassbinder's radical ambivalence responds.

Whity, in which Kaufmann stars as a slave to a white family, too produces an ambivalent critique. Adopting tropes of the Hollywood Western, the film's theatricalization of race is highly critical, but its violent negativity fails to propose any liberatory possibilities. Kaufmann's titular character is served with some very harsh treatment; his acquiescent subservience contributes to his own oppression until finally, in "a sudden violent *élan*,"[58] he murders his oppressors. The film exaggerates class exploitation in this microcosmic Western town. The genre's conventional characters, from the saloon-singing prostitute played by Schygulla to the brawling cowboy Fassbinder plays himself, all perform identifiable roles, and are unable to transcend their socially proscribed positions.

Figure 3.4. Harry Bär and Günther Kaufmann in a still from *Whity*, R. W. Fassbinder, 1971.

The violence they enact on one another is finally overcome by Whity's own outrageous violent act, when he shoots the entire family that had been exploiting him economically and sexually. While this violence frees Whity and his sex-worker girlfriend from the inevitability of their social positions, it provides them with no real alternatives. The pair end the film in an embrace as they stand alone in the desert. Their freedom from society's restraints means there is no longer any apparatus to sustain them. Their revolution may produce momentary pleasure, but it has no future.

Whity is Fassbinder's most direct appraisal of race. While Kaufmann always mobilizes racial dynamics and serves to radicalize the other films he appears in, his race is the central dramatic fact in *Whity*. His blackness structures the narrative, providing the catalyst for action. While Whity's blackness corresponds with Kaufmann's actual appearance, *Whity* is the Fassbinder film in which race is most theatrically demonstrated. This theatrical demonstration renders race a highly conspicuous spectacle, while distancing its performance from any notion of realism. Kaufmann's lips are sometimes whitened for uncanny emphasis, and several of the other actors wear makeup to emphasize their characters' racial differences, not only using blackface but also whiteface, grayface, and even greenface to occasionally signify the corrupt decadence of the elite. The starkness of these visual differences matches the bold relief of the narrative, with its excessive murder plots, abusive reprisals, and episodes of sexual domination. *Whity* is particularly unsubtle.

The high racial stakes are evident from the beginning of the film. The first shot shows Whity lying face down in the dirt, motionless, his visible cheek glistening with sweat and tears. The film's sadistic attitude is clear from this first sequence, as the credits appear around Whity's abject body. Everyone who worked on the film is named in the credit sequence, including Fassbinder, whose lengthy name spreads across Whity's body rather than appearing above it or below it. At the end of the sequence, the text reads, "Günter Kaufmann . . . is . . . Whity."[59] Singled out in this final position, his first name curiously misspelled, Kaufmann is both specially designated and the last to get credit. This treatment forecasts his role in the film.

The setting changes to a Spanish-style kitchen where a white actress painted black and wearing a messy black wig stirs something in a bowl while a caged chicken watches. At first she is seen only in a shadowy close-up, but the camera soon catches the edge of the makeup on her neck as it begins to give way to light skin, and starts to wear off on the white collar that surrounds it. Flies buzz. Kaufmann enters through a dark wood door in a bright, crisp red suit and white gloves. He complains to the cook, who turns out to be his mother, that they have not done enough to please their masters. Though the dialogue is in German, the cook begins to sing an English language conflation of "Battle Hymn of the Republic" and "When the Saints Go Marching In" as she stirs. The song is comically strange in her accent; though playing a stereotypical mammy, she pronounces the word *halleluja* in a particularly German way. The dissonance of this accented song with her disturbing appearance makes clear that this is a film where race is relentlessly performed. Whity responds to her: "You shouldn't sing songs like that." "What songs?" she asks. "Black songs."[60] Whity emphasizes in this first scene his interest in suppressing his blackness, and in appealing to his masters' white sensibilities, even while in the act of serving them. Though a racially aware viewer might also wonder if this cook really should sing songs like that, because she obviously is not black and it is ridiculous and probably offensive for her to pretend in this way. But there is no politically progressive solution to this scene; in this conflict between mother and son, blackness can be either totally suppressed, or performed outrageously. In the end, the cook spits on Whity's face and draws out his name derisively, "Whi-ty." In a slow, gestic manner, he wipes away his mother's spit with a gloved white hand. The opening scene introduces a film that expertly choreographs racial ambivalence. Fassbinder recalled some of his process in making *Whity*:

> Before I made *Whity*, I looked at several Raoul Walsh films, especially at *Band of Angels* (1957, with Clark Gable, Yvonne de Carlo and Sidney Poitier), which is one of the loveliest films I've ever seen. A white farmer dies, leaving behind the daughter he's had with a black woman. The girl looks completely white, but as soon as the old man is dead she is sold, to help clear his debts. Clark Gable plays the slave trader who buys her: he knows she is a negro and she knows he is a slave trader. Then the Civil War starts. Sidney Poitier plays the slave trader's faithful servant and, even though he is fighting on the other side, he helps his master to flee with the girl. So everything works out fine. Or does it?[61]

Adapting a Hollywood source, Fassbinder tapped into an American system of representation, one in which blackness serves predictable plot purposes, while politicizing the situation with radical possibilities. That this over-the-top narrative produces "one of the loveliest films" Fassbinder had ever seen indicates the complex pleasure he derived from explorations of exploitation. His ambiguous question about the film's finale—is the happy ending truly happy—suggests the critical reversals Fassbinder applies to the Western genre in *Whity*. That ambiguity is embedded in the difficult contradictions invoked by racial representation in films like *Band of Angels*. While Walsh was known as a director of Westerns, a genre that *Whity* mimics, *Band of Angels* is itself a colorful Southern melodrama, like its successful predecessor *Gone with the Wind*, narratively organized around racial politics. In the beginning of the film, the slave-owning father playfully asks his little girl what she is made of, eliciting the clichéd response "Sugar and spice and everything nice." After her favorite slave is sent away for revealing the child's mysterious black maternity, her father tries to appease his daughter by repeating his cute question. This time, as music swells, the girl responds tearfully: "I don't know, Father. I don't know."[62] This is the ambiguity that propels that film's narrative, leading to tangled and contorted ethical conundrums, such as the choice the Union soldier played by Poitier must make to help his former owner escape with his mixed-race, white-identified girlfriend. In *Band of Angels*, race propels the melodramatic mode. In *Whity*, which makes a campy combination of the Southern melodrama and Western genres, race theatricalizes Fassbinder's radically ambivalent mode.

And again, sexuality and gender complicate the race-based class arrangements. While Whity's main sexual interest is in the prostitute played by Schygulla, he is a sexual object in the incestuous household where he works, subjected to ritualistic attention by his owner and father, who whips him sadistically from behind; by the master's wife, who tends his wounds erotically; and by the eldest son of the family, who wears women's lingerie in an attempt to seduce Whity. These characters are trapped in their own hierarchical scenarios; the mother and the son are both trying to get Whity to kill the father. At the same time, they abuse Whity and derive pleasure from it. In one scene, the mother and eldest son relentlessly taunt Whity while groping each other. They repeatedly ring a bell for service and call for things they do not want. They laugh at Whity's subservience and at their own power over him. However, they ring the bell one time too many; the master finally emerges from the kitchen instead of Whity and his presence puts them in their place. His wife, chastened, apologizes. The son is suddenly silent. Each character is dominated by another in a vicious system of power. The master/father dominates the entire network.

Kaufmann's regular acting partner Harry Bär plays the youngest son, Davie, whose mental disability leaves him mostly catatonic. Whity is fond of Davie, the least powerful member of the household beside him. Performing his own subservience, Whity is whipped in Davie's place. Davie had spied on his parents in bed the night before and had witnessed his father's impotence, stoking his fury. As the father angrily whips Davie, Whity offers to be punished on his behalf, removing his shirt, and straddling the deflated Davie, who lies on the ground. As the rest of the family watches with ecstatic pleasure, Whity smiles as he is being struck, until his master commands him to yell out. When Whity finally screams, the master declares with satisfaction, "That was pretty good, Whity," making up for the previous night's failed sex. Whity is fully complicit in this abusive relationship. He readily admits this to his girlfriend in the brothel when he claims he is happy with the family and rejects her suggestion that they run away together. His complicity is

tied to his own sexual desire as well; in an eerily tender scene that precedes the whipping, Whity puts Davie's hand in his as they slowly brush
a horse together. Davie falls to his knees, his face in front of Whity's
crotch, as Whity slaps him gently. Then falling to his knees, Whity kisses
Davie over and over again. Davie's gray-green makeup rubs off on his
face. Whity's sexual encounter with his disabled half-brother and his relationship with the prostitute depict a kind of love among the exploited,
situating Whity's own exploited sexuality.

While the distancing enacted by the makeup and the film's alienated
acting suggest some of the Brechtian influence mentioned above, the
film's lack of political clarity and complex sexualities suggest something
more is at play. A comparison can be made to Jean Genet's 1957 play *The
Blacks*, which enjoyed a popular run in New York in 1964. Fassbinder,
who certainly knew *Querelle*, was likely familiar with this well-known
work of Genet's. *The Blacks* also theatricalizes race, using masks and
grotesque exaggerations, while providing no liberal relief to the tense
racial conflict invoked onstage. It figures as an important iteration of
a queer European sensibility that foregrounds the artifice and ritual of
social interactions. Though Genet's work precedes the literature on the
term, the American concept of camp begins to address the kind of artificial, ironic presentation evident in both *The Blacks* and *Whity*.

Richard Dyer has associated camp with Fassbinder's investment in
sexuality, a consideration that tends to fall out of the Marxist approach,
claiming "it is Fassbinder's camp that has allowed him to develop the
kind of foregrounding techniques which critics have usually preferred
to ascribe purely to Brechtianism."[63] Case bolsters this association when
she describes Fassbinder's "sense of camp and its distance from the
real."[64] While his perspective as a gay filmmaker enables arch representations that defy naturalism and satirize normative roles, camp is seen
by Dyer as fraught with complications:

> Camp is an enormously ambiguous phenomenon, ambiguous in its own
> right as a particular sensibility, and even more so in relation to the ho-
> mosexual sub-culture. On the one hand camp is relentlessly trivializing,
> but on the other its constant play with the vocabulary of straight society
> (in particular, the excesses of male and female role-playing) sends up that
> society in a needlingly undermining way. In the last analysis, gay politics

and culture are going to have to move beyond the limitations of camp; but we still have to appreciate how central and almost instinctive a feature of the male gay subculture it is, how much many gay men feel at home—for once in their lives—with the camp sensibility. Fassbinder's work is caught up in these ambiguities, and I feel I want to defend his involvement in camp even while acknowledging its problems. The latter include the extreme ambivalence of his/camp's depiction of women . . .[65]

The abuse of women is mentioned by Dyer, whose fascinating read of Fassbinder is an ambivalent mix of criticism and praise. He bristles at the director's representation of violence against women, as in the instances in which women are slapped in the face in all of the films discussed here. These scenes tend to parody the normative relationship between men and women in an "undermining" way, drawing on the queer sensibility Dyer identifies as camp. Still, he has difficulty defending this queer sensibility in any respect other than for its useful social function. Camp does not offer a clear critical apparatus; it turns presumed social realities into heightened mixed messages.

Dyer, whose writing portrays an investment in radical social action, can't arrive at a political resolution with these works. He recognizes that the problem of sexuality, desire, and difference tend to produce unsatisfying images of political liberation, lacking the scientific clarity of class-based analysis. While Dyer is discouraged that "the emphasis in Fassbinder's films on people as victims of society and history implies a model of social change that is unable to indicate how people can be actively involved in that process of change,"[66] he equivocates, stating that "Fassbinder's films often provoke better discussion of sexual political issues than some films that I would argue are more ideologically acceptable."[67] Dyer's focus in these comments is on the ways sexuality and gender camp up the critique in Fassbinder's oeuvre; he neglects to incorporate any sense of race into this criticism, despite its consistent presence in the work. In films like *Whity*, Fassbinder achieves what so many theorists, scholars, and critics are unable to: he critically manages race, gender, sexuality, and class all at once. The most radical aspect of *Whity* is the unusual criticality its queer camp sensibility brings to emphasizing the artifice of race. Race is done like gender might be done in drag: its hierarchies are hyperbolized and its biological premises are lampooned.

Whity's camp borrows from queer theatrics not only to obviate the problem of racial oppression, but to declare the performativity of race.

As discussed earlier, Dyer has used the term "left-wing melancholy" to describe Fassbinder's political position, a term that suggests
a post-Marxian criticality embedded in a personal psychology of desire. This position becomes legible to Dyer when he identifies with it
generationally:

> [T]here are worse things in this world than left-wing melancholy. We are
> living in a period in which capitalist recession is not visibly being greeted
> by working-class revolutionary struggle (though there's always plenty of
> resistance), and which is for artists and intellectuals a retreat from the
> hopes of May 1968. Moreover, Fassbinder is living in a wealthy country
> of quite exceptional political repression, which has seen, as in Britain, a
> disturbing resurgence of fascist politics (with considerable working-class
> support). On the terrain of sexual politics, I acknowledge the force of a
> line Petra von Kant is given to say: "People need one another, but haven't
> learned how to live together."[68]

Dyer indicates the limits that were visibly erected around the possibility
of Marxist resistance in wealthy Western countries after the major student and civic protests of the sixties, and acknowledges that the sexual
revolution of that time had been less transformative of dominant morality than might have been hoped for. Fassbinder, who was himself in Paris
during the May 1968 student uprising, experienced both the energies of
the era's social and sexual movements and the repression Western states
initiated against these transgressions. Dyer quotes from Fassbinder's
play and film *The Bitter Tears of Petra von Kant*, which depicts a sado-
masochistic lesbian relationship, and which Fassbinder claimed was a
representation of his own relationship with Kaufmann, as an expression
of the fracturing pressures of social forces Fassbinder deploys but never
resolves. Here Kaufmann is invoked again, as a symbol of the contradictions of social experience.

Though Fassbinder uses Kaufmann as the subject of racial oppression, he also simultaneously presents him a source of political energy. In
The Niklashausen Journey, a 16mm film that was made for television by
the antiteater in 1970, Kaufmann recites from the Black Panther mani-

Figure 3.5. Günther Kaufmann in a still from *The Niklashausen Journey*, R. W. Fassbinder and Michael Fengler, 1970.

festo, reads aloud from a newspaper about the shooting of Black Panther Party members Fred Hampton and Mark Clarke in Chicago, and finally leads a violent revolt, machine gun blazing. He mobilizes a black revolutionary power, the image of which was in wide circulation in leftist movements at the end of the sixties. The film captures an important dynamic between Marxist revolutionaries and black radicals of the time. Kaufmann's performance intensifies the Marxist struggle with a contemporizing blackness.

Kaufmann serves as a member of a radical cell in *The Niklashausen Journey,* which conflates a medieval German messianic movement with a sixties communal revolutionary plot. Peer Raben later described the film as "the only existing valid document about life in the late sixties."[69] Fassbinder himself claimed he "wanted to show how a revolution fails."[70] In the film's narrative, a Christian visionary is adopted as a figurehead by a vanguard of radicals led by Fassbinder's own character. In the opening scene, a few of the radicals rehearse their rhetoric while pacing in front of a brick wall. Fassbinder's monk, with his back to the camera, quizzes his comrades:

> THE BLACK MONK: Are [revolutionaries] allowed to stage a
> revolution?
> JOHANNA: That is impossible.
> THE BLACK MONK: Are they allowed to make use of theatrical effects,
> for example, to agitate more effectively?
> JOHANNA: Yes. Of course. Yes.[71]

Theatrical effects are eventually put to use, as ideology soon gives way to image. Reflecting one critic's description of *The Niklashausen Journey* as a "revolution in costumes,"[72] Schygulla's Johanna poses as the Virgin Mary so that she may speak on her behalf in favor of the political movement. Exposing the theatricality of this ploy, Fassbinder's monk tests her on her political speech as she prepares her hair and makeup. In another, Fassbinder's monk and another radical dressed in a feudal style argue about value. While their dialogue mimics the mathematical terms of Marx's "The Commodity," the first chapter of *Capital*, Fassbinder is unable find the right formulation. Rather than the linens and coats Marx uses as exemplary commodities, Fassbinder reflects his Southern German origins as he determines emphatically to analyze the exchange values of bears and wolves. Following this episode, the group surrounds their prophet as he quotes correctly from "The Commodity" while standing at the rim of a giant, empty, quarry. There is no public here, simply a rhetorical theory with no practical possibility.

The film is perhaps Fassbinder's most perfect expression of left-wing melancholy, as it follows a disheartening movement from revolutionary fervor to spectacle to fascist reprisal. The radical cell is eventually put down by the military and church. The vanguard agitators disperse, having provoked a violent outburst, but prompted no real structural changes. While Kaufmann's presence provides urgency, black power isn't enough to reanimate Marxist resistance to fascist power. Still, Kaufmann's character excites the proceedings by offering a spectacle of resistance: killing military police, throwing bombs, and spinning around in circles while aimlessly firing a machine gun as he laughs in his typically gleeful manner. This extreme posture, paired with the naked pose in *Gods of the Plague*, demonstrates the excessive possibilities Kaufmann brought to the Fassbinder imaginary, both politically and sexually.

Conclusion

While there is a crucial fluidity between the antiteater's film and theater projects, it's worth finally noting the differences between these two forms in the ways they concretize difference, and how a progression from one to the next establishes a performative repertoire. While the filmic close-up simultaneously spectacularizes and naturalizes an actor's features, including his racial appearance, the cognitive distances of alienated theater make Fassbinder's racial play possible. The films, through strategies like the close-up, raise identificatory possibilities that intensify the historical space of theater. Television, the third term in this production, with its powers of dissemination, appropriates a broad cultural space across which to perform this alienated desiring apparatus. Among the works in which he appears, it is in the theater piece *The Coffeehouse*, shot on video for television in 1970, where Kaufmann fully confounds racial conditions, playing a European count with a lacy collar in an adaptation of Carlo Goldoni's eighteenth-century play. Still, while Kaufmann plays against his race in this production, his aristocratic costume heightens a dissonance between his role and his person. That dissonance is an event of imaginary freedom. Even in this event, Kaufmann's appearance distinguishes him from the rest of the group as something different. Like so much in Fassbinder's work, blackness is delivered, through Kaufmann, as a radically ambivalent force.

4

The Cockettes, Sylvester, and Performance as Life

California offered itself to me. It seemed to present the pos-
sibility of creating a life or finding one. It would be mine and
I would slip it on like a glove.
—Elaine Brown

Any time you enter a region where there is a strong revolt
forming you are immediately struck by the common manner
of dress, gesture, and modes of relating and communicating.
Jean Genet, for example, remarked that what characterized
the Black Panthers was primarily a *style*—not just the vocabulary, the Afros, and the clothes, but also a way of walking,
a manner of holding their bodies, a physical presence. These
elements of style, however, are really only symptoms of the
common dreams, common desires, common ways of life,
and common potential that are mobilized in a movement.
—Michael Hardt and Antonio Negri

The world for the most part is shit . . . with the wars and the
banks and the corruption and the lies and the malls. Forget
it. Just give me a torn dress, a hit of acid and let's go to the
beach. That's enough. That's a lot.
—Reggie

Introduction

California in the late sixties set the scene for a number of revolutionary efforts, from the fervently political to the ecstatically sexual. While
many of these movements were engaged in a larger context of leftist
resistance, they were shaped by the local situation of California, the
home of hippies, love children, black radicals, labor organizers, activist

student groups, and advocates of gay liberation. Though different from each other, the participants of these diverse movements each facilitated a dynamic practice of personal reinvention.

Even in this energetic context, the transformational performance strategies enacted by the troupe known as the Cockettes were exceptional. Between 1969 and 1972, the group's celebratory excess, or excessive celebration, was presented vividly in stage revues and short films, and continuously enacted in the spaces of the participants' public and private lives. The communal performance troupe activated an empowering countercultural visibility through constructed dress, speech, and physical action. These tactics allowed the group to radically restage the notion of sexual and gender identity in campy performances, and their life-as-performance approach made everyday practices into radical antinormative spectacles. These performances theatricalized their distance from authority, staking out an imaginative eccentric position. Altogether avoiding regular roles associated with work, family and citizenship, this marginal location was a space where cultural hierarchies could be temporarily suspended amid the play of camp humor, the pleasures of queer sexuality, and the altered perceptual terrain of psychedelic drug use. Sylvester, the group's best-known member, contributed significantly to the language of difference deployed by the Cockettes. While the troupe's communal efforts were non-doctrinaire, Sylvester drew on conventions of black American performance, and their transnational discursive sphere, while pursuing a self-styled individualhood. Harnessing the transformative potential of their historical moment, Sylvester and the Cockettes performed an artful negotiation of race, gender, and sexuality in the space between subjectivity and historicity, temporarily outmaneuvering the punishing fixities those terms ought to have proposed.

The Travesty of *Tricia's Wedding*

The Cockettes' ambivalent drag performances constructed a provisional world to live in, while also critiquing the normative social world and its regulating images. A primary example is the short film *Tricia's Wedding*, which imaged and imagined a negation of ruling order, using satirical doubling and the violation of taboos to terrorize the notion of the paternalistic state. Shown in theaters on the day in June 1971 that President

Figure 4.1. "Tricia's Wedding" promotional poster, Todd Trexler, 1972.

Richard Nixon's daughter Tricia had been married at the White House and on national television, the Cockettes' alternate version, directed by Sebastian, mercilessly ridiculed the ruling elites with disrespectful impressions. As the large group of costumed performers enact their idea of a White House wedding, they at first appear to relish the pretense of importance they are mimicking, an act of class drag that exaggerates their own social status. Soon, though, the pious wedding ceremony descends into the narrative's bacchanalian climax, desecrating the pious order of Nixon's heteronormative ritual.

Television news broadcaster Barbara Walters recalls the real Rose Garden ceremony as being "beautiful" if formal: "I remember . . . I remember—it was so strange—Richard Nixon and his wife dancing, and she put her arm around him, and he stiffened. Strange. It was a beautiful wedding. Tricia Nixon was a fairytale bride, long blonde hair, she looked like a princess. . . . We covered the wedding in the afternoon, we replayed it at night, it was such a big event."[1] The ceremony was a public spectacle, confirming the head of state's private family order for a television audience, broadcast live and in rerun later the same day. Nixon himself joked that it would be the last time he would dance in the White House, attributing his discomfort during the broadcast to his Quaker upbringing. The president's poor performance aside, newspaper reports from the time confirm the sense of a distant ideal, echoing Walters' appreciation for the strange beauty of blonde fairytale princesses. Tricia Nixon's role as the princess bride codified a perfect image of white femininity, contained by the family order of powerful men, and magnified by a rich, costumed display. According to a report in the *Los Angeles Times*, "Tricia wore a sleeveless, organdy dress appliquéd with Alecon lace and embroidered with lilies of the valley, over a white crepe underslip. She wore a small sculptured Juliet cap appliquéd to match the gown, and carried a miniature bouquet of lilies of the valley, small white sweetheart roses, baby's breath, and Baker's fern. Around her neck was an heirloom diamond and gold pendant, a wedding gift from her groom."[2] The excessive attention paid by a source of official public discourse to the details of attire—the gown's material, structure, and relationship to the bride's wearing body—suggest the hyper-importance of costume in confirming this feminine performance, a hyperbole ripe for drag satire. The description emphasizes everything's status as "under-"

or "-less"; the diminutive pretense of "a miniature bouquet" of "small white sweetheart roses and baby's breath" exaggerates the fragility of this florid femininity. The groom's heirloom has this bride by the neck. Tricia Nixon, who, along with her mother and sister, had for several years been the subject of newspapers' hemline analyses, had been framed in the public imagination as an ideal young woman made by costume. In 1968, shortly after Nixon's first successful presidential election, which had exploited the candidacy of Southern segregationist George Wallace, one *Los Angeles Times* analysis bore the headline "Nixon Gives Wife, Daughters Fur Coats": "Tricia Nixon's coat is a white sheared lamb, doublebreasted with silver filigree buttons. It is made princess style with a cinched-in waist. With it she wore a white lamb beret Sunday."[3] Draped, in this case, in baby sheep, Tricia Nixon's small white status was a matter of public record, a national performance that was perfected in her White House wedding.

Goldie Glitters, the Cockette who plays Tricia Nixon in *Tricia's Wedding*, also wears a white gown, but by the end of the film, her penis is showing. The film is irreverent from the first scene, in which the president and his wife plan the nuptials from their bed, insisting against hope that it will be a dignified affair. Static shots of individual characters in exaggerated costumes signify the arrival of guests, each of whom delivers a one-liner. Golda Meier, breasts hanging to her waist, makes a Jewish mother joke; Rose Kennedy is delusional in her wheelchair; Phyllis Diller laughs ridiculously; Lady Bird Johnson is loud and abrasive; Jackie Kennedy complains that the White House décor is "tacky." After the arrival of an African ambassador, played by Sylvester in a one-shouldered gown with leopard-print accouterments, another guest complains that there ought not be so many "nigras" in the White House. The film uses these caricatured celebrities and other figures of the imagination to articulate the capriciousness and hypocrisy of the political ruling class.

The film's version of the guest list is far more colorful than the Nixons' own. At the official event, the most well known figures were members of the president's cohort, including war enthusiasts Henry Kissinger, George H. W. Bush, and Donald Rumsfeld, other government officials, and a few celebrities including entertainers Red Skelton and Ethel Waters, who was an atypical black guest—the former vaudeville, Broadway, and Hollywood star had by this time become a conservative Christian

Republican. While generally glamorizing the guest list, the Cockettes were indeed correct in depicting the attendance of Mamie Eisenhower; in her film portrayal, the frumpily attired actor mocks both the elderly former first lady and Nixon's outrageous six-tiered "towering wedding cake" by collapsing face first into the frosting. None of Nixon's actual guests were quite as theatrical as Eartha Kitt, for example, who, played by Reggie in a low-cut, draped mini-dress, spikes the punch bowl using a bottle boldly marked "LSD."

Kitt, the singer and actress whose condemnation of the Vietnam War at a Johnson-era White House function had damaged her career irreparably, is used here by the Cockettes as a black radicalizing agent. Dunnigan offers mischievous sidelong glances as he pours the bottle's contents into the bowl, transforming the staid affair into an outrageous orgy. The black performers each enact some iconic image of American blackness, complicating the scene of the white wedding. Sylvester acts a dual role, arriving as the fashionable ambassador of some newly independent African state, but also portraying Coretta Scott King in a state of perpetual mourning for her slain husband, the civil rights leader. As Sylvester's King concludes the antique love song "Because You Come to Me" in his proficient falsetto, he delicately wipes tears from his eyes. His last sustained notes bends awkwardly flat as he casts his eyes down. This dual role—ambassador and widow—enacts both the cosmopolitan, utopian glamour and the dramatic realism of American violence imagined through black liberation projects. Sylvester contributes both a transcendental exoticism and some civil rights gravity to the mock affair.

Sylvester's own dual role underscores the carnivalesque quality of the film, a quality that circulated generally through Cockettes performances. In the case of *Tricia's Wedding*, clowns become kings, as hierarchies are inverted amid laughter, and bodies lose their singular meanings while they reveal their lower strata. While practically concerned with an image of folk culture from the European Middle Ages, Mikhail Bakhtin's theory of the carnivalesque is itself a critique of modernity. The Cockettes' performances resonate with its emphasis on "exaggeration, which always tends to transgress its own limits."[4] For Bakhtin, these transgressions are both positive and negative at once, maintaining the indispensable trait of ambivalence, a power that both elevates and debases. This sense of ambivalence destabilizes established order within the "gay time" and

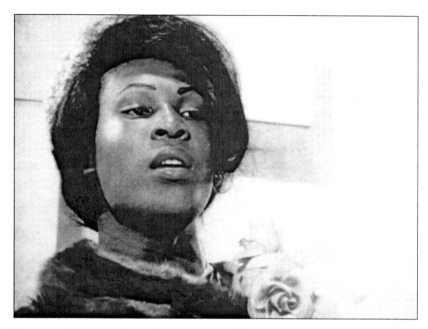

Figure 4.2. Sylvester as Coretta Scott King in a still from *Tricia's Wedding*, Sebastian, 1971.

space of festival culture. Signs are read multiply in this world of grotesque transformation and exaggerations hold multiple meanings together, speaking in heteroglossic terms.

Ambivalence is linked here to the critical power of the carnivalesque, which associates with "forms that would make possible and would justify the most extreme freedom and frankness of thought and speech . . . often enough words and thoughts were turned around in order to discover what they actually were hiding, what was that other side."[5] In *Rabelais and His World*, Bakhtin explores a history of "festive comic images" used by non-elites "to express their criticism, their deep distrust of official truth, and their highest hopes and aspirations . . . it was the thousand-year-old language of fearlessness, a language with no reservations and omissions, about the world and about power."[6] While generalizing broadly, Bakhtin posits a critical function available in ambivalent representations, a function that boldly interrogates power relationships, as *Tricia's Wedding* does. This ambivalence inverts the ruling order, or negates that order altogether and evades its normalizing structure, a possibility Stallybrass and White locate in the carnivalesque.[7] What emerges in the carnivalesque, then, is a fungibility of statuses. This fungibility can be read as a liberatory possibility in the face of entrenched disciplinary authority. Particularly relevant to the Cockettes is Bakhtin's notion of the grotesque body, which is incomplete, changing, and symbolized in the "lower bodily stratum." The Cockettes' broader social project of communal living, sexual availability, and amorphous displays of these traits all celebrated the transformative possibilities of bodies in groups. The carnivalesque and its subset of the grotesque are textual strategies for elaborate displays of difference. In the carnivalesque, as in the Cockettes' own radically ambivalent mode, difference becomes legible across the bodies it marks.

This grotesque critical mode is deployed throughout the film. Drag performances make travesties of the revered figures of the elite class who are participants in the state-sponsored sanctification of heterosexuality. The visibility of revelry is what undoes the oppressive White House ceremony, as writhing performers tumble around the room with their genitals exposed. The critique resonated: "the White House was basically humiliated by that," remembers John Waters.[8] Douglas Crimp sites Nixon advisor John Dean's memoir to show that key members of the administration viewed the film in a special bunker set up to monitor dissent. Crimp muses, "Imagine all those buttoned-up Nixonites huddled together in the East Wing watching the Cockettes send up the White House wedding—and trying to figure out how to put a stop to such dangerously subversive activities!"[9] In this anarchic instance, marginal actors spoke directly to the center of power, revealing absurdity on all sides.

Despite the film's social non-compliance, the black actors, and particularly Sylvester, resist the total dissolution that many of the white performers finally undergo; Kitt, King, the lady ambassador, and another performer's Mahalia Jackson all escape the most vicious parodying enacted by the troupe. While Pat Nixon ends the wedding with hilarious, hysterical screams, her blouse open, and Richard Nixon is seen finally coupled with a young man, Sylvester never quite dissolves into the abandoned state of ecstatic mockery some of the white actors are able to reach, maintaining a level of respect for the figures he portrays. The troupe's black performers, who are performing other black performers, appear to be aware of the visibility that has already constrained their figures, and seem less committed to a politics of total exposure. While Goldie Glitters attempt is to reveal a true body that overrules the makeup and costume of holy matrimony, Sylvester's thoroughly conscribed body offers up no truth more revelatory than the costumed presence of an African ambassadress. Even within the Cockettes' communal ethos, black bodies and white bodies appear to perform differently in relationship to the ordered femininity and masculine authority to which *Tricia's Wedding* responds.

The California Context

Various imaginative transgressions were enacted during this period in California. Fassbinder collaborator Kurt Raab recalls a visit to the state in the early seventies, where he was a witness to unusual gender performances acted out in daily social life. He describes the gay scene:

> In San Francisco we were met at the airport by a dozen leather freaks in fabulous polished-steel-studded getups. They took us everywhere. On one sightseeing tour, they showed us an entire neighborhood for homosexuals only, and we went to all the bars and saunas. By the time we got to Los Angeles, though, I was bored with the whole scene. Going around with all those people just didn't suit my personal tastes. I didn't want to offend our hosts, but finally Fassbinder explained my long face. I saw one of them smile and say, "Oh, he's a chicken hawk," and we then proceeded to make the rounds of bars that featured the underage set.[10]

Raab's anecdote describes subcultures that arose in California out of different inventive identifications and their overlapping affinities, gathered in their anti-normativity, operating in public spaces, extending to organize freaks, homosexuals and, apparently, pedophiles, into a network connecting San Francisco to Los Angeles. While Raab describes a moment in the early seventies, such practices of visibility were set in motion by the social experiments of the late sixties. Gay rights and black liberation movements had emerged in the state by the middle of the decade, while white heterosexuals themselves were reimagining their lives, as was evident in 1967, when one hundred thousand hippies gathered in the Haight-Ashbury neighborhood during San Francisco's so-called "summer of love," celebrating their own notion of sexual liberation. In those years, political tension was expressed across the state through frequent conflicts between law enforcement and urban populations on one hand, and student groups in the state's two public university systems on another. Demonstrations against the war in Vietnam and for various social freedoms were commonplace and widely publicized by media. These conflicts were broadly visible and formed a dramatic public antagonism between authority and its dissidents. Former film actor and California governor Ronald Reagan performed this authority through a televised campaign denouncing the counterculture and by using state powers against demonstrators. As for reformed sexualities, San Francisco had earned a national reputation as a "homosexual city," influenced by the radical community of writers and artists who had gathered there since the fifties. The popular use of marijuana and LSD served to emphasize personal subjectivity, estranging experience from the compulsory regimes of family and nation that figures like Reagan promoted.

Sylvester reached maturity in Los Angeles during the politically charged sixties. Expelled from his family's church after an alleged affair with a male choir-leader, Sylvester began "dressing up" with a community of black drag queens, who organized themselves into a gang. The Disquotays performed highly visible gender transgressions both in their private homes and in the public space of Watts, a predominantly black area of Los Angeles. Sylvester biographer Joshua Gamson quotes Sylvester as he recalls the 1966 civic disorder in Watts: "while everybody else was burning and looting, me and my friends were grabbing wigs, hairspray, and lipstick. No food or TV sets—just fun stuff."[11] Sylvester and his friends used a civic racial crisis as a platform for gender play. Pleasure is asserted in the act of "dressing up," a pleasure Sylvester distinguishes from more aggressive forms of protest. Still, the group participated in the unrest, acting out against principles of private property. Gamson's account reports: "while the neighborhood burned, the Disquotays ignored curfew at a house party. They only stopped dancing when the National Guard came pounding on the door."[12] This performative community's costumed transgression confronted the regime's agents in the form of a party. In this example can be found an approach to politics that enacts resistance in festive rather than disciplined modes.

Sylvester arrived in San Francisco at a particularly transformational moment within this transformational era. In the mid-sixties, the hippie scene had been initiated by a white, heterosexual set of relations. Alice Echols describes the historical context in her study of the 1960s, tracing the differences between the Beat generation of the 1950s and the hippies who followed:

> Race, sexuality, and gender played themselves out differently. . . . For Beats, blacks had signified hipness; the new bohemians, whether out of choice or necessity (by the mid-sixties, black power was beginning to eclipse fantasies of integration), insisted on their own hipness—[Ken] Kesey claimed to have "outniggered" blacks, as he put it. . . . [T]here was virtually no connections between San Francisco's black community and white counter-culture. And whereas the Beat scene had been, if anything, queer-inflected, the hippie counterculture was relentlessly straight, even homophobic. All the talk of free love brought lots of gay people to San Francisco, but the Haight was "overwhelmingly heterosexual." Timothy Leary even proclaimed LSD "a specific cure for homosexuality."[13]

Echols, who goes on to identify the ways that women's roles were curtailed in hippie culture, shows some of the paradoxes of the "free love" and "drop-out" mandates: even while escaping mainstream social structures, they tended to reaffirm the authority of white experience and patriarchal hierarchies. Leading counterculture figures like Kesey and Leary are shown to rely on racist and homophobic notions in the affirmation of their white male originality. Unlike the beats, whose more cynical, urban vernacular accommodated some sexual and racial differences, the hippie scene tended to resubstantiate the white, straight, male actor as the agent of freedom. By 1970, the energies of this previous moment had been dispersed and distorted, limiting the revolutionary possibilities of the drop-out position, but also destabilizing its gender arrangement.

By 1970, when Sylvester moved to San Francisco, a prominent gay community had formed in the Castro neighborhood. That area of Eureka Valley had attracted middle-class gay men who gravitated toward the large Victorian houses that had become available as a result of suburban migration, as well as others gay men who drifted in from the counterculture scene in the nearby Haight district. The utopian hippie sensibility that had emerged there in the mid-sixties had been transformed by national publicity, an incredible influx of "drop-outs," violence and profiteering associated with a drug culture that had moved from psychedelics and marijuana to speed and heroin, tensions with the black population in the nearby Fillmore district, and increased harassment from the police, who typically swept the area searching for runaways. The heyday of the Cockettes performance collective, which formed in 1969, occurred after the Haight's climactic moment, but before the gay subculture's golden age in the seventies. In the space left by the denouement of hippiedom, and amid the rising action of gay culture, the Cockettes enacted an unusual character that portrayed elements of both sensibilities.

Unlike within the hippie scene or the emerging gay male subculture, gender was performed loosely by the troupe, who each deployed various states of excessive drag and undress. It is difficult to describe the genders of the group's member without reaching the limits of one historically inscribed terminology or another. Many could be described as gay men who liked to dress up. Others might be described as transgender women or as gender nonconforming, while others were cisgender women, and at least one other was a straight man in drag, though the troupe's excessive theatricalization of gender disturbs all of these categories, and in a time before language had been carefully articulated to address these differences in public. Regardless of these distinctions, the Cockettes performed—onstage, in their domestic spaces, and in the street—resistance to the identities their apparent bodies would have authorized.

Still, hippie attitudes toward race circulated in the troupe. The Cockettes included other black members besides Sylvester, notably performers Reggie (a.k.a. Anton Dunnigan) and Lendon Sadler. Blackness, however, was distinctly minoritarian within the group's mostly white throng. Part of the broader Cockettes project of freedom was the abolition of identificatory categories such as gender and race. Gamson describes the prevailing attitude:

> The Cockette utopia was one in which the love party erased any differences: we are all freaks under the skin, sisters in glitter. "We didn't even look at differences," Scrumbly Koldewyn says. "Nobody ever talked about

race," says Fayette [Hauser]. . . . Still, that Sylvester's screaming-Josephine
persona was specifically and matter-of-factly black further distinguished
him from the Cockettes. Although he was not an overtly political sort,
Sylvester's utopia was one in which blackness, his blackness, large and
silky, was looked at and attended to, applauded, and set off beautifully
against a white background. Sylvester was a Disquotay in Cockette drag.
He would be inimitable and unavoidably black.[14]

Sylvester's racial difference from the white norm was one of the features that magnified his significance within the troupe. Though also
utopian, Sylvester's ideal was a world in which blackness amplified
presence. Using an imposing black body as a scaffold, and rooting his
performance in a black American subjective experience, Sylvester's
constructed performance accentuated his racial difference through stylized costume and voice. As even the *New York Times* acknowledged,
Sylvester's virtuosity as an entertainer was far in excess of the Cockettes
standard, a proficiency bolstered and mystified by his unusual blackness, which would stereotypically suggest aptitude in entertainment and
other physical techniques. Sylvester's proficient voice sang jazz, gospel,
and R&B phrasings, genres associated with black American interpretive
forms. His style of dress implicated the distinctness of his diva performance, a performance paralleled in the reference to Josephine Baker
above. As was the case with Baker, Sylvester's dress, voice, attitude, and
body colluded in the invention of a black queen.

Many of the white members of the Cockettes had themselves chosen
to "drop-out" of straight white society, and attempted to reject its racial conditioning. That white world, however, was already configured
around Sylvester's permanent exclusion. Racial difference raised different problems for Sylvester. Cockette Fayette Hauser claimed that "Sylvester was never a hippie like we were. He didn't want to toss it all away.
He wanted to sing in drag, and that's what he did with the Cockettes. He
was interested in being an artist."[15] Though everyone was expressive,
Sylvester's proficiency as a singer and discipline as an artist contradicted
the anti-disciplinary ethos established by the group's first leader, Hibiscus, who emphasized a pure creativity free from societal constraints.
In one instance Sylvester and Hibiscus even came to blows backstage
over this difference; Sylvester's transformative presence and Hibiscus's

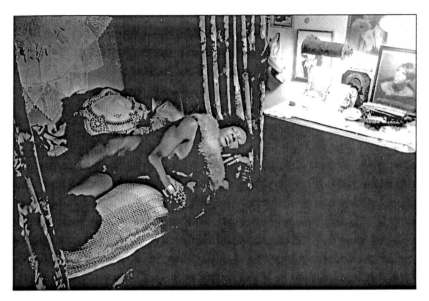

Figure 4.3. Sylvester in bed. Photo by Bud Lee.

transcendent originality were of such contradictory registers, they occupied the same stage with occasional difficulty. Contradictions such
as this one served the Cockettes' radically ambivalent project. As in the
Cockettes' mode of drag that revealed both bodily and constructed elements, the troupe's effectiveness as an anti-normative display depended
upon the simultaneous performance of irreconcilable differences. Racial difference came to play an important role in the troupe's ambivalent
presentations.

Genre and Resistance

While their performances never ended at the stage door, the Cockettes'
stage shows were a central focus of their phenomenal presence in San
Francisco. These performances reconfigured familiar elements of theater
and film genres, rehistoricizing the nostalgic materials of the American
stage and screen. Those genres' attendant racial and sexual stereotypes
were necessarily reinterpreted, and became potent sites of reinvention.
The troupe's white slavery melodrama *Pearls over Shanghai* for example, which premiered in November 1970 and included the numbers

"Jaded Lady" and "Endless Masturbation Blues," deployed Beijing opera costumes and fake Cantonese dialogue, hysterically reenacting, and thus lampooning, some of the orientalist fantasies that haunted early Hollywood. *Gone with the Showboat to Oklahoma* collapsed three American classics, *Gone with the Wind*, *Showboat*, and *Oklahoma!* into one Southern pastiche. The musical was performed in May 1970. In these collapsed genre pieces, an intertextual strategy becomes evident. The collective troupe portrays a decentered set of narratives, displacing any monologic claims to meaning. By bringing various texts into contact, the performance produces meaning by negotiation differences, rather than from within a particular grand narrative. Lacking true protagonists, individual characters' moral perspectives are less important than thematic coincidences, suggesting a normative narrative order against which the performance agitates.

This strategy of intervening against a text's norms by ridiculously reenacting it was one of the ways race was approached by the troupe. While the textual differences between *Gone with the Wind* and *Showboat* are significant, they both dramatize the tragedy of black sexuality. Among the racial problems raised by *Oklahoma!* is the Native American subjugation the narrative elides with manifest destiny. In 1970, shortly before joining the Cockettes, Sylvester saw the production while visiting San Francisco. As Gamson reconstructs it:

> That weekend, a couple of Sylvester's friends took him to the Palace to see the Cockettes' latest, *Gone with the Showboat to Oklahoma*, a promiscuous mix of musical Americana that included a Mammy drag queen in a bandana, who was servant to a Scarlett O'Hara played by a pale young man named Johnni. Johnni, the ex-Cockette Martin Worman recalled, had "natural Scarlett O'Hara ringlets," and was wearing a see-through hoop skirt and "just the lower half of his bloomers, jauntily revealing his fat cock and balls and succulent buns." The show started late, but no one seemed to notice. The audience was noisy, giddy, standing on the seats calling out and screeching and making their own fun and only half paying attention to the stage. . . . Later, the Day-Glo *Show Boat* set collapsed, to the audience's delight, just as a line of chorus girls moved downstage singing, in multiple keys, "Life Upon the Wicked Stage." Upstairs in the balcony, some people seemed to be having sex. Sylvester had never seen

anything quite like it, not even in church, where in a different way, people could get carried away. He was excited, and put off. "I was really, really scared," he said later. "It was nothing I wanted to be part of."[16]

Incongruities break open the text and reveal its dissonances. That an actor could simultaneously possess "natural" Scarlett O'Hara curls while also displaying his "fat cock," suggests a critique of the natural-izing language through which gender is normatively purveyed. There is an ambivalent attitude toward form: men are partly women, sets are erected and collapse, songs are sung in many keys, seats are for standing on, attention is half paid. This ambivalence is performed in the spaces opened up by a lack of fidelity to the text. The play, like the bodies of its performers, is a site for constant reinvention.

Despite his own apparent ambivalence, Sylvester joined the Cock-ettes, knowing the extent of racial travesties many in the group intended to perpetrate. In *Midnight at the Palace: My Life as a Fabulous Cockette*, performer Pam Tent describes the proceedings, which starred many Cockettes regulars:

> The show itself was high camp: a combination of two musicals with a bit of dialogue from Uncle Tom's Cabin thrown in. Hibiscus sang "Can't Help Lovin' Dat Man of Mine" and "June Is Bustin' Out All Over," while the gals threw their chests out for emphasis. Rumi played Belle Watling, the town whore. And never having heard the term "politically correct," Kreemah and Link did the show in blackface. Link tied strips of rags into pink bows all over his head and played "Prissy" from *Gone With the Wind*. Made up with a cork face and white lips, Big Daryl sang "Ol' Man River" while outfitted in a feather boa. Their effrontery got some members of the audience riled up, including Big Daryl's mother, who sat in the audience glancing over her shoulder, afraid that the police would burst in at any moment and arrest everyone. In the lobby after the show, a very large black man approached Big Daryl and picked him up by his shoulders. "You're not going to do blackface no more, are you?" he asked. Big Daryl squeaked out a "no" and kept his word. From then on, any kind of racial satire—and indeed there was some—was done by our own black cast members, whose humor was predictably irreverent and spared no one.[17]

The practice of combination, of costume styles, of texts, of registers of matrixed and non-matrixed performances, effects an intertextual strategy, a process that works in and among differences. This intertextuality works as a critical tool, drawing more attention to generic conventions than the narratives they facilitate. A white man sings "Ol' Man River," a song associated with the black actor Paul Robeson, whose own performance traced a route from American slavery to international communism. In this performance, not only is the slave song travestied through blackface, but camped up with a feather boa, a transgression that was imagined to attract police reprisal. The Hollywood musicals and melodramas to which this production referred were loaded with racial stereotypes, ideas about representation entrenched in American images, images that were immediately relevant to the racial antagonism and violence that had served to politicize the era. While those original texts make specific claims about the nature of black people, the parodic interpretation of these genres emphasizes the fictitiousness of these claims. The genres define loose boundaries in which to play, and in such play, all reliable representations have already been dismissed.

From the start of Tent's description, the musical genre is given a camp treatment, one in which values are inverted and signs are estranged from what they signify. "Can't Help Lovin' That Man of Mine," in its original *Show Boat* context, posits an inescapable black femaleness that bears essential control over the tragic mullato it narrates. In this instance, the melancholy song is sung by an ecstatic blond man in outrageous drag, distorting the reliability of those essential categories. The various gender masquerades alluded to here, including the fake bosoms that the "gals" pushed forward to illustrate "June Is Bustin' Out All Over," are paired with racial masquerades. This performance of blackness is a normative formal element of the genre being dissected, but in this context, these travesties emerge as dangerous, both politically and physically, according to Tent's account. The Cockettes traipsed into the spaces of difference that the genre opened up. There is where the troupe makes recognizable an incongruity between image and meaning, and there is where a critical intervention is made possible.

Playing with textual precedents creates meaning apart from the texts themselves. This meaning is generated in distinction to the conventional meanings associated with the appropriated genres. Linguistic anthropologists Charles Briggs and Richard Bauman have explored a notion of intertextuality made evident in genre, describing the gaps that necessarily exists between an utterance and the generic model to which it is linked. Those intertextual gaps may be intentionally and critically heightened, as strategies for "building authority through claims of individual creativity and innovation . . . , resistance to hegemonic structures associated with established genres, and . . . distancing oneself from textual precedents."[18] While the members of the Cockettes were fans of their textual precedents, their innovative and resistant mode of performance maximized the intertextual gaps produced in their generic homage. Briggs and Bauman address musical satire directly, insisting that it generically emphasizes these gaps. "The use of music in Parody and Satire (as in Brecht's plays) points contrastively to its potential for foregrounding intertextual gaps . . . musical features can simultaneously create intertextual links to generic precedents and to quite different types of discourse."[19] The authors identify an ambivalent force in musical features, one that at once points to and away from their generic precedents. Invoking Brecht in this context, they suggest methods of estrangement that also maximized intertextual gaps.

In his essay "On Music in Epic Theater," Brecht relates his politically engaged theatrics, which he describes as gestic, in opposition to imitative Aristotelian theater, which minimizes such gaps between texts.

> In short, the spectator is given the chance to criticize human behavior from a social point of view, and the scene is played as a piece of history. The idea is that the spectator should be put in a position where he can make comparisons about everything that influences the way in which human beings behave. This means, from the aesthetic point of view, that the actors' social gest becomes particularly important. The arts have to begin paying attention to the gest. . . . To put it practically, gestic music is that music that allows the actor to exhibit certain basic gests on the stage. So-called "cheap" music, particularly that of the cabaret and the operetta, has for some time been a sort of gestic music.[20]

In Brecht's method, music is used to create irresolvable formal differences, differences that allow critical comparisons to be made. This approach politicizes theatrical presentation by denaturalizing it, using elements including musical numbers that disrupt the authenticity of the narrative in order to make the audience face the material in a critical manner. Members of the Cockettes may or may not have been familiar with Brecht. Most were certainly aware of the local political street theater of the time that employed Brechtian tactics, particularly the San Francisco Mime Troupe, out of which pedigree the Sutter Street Commune evolved, a primary ideological influence on the Cockettes' own commune. In the terms of experimental theater canons, the antidisciplinary performances proposed by Antonin Artaud would be just as relevant to the Cockettes, were it not for their fidelity to an idea of a text. Regardless, in performances such as *Gone with the Showboat to Oklahoma*, the Cockettes promiscuously brought together different influences in a celebration of critical reinvention. All at once, the Cockettes would have been invoking the glamorous floor shows and Broadway spectacles that served as a primary influence, the particulars of the Southern nostalgia genre of musicals, a history of detached modes of performance with roots in political theater practices of the twentieth century, along with older traditions of carnivalesque revelry. By denaturalizing these texts and their relationships, the Cockettes' outrageous performance achieves a critical function.

Reworking Bakhtin, Briggs and Bauman offer that genres are always situated historically, and invoke historical situation. A critical approach brings historical context to bear on any generic utterance, disturbing any reading of genre as an eternal configuration.

> Invoking a genre thus creates indexical connections that extend far beyond the present setting of production or reception, thereby linking a particular act to other times, places, and persons. . . . [G]eneric features thus foreground the status of utterances as recontextualizations of prior discourse. . . . [G]eneric intertextuality points to the role of recontextualization at the level of discourse production and reception. Genre thus pertains crucially to negotiations of identity and power—by invoking a particular genre, producers of discourse assert (tacitly or explicitly) that they possess the authority needed to decontextualize discourse that bears these historical and social connections and to recontextualize it in the current discursive setting.[21]

This reading posits a provisional agency within the act of genre performances. The Cockettes demonstrate a certain power over the genres they manipulate, acting, in the intertextual gaps, against the systems of power they have historically substantiated. The idea of blackface performance, for example, which was compulsory for black performers in the eras of minstrelsy and vaudeville, and which allowed white performers to assert power over the black subjects they represented, is destabilized by the recontextualization into queer San Francisco of the late sixties. In the example from *Gone with the Showboat to Oklahoma*, the performance of blackface was not compulsory, but a voluntary accentuation of a generic feature bound to another time and place. Blackface is presented out of place, making the practice strange rather than essential. This estrangement puts the practice in some manageable context: It was a black audience member who asserted his own agency by intimidating the white performer into giving up the practice. This recontextualization of blackface resulted in a critical intervention that subverted the racist power of that practice. This kind of intertextual play rehistoricized the very texts through which race, gender, and other identifications have become legible.

Private Parts in Public Spaces

Despite the richness of their stage shows and the films in which they appeared, Cockettes performances are best understood in terms of a continuity among standard performance contexts, public spaces, and private life. These performers effectively destabilized the differences between these various notions of space, and the constraints that govern them. While the Pagoda Palace Theater in the North Beach district of San Francisco was the official home to the Cockettes' stage revues and film screenings, their excessive antics were also acted out in public demonstrations and in their communal domestic spaces. The troupe members commonly used LSD in their daily lives, an effect of which may have been a decreased sensitivity to preserving the disciplinary distinctions between various spaces. The use of costumes certainly did not end at the theater door. As Sylvester put it, "Everyday life with the Cockettes . . . was like living on stage. I mean, you lived in glitter and you ate glitter—the whole thing was glitter."[22] Cockette John Flowers claimed,

"Glitter covers a multitude of sins,"[23] amplifying what poet Allen Ginsburg had to say about his friend and onetime lover, the troupe's first leader, Hibiscus: "I know his bed was a little gritty because he had a lot of sequins in it. And it was difficult to sleep on the sheets because there was this sort of like difficult glitter stuff there. And it was always in our lips and in our buttholes. You know it was always around. You couldn't quite get it out."[24] The pervasive glitter in these comments acts metonymically, standing in for a performative lifeworld in which the Cockettes were enmeshed. This glitter circulates between the broad stage and intimate bodily orifices, lending its transformational decorative quality to the experience of performing a transforming body in the theater, in bed, and everywhere in between. This transforming body exceeds classical categories, resisting the normalizing force of dichotomous arrangements like public and private, imagining a way of being uncontained by disciplinary hierarchies.

Just as public and private spaces regulate modern social experiences, the Cockettes demonstrate the ways that misused spaces can create momentary radical challenges to normativity. As Michael Hardt and Antonio Negri describe in *Multitude*, the dominant notions of public and private are themselves fallacious conflations, combining on one hand the private operations of the body and its performative actions with the economic idea of private property, and on the other hand an idea of the common with spaces controlled by the state.[25] The Cockettes troubled this fallacious distinction, queering both public and private realms. Lauren Berlant and Michael Warner's article "Sex in Public" offers some useful perspective on the counterdiscursive possibilities exacted through an idea of queer space. Crucial here is an analysis of normativity, as it informs the separation of public from private that undergirds modern life. Following Habermas and others, Berlant and Warner describe how this separation has institutionalized the bourgeois family through a reciprocal process. The public realm has legislated and monetized the privacy of its citizens while granting autonomous personal space; the personal realm has marshaled the intimacy of sex acts that produce the private citizens of the future, a future that validates the public project. Privacy exists in a dialectical relationship to the public. Berlant and Warner unveil a history in which private intimacy "grounded abstract, disembodied citizens in a sense of universal humanity."[26] This universal sense is heterosexual: "A complex cluster of sexual practices gets confused, in heterosexual culture, with the love plot of intimacy and familialism that signifies belonging to society in a deep and normal way. Community is imagined through scenes of intimacy, coupling and kinship; a historical relation to futurity is restricted to generational narrative and reproduction. A whole field of social relations becomes intelligible as heterosexuality, and this privatized sexual culture bestows on its sexual practices a tacit sense of rightness and normalcy. This sense of rightness—embedded in things and not just sex—is what we call heteronormativity."[27] Berlant and Warner use this definition of heteronormativity to contextualize the "counterpublic" enacted by queer space: "Queer and other insurgents have long striven . . . to cultivate what good folks used to call criminal intimacies. We have developed relations and narratives that are only recognized as intimate in queer culture . . . Queer culture has learned not only how to sexualize these and other relations, but also to use them as a context for witnessing intense and personal affect while elaborating a public world of belonging and transformation."[28] The Cockettes community effectively elaborated their own world of belonging and transformation, using sexual differences within overtly sexualized performances, announcing a queer counter-public. This counter-public reveals its private parts, destabilizing the very sense of humanity regulated by this legacy of public/private partnership. The transformational performer publicly expresses a present subjectivity rather than the futurity of family and state that is imagined through the private citizen subject. Even reproductive Cockettes, such as Dusty Dawn, who would sometimes breast-feed her infant son during performances as semi-nude drag queens danced around her, exceeded the proscribed terms of familial reproduction. In *Tricia's Wedding*, this baby wears exaggerated makeup like everyone else. In Cockettes performances and in the everyday of their communal experience, drag, androgyny, nudity, and a broad set of provisional intimacies agitated against a privileged and punishing heteronormativity.

This agitation was anti-disciplinary. As a group of performers, the Cockettes did not act in accord with an ideological platform or a social activist agenda. The political resonance of their performances was indeed viewed as radical and liberatory by the audiences who enjoyed them. As Gamson points out, comparing the troupe to some of the more organized activist groups in California at the time: "Their project involved very little of the meeting, organizing, and comprehensibility, and involved a whole lot of the singing, dancing, and fucking. If communes, hippies, drugs, homosexuals, and drag queens were increasingly unremarkable in San Francisco at the time, the Cockettes nevertheless combined them all into an unprecedented stew. 'The weirdest thing was that they were Communist drag queens,' says the filmmaker John Waters. 'Bearded, transvestite, drug-crazed, hippie Communists.'"[29]

Their collective's combinatory project worked against formal and institutional distinctions, enacting a theatrical sense of performance in public and private life. Though disorganized, these performances suggested a political sensibility aware of a broader political context for this intervention. Pam Tent describes the influence that confrontations between state authorities and a resistant population had on artists, intellectuals, and political radicals of the time. Responding to an array of culturally significant events she had witnessed, from the violent demonstrations in 1968 in Chicago around the Democratic National Convention, to instances in California that year and the next during which Governor Reagan called out the National Guard to quell protests, Tent recalls a sense that "student unrest and radical politics were here to stay—it felt like a revolution was imminent."[30] This anticipation of revolution informed many of the troupe's members. Many participants had worked in emerging gay liberation political movements, particularly on the University of California, Berkeley, campus. Others, including Hibiscus as well as Tent, had been trained in the "ideologically serious" Sutter Street Commune under the strict guidance of writer Irving Rosenthal, who advocated radical experimentation in collective living.[31] Others were in the vanguard of open expressions of sexuality that had only recently been made possible by the emergent queer space of San Francisco. Performer Bambi Lake, a member of Hibiscus's Angels of Light troupe, describes the process of coming out to her mother:

> I told her on the way to the Oakland Induction Center. It was 1968, the height of the Vietnam War, and I had to stand in line in my underwear with all the other draft age boys like lambs to the slaughter. I wrote on my clipboard in large bold letters: I'M GAY. My mother pretty much wrote

me off after I told her. I moved to the Twin Oaks, a sort of sleazy hotel in San Francisco's Tenderloin. I was thrown out a week later for doing drag. Fortunately, one of the Cockettes, Hibiscus, was forming a new group called the Angels of Light and had an opening at the house where they lived at Church and 17th Streets. So, at the tender age of twenty, I moved into what an alternative paper at the time called, "A hotbed of screaming faggotry." It was 1971 and graffitied on the side of the house was a slogan which has kind of stuck with me: Sisters, Rise Up![32]

This personal account represents a politicized set of private choices that resonated throughout the culture. Referring to the troupe Hibiscus formed after falling out with the Cockettes, Lake describes liberatory possibilities engendered in performance, where real-life gender transgressions can be rehearsed. These radical gender performances were elements of a culture of resistance: to the war in Vietnam, to patriarchy, and to sexual regulation.

Rather than an orthodoxy of action or critique, the individual members of the Cockettes brought together subjective experiences that were the political foundation of their work. In addressing the troupe's lack of organized doctrine, troupe members Scrumbly Koldewyn and Maude Mormon recall in a 1977 public radio interview a politics of excess:

MAUDE MORMON: One thing the Cockettes always did was be outrageous, but underneath the outrageousness was a sense of social consciousness.

SCRUMBLY KOLDEWYN: . . . I think it was pretty unconscious . . . one of the criticisms from some people was like "its unconscious." And, and what we were dealing [with] was exploding sexual types—more than having any other kind of analysis . . . exploding . . . the myths of sexuality and the roles that we had been given. It was real sexual role confusion. And even though we didn't collectively say yes we're dealing with that stuff, . . . unconsciously we were being conscious.

MAUDE MORMON: We looked at our fantasies and by accident there was a lot of social comment.

SCRUMBLY KOLDEWYN: The fact that it was public outrage and public spectacle made it inevitably political.[33]

THE COCKETTES, SYLVESTER, AND PERFORMANCE AS LIFE | 159

The notion of public spectacle, anathema to twentieth-century middle-class American mores, articulates a mode of transgression with political effects. The performers' outrageous costumes indicated, publicly, ways of organizing individual life experience that were in excess of normative requirements. As Koldewyn indicates, prescribed sexuality was taken as myth, a set of roles to be performed or unperformed.

The politics of public spectacle that Scrumbly Koldewyn described above are the basis for the Cockettes' radical project. Koldewyn's notion, perhaps coincidentally, deploys Guy Debord's terminology, echoing the Situationist critique that comingled with the 1968 student revolts in Paris. Without overstating the similarities between Paris '68 and San Francisco '68, recognizing a shared superstructure of international capitalism emphasizes commonalities in the deployment of images across the West's commodity world. To combat the commodity image, Debord and the Situationists called for "situations" rather than bourgeois art, or "the concrete construction of momentary ambiances of life and their transformation into a superior passional quality."[34] This call, which encouraged heightened, momentary interactions with the everyday world that might include playful misuses of public space and revisions of mass images, resembles the anti-bourgeois, transformational performance of the Cockettes. *Tricia's Wedding* resembles a kind of Situationist *détournement*. But the difficulties of applying a Situationist critique to the work of the Cockettes are first that Situationist critique, like most Marxist projects, tends to be heteronormative, and second, that the Cockettes would never disavow spectacle. Spectacle was a means of visibility for the Cockettes, a means of sustaining prohibited life possibilities.

Decidedly unrigorous, the group played flexibly among political analyses. Their anti-disciplinarity allowed its members to mix and match political attitudes, which included donning attributes of Marxism without adhering to its totalizing analysis. In the film *Elevator Girls in Bondage* (1969), performers from the troupe enact a narrative in which elevator operators dressed in mini-skirted uniforms from the twenties, discovered at an MGM costume sale, revolt against their workplace oppression. In one scene, the "girls" surround a large portrait of Karl Marx. The ringleader instructs, "The Great Karl Marx said, 'From each according to his abilities, to each according to his needs.'" Another perplexed elevator operator blankly asks, "What does that stand for?" A third asserts, in an unfocused close-up, looking directly into the camera, "It means you can do whatever you want and you get what you need."[35] At this, the rest break out in a cheer of mock enthusiasm. This alienated performance, framed by unrealistic acting in unconvincing drag with amateurish camerawork, broadly indicates the various incomplete performances being undertaken: the failed performance of a true feminine gender as well as the loose performance of Marxist politics. While critiquing these possibilities through these discrepancies, this example nonetheless confirms the politicized milieu in which the troupe's ecstatic performances played out, and an awareness—if not a fully developed consciousness—of a leftist social project their sexual radicality complemented.

Other Black Energies

This leftist orientation also exploited the image of black radical activism that circulated around the era's politicized milieu. *Elevator Girls in Bondage*'s director, Michael Kellman, recalls the social context for the film's narrative conflict: "Fortunately what was going on in the news provided me with all of the material I needed. There was a raid on the Black Panther Party where the Black Panthers were stripped and guns stuck up their ass, so I just said, fine, we'll have that happen to the elevator girls."[36] This does happen in the film, as an intruding agent in a trench coat lifts an elevator operator's skirt from behind as she stand spread-eagled against a wall. In a close-up shot, the agent pokes a hairy butt with his weapon. This action playfully mimics real instances of violence. The Black Panther Party was frequently in the news at this time; the group's most intense period of activity, marked by violent clashes with law enforcement institutions, coincided with the active years of the Cockettes, their Bay Area neighbors. In this film, the Cockettes associate their own anti-normativity with the fight of the party, borrowing from its black resistant energies to ironically reframe their own outlaw situation. There were strange affinities between the two groups: the Panthers too used affected speech and dress to represent imaginative possibilities of belonging, their transforming bodies performing a vision of liberation. The eerie parallels of their members' violent demise—through police assassination on one hand and through drug overdoses and AIDS on the other—would not yet have been understood by the Cockettes in 1969. Still, Kellman's comments suggest a recognition of radicality that transcended the stark differences between the black political party and the queer performance troupe.

The Black Panthers' visibility was a sign of the times, as it were; the assassination of Chicago party member Fred Hampton, for example, affected a wide audience of interested dissenters. This highly publicized, extremely violent event was a stark indication of the conflict between state authority and organized resistance. Black Panther Party leader Elaine Brown describes the scene in her autobiography, having met shortly after the attack with Hampton's wife, Deborah: "She had been in bed in the back of the house, next to Fred, whom she could not wake, not even after they kicked in the front door. As she had struggled to wake him, her nineteen-year-old body had been rocked with the forty-two rounds that were pounded into the bed. Her body had been stained by his blood. Not one bullet hit her. It was a premeditated assassination."[37] As described in the previous chapter, the resonance of this violent event was wide enough to have reached the set of Fassbinder's film *The Niklashausen Journey*, in which Günther Kaufmann reads the account of the murder out loud from a German-language newspaper. These vivid examples of resistance and reprisal informed both communal troupes, the Cockettes in San Francisco and the antiteater in Munich, who both attempted to deploy the Panthers' radical black energies in alienated performances of resistance.

The Black Panthers, whose main chapter was across the San Francisco Bay in Oakland, also tended to use dress and voice as symbols of a radically transforming social situation. Their tactics for visibility were widely observed. While the Panthers' political influence has been acknowledged, their performance strategies have not been fully unpacked. As the Cockettes were appropriating Panther politics, they were also adopting a confrontational Panther style. Even in this much more serious political enterprise, the public performance of an empowered self can be seen in an artful arrangement of racial and gendered signs.

Black expressivity was seen in the BPP context as a proscribed political freedom, as party leader Huey Newton explained using the artistic notion of creativity: "In America, the true basis of creativity is suppressed. Returning to my basic premise, the value of man, the purpose of man is to be free and to engage in productive creativity. This is the freedom we are talking about; this is the freedom that makes life worth living."[38] Leaving aside momentarily the masculinism of this rhetoric, the idea of black expressivity was amply demonstrated by party members in their publications, which often included poetry; in their various memoirs; in their oratory, which radically adapted the artful cadences of the black pulpit; in their distinct manner of dress; and, notably, in their public demonstrations. These politicized expressions contributed to a sense in California that asserting a self through voice and dress could agitate against authoritative oppression. This mode of performance included a revisionist style of presentation. Black radicals in California and elsewhere had begun wearing the natural Afro hairstyle during this time. Former Communist Party member Angela Davis remembers in her autobiography that this hairstyle "identified me as a sympathizer with the Black Power Movement."[39] During this high moment of militant black radicalism, other groups such as Ron Karenga's US Organization wore demonstrably African attire such as dashikis, while the Black Panthers, whose communist doctrine was critical of such essentializing African nostalgia, preferred a contemporary counter-state nationalist uniform consisting of black pants, a blue shirt, a black leather jacket, and a black beret. Firearms often accessorized this look.

While much of the Panthers' rhetoric circulated around images of "the black man," women played important roles in the organization, and adopted variations on the signature look, mimicking the masculinist uniform. Unlike the Cockettes' excessive masquerade, this uniform visualized a militant solidarity, resembling in some ways the gender obfuscating uniform of the Chinese Communist Party, which the Panthers admired. In *Multitude*, Hardt and Negri muse, "It is hard to imagine . . . what the Black Panthers had in mind when they sold copies of Mao's little red book on the streets of Berkeley."[40] Rather than wonder, an answer can be apprehended by asking a Black Panther: Elaine Brown suggests in her autobiography that Mao's book internationalized their movement, and that mandating it implemented party discipline.[41] Among its disciplinary practices, international communism rejected decadent gendered costumes in favor of masculinized uniformity.

Women associated with the black power movement often reenacted male-identified forms of oratory in their speeches. Davis was known for her public speeches, which put her at odds with what she called the "Nixon-Reagan clique,"[42] and set her on a widely publicized course toward jail. While incarcerated in New York, she gave an interview that was released in 1971 by Folkways Records as the spoken-word album *Angela Davis Speaks*. On this recording, as in her public speeches, Davis employs her signature vocal style, delivering radical analyses in long sentences. The content of her commentary is informed by her expertise in European philosophy, but formally it rings of the American South's black pulpit tradition. Davis's drawn out cadences achieve a sing-song quality. She maintains a tone of knowing authority, enacting a constructed vocal position that is neither distinctly feminine nor masculine. Her later body of writing pays considerable attention to historical connections among race and gender and sexuality, and reveals her own lesbian identity. In this interview, she pays particular attention to the ways women are treated in prison, bringing a feminist dimension to her black power activism.

Davis rose to prominence through an outlawed lecture in 1969 at UCLA, which led to a long speaking career. As in other movements, public speeches served important functions in the Black Panther Party. Elaine Brown's autobiography opens with a scene from Oakland in 1974 in which she announces, from an auditorium stage, that she will replace Newton as party leader. As she speaks to a mostly male group of representatives from different national chapters, she describes stylized gestures and vocalizations calculated to intimidate. "I began to walk up and down the stage," she remembers, "purposely emphasizing my words with the sound of the heels of my black leather boots."[43] Her reminiscences recall the creative ways her gender was performed within a male-dominated party that, despite a prevailing anti-sexist agenda, had difficulty overcoming gender differences. Brown's colleague Ericka Huggins also played an important leadership role in the party. While contextualized and sometimes marginalized by their heterosexual relationships with male party leaders, both activists resisted standard support positions, playing out improvisatory positions of authority.

The performance of such a position is substantiated in Brown's musical recordings that she made as culture minister of the party. Her record *Seize the Time*, recorded in 1969, has a cover designed by BPP artist Emory Douglas, featuring an illustration of an androgynously uniformed figure seen from the chin down, holding a machine gun.[44] The only sign of gender costume are the conspicuously red fingernails on the hands holding the gun. The image suggests a woman posed for military action, but its ambiguity leaves open the possibility that it is a man wearing fingernail polish. This gender confusion extends to the content of Brown's original activist songs, as communicated through her female voice. At the formal level, her piano playing and singing more resemble American folk music than the sound of black soul; her voice extends notes using a clear and even vibrato, unlike popular singers of the era who elaborated on gospel and blues phrasings. Her piano playing uses regulated rhythms and standard chords, avoiding the complex revisions of jazz. While these formal elements are fairly conventional, and don't necessarily rely on a performance of blackness, the songs' explicit content radicalizes the enterprise. Her stirring ballad "The End of Silence" returns again and again to the strident refrain:

> Well then, believe it my friend
> That this silence can end
> We'll just have to get guns and be men[45]

This image, like Douglas's cover image, arrives at an empowered position through a convoluted gender situation. Brown sings in the third person about becoming men. This plural masculinity is accomplished through the acquisition of a phallic prop, the key instrument of armed resistance. The "we" implicates an imagined black listener, rendered mute under the "silence" of racism. Blackness gains a voice through manhood, a proposition announced by Brown's feminine vibrato. Race and gender are, as always, collaboratively ensnared.

Responding both to a Nikki Giovanni poem and to Brown's lyrics, which were printed as a poem in the party newspaper, Regina Jennings critiques these women's gender attitudes: "Both female artists assume male personas when urging the need for revolutionary action. What this poetry demonstrates is that during the 1960s, in certain areas, women had not thought out their roles."[46] Brown's entire album is consistently focused on man and men, and does not launch a feminist critique. Her inexplicable gender position leaves much to be "thought out." However, her own voice brings a gendered depth to the lyrics. A woman assuming a male persona, if that's what she's doing, is a practice with some transformational potential. This performance of transformation agitates against fixity. As Jean Genet wrote in one of his several essays in defense of the Black Panther Party: "I have hope for the Black people and for the revolution undertaken by the Black Panther Party. First of all, all the peoples of the third world are increasingly conscious of the revolutionary necessity; secondly, the Whites, and even the Americans, and even Johnson and what has come after, can transform themselves."[47] The notion of transformation is projected as a revolutionary force. Changing bodies can change society. While Genet's own zeal at this time was oriented around the prominent imprisonment of party leader Bobby Seale, his writing makes no mention of Ericka Huggins, who was also imprisoned. While Genet's complex interest in revolutionary men is well documented, Huggins is marginalized in this aspect of the mythology. Just as gender difference tends to impose invisibility, gender performance serves as a way to be seen. In the Cockettes, gay men wore drag to become spectacular. In the black power movement, women performed masculinity to become visible.

Unlike the Cockettes, the Black Panthers were not queer. Despite some evidence of gay Black Panthers, heterosexuality was the dominant norm within the movement. Brown's own attitude toward gay people in her autobiography is somewhat disparaging. But among the party leadership, there was a doctrinal acknowledgment of solidarities among various differences. At their 1970 Constitutional Convention, the party put gay rights on the agenda. Huey Newton wrote:

> We have not said much about homosexuals at all, but we must relate to the homosexual movement because it is a real thing. And I know through reading, and through my life experience and observations that homosexuals are not given freedom and liberty by anyone in the society. They might be the most oppressed in the society. We should be careful about using these terms that might turn our friends off. The terms "faggot" and "punk" should be deleted from our vocabulary, and especially we should not attach names normally designed for homosexuals to men who are enemies of the people, such as Nixon or Mitchell. Homosexuals are not enemies of the people. We should try to form a working coalition with the gay liberation and women's liberation groups. We must always handle social forces in the most appropriate manner.[48]

Figure 4.4. Cover of Elaine Brown's *Seize the Time*, 1968. Cover art by Emory Douglas.

While this statement does little to acknowledge sexual diversity within the party, it attempts to find solidarity with the "homosexual movement" going on across the bay. As E. Patrick Johnson has shown, Newton had also cast doubt on former collaborator Eldridge Cleaver's heterosexuality, a discrediting move that inadvertently revealed strains of queer melancholy within the masculine discourse.[49] Despite these heterosexist limitations, the statement above signals an awareness that resistance is not a singular movement or analysis, and of the many differences that had come to characterize the left by the end of the sixties. The Cockettes, like much of the nation, were watching the Panthers, and to some extent, the Panthers were watching the gays.

"As for the Black Panthers," reports Gamson, "the Disquotays main interest was in the ones they dated, 'on the QT side.'"[50] While Sylvester grew up in a Los Angeles neighborhood that was a center of black radical activities, most of the Cockettes would not have had contact with the agents of the Black Power Movement. For Sylvester and the Cockettes, sexual freedom superseded political doctrine. Despite these limitations, in performed episodes like that of the elevator girls, the Cockettes demonstrated a sense that racial oppression has something to do with their own playfully critical attitude, and that black radicality can in some distorted way represent their own. In their public performance of difference, Marxism, Black Power, and MGM costumes all provided signs that could be tried on and rearranged.

Drag Personae

Cross-gender costume is a deep and broad theatrical convention, and it has played a particularly significant role in performances associated with queer spaces. While attention to these histories reveals important critical strategies, drag's effectiveness as a critical tool is itself contingent and situational. Gender performances such as the phallic Scarlett O'Hara may tend to disrupt a viewer's idea of gender as correlated to sex. Judith Butler's discussion of drag performance in this context is well known. Butler illustrates a difference between the expression of gender as the reflection of a prior-existing sex and performances of gender that themselves "constitute the identity they are said to express or reveal."[51] She elaborates: "[I]f gender attributes and acts, the various ways in which a body shows or produces its cultural signification, are performative, then there is no preexisting identity by which an act or attribute might be measured; there would be no true or false, real or distorted acts of gender, and the postulation of a true gender identity would be revealed as a regulatory fiction."[52] Drag performance is a useful example here because it can fully separate sexual difference from the trappings of gender, its costumes, gestures, and postures. As in Hibiscus's tragic mulatto performance in *Gone with the Showboat to Oklahoma*, reproductive organs and other biological materials are freed from the regulating apparatus of surfaces.

Drag does not, of course, automatically abolish gender hierarchies, and often capably expresses the misogyny embedded in conventional representations of women. A Foucauldian understanding of discourse insists that drag performance—in fact all performance—is itself already a function of the social regime that precedes the subject. Complicating the historical context, Butler addresses the heterosexist constraints that contain drag's "play *between* psyche and appearance," suggesting limits set by the unconscious on possible externalization.[53] In her essay "Miming the Master," Mary Kelly points to the phallically inscribed feminine position that acts of masquerade emerge from and resubstantiate.[54] Drag in this sense is a dance of seduction for a dominant viewer, an attempt to catch the attention of male power with the trappings of feminine costume. Locked into the terms of gender difference, drag produces limited possibilities for resistant acts and does not represent a mode of agency in and of itself.

Still, the anti-authoritarian Cockettes performances described above align with a radical queer tradition more invested in destabilizing gender categories than substantiating the discursive terms of femininity. Along these lines, José Esteban Muñoz distinguishes the radical, "terrorist drag" of performer Vaginal Davis from what he calls "commercial drag," which "presents a sanitized and desexualized queer subject for mass consumption."[55] Davis's example is particularly apt, as her persona—named in an inversion of Angela Davis—complicates gender, race, and sexuality simultaneously, hyperbolizing each to press against the others, exceeding the boundaries of sensible, commodifiable drag performance. Davis continues a tradition of countercultural gender performance innovated by the Cockettes. Muñoz's focus on Davis is set against a liberal pluralist backdrop in which a "sanitized queen is meant to be enjoyed as an entertainer who will hopefully lead to social understanding and tolerance."[56] The actors described here maintain less politely progressive aims.

Still, even the queerest drag is constrained by a millennia-long Western tradition of cross-dressing performance, through which gender has been elaborated. Attention to this history shows oppressive regulation, as in Sue-Ellen Case's analysis "Classic Drag: The Greek Creation of Female Parts," which demonstrates how performances of womanness were used in that tradition to confirm the political project of containing women and maintaining patriarchy.[57] Far from out-lining the fictions of gender for their ancient audiences, Case argues that cross-dressing performances on the Athenian stage served to substantiate discursive norms, effectively reinforcing gender struc-tures that were expedient for the city-state.[58] Amy Richlin's study of Plautus, on the other hand, has located some ambivalent potential in the drag canon. Richlin focuses on the role reversals, vulgar actions, and drag performances in Plautus's works, which are key contribu-tions to Western comedy. Their performances spoke across classes of masters and slaves to the mutual ridicule of all.[59] According to Rich-lin, the languages they used were less universalist and more specific, often representing local dialects and class situations familiar to the audience, even at times speaking multiply to different sections of the audience. This comedy, in its locality, engaged with culture at the low-est levels, and was capable of sending mixed signals about class, gen-der, and ethnicity. [60] Richlin further suggests that, despite common arguments to the contrary, the concept of drag is applicable to these Roman cross-dressing practices, in that "the actors' transgressive skills were viewed as risqué," pushing the boundaries of sexual normativity when permitted onstage.[61] In her account, this theater, which likely also included slaves as performers, offered critiques of the culture it represented while also upholding that culture's political project.[62] Just as Butler's drag performer is both beholden to and critical of the ap-paratus of gender, the performances Richlin describes provided mo-ments of criticality. This long history helps to illuminate the resistant possibilities inherent in the Cockettes' main performance strategy, drag. While drag's ability to foster agency is limited, the possibility of provisional resistance cannot be closed altogether. This frames drag as ambivalent at best, which is better than nothing.

As discussed above, drag costume combined with voice in the con-struction of Sylvester's persona. His highly developed personal style was of immediate interest to the Cockettes, whom he joined in 1970. Resem-bling the sort of attention paid to Nina Simone in New York, references to Sylvester frequently described the outfits he wore. Exemplifying this relationship, the poem "Nubian Goddess" by Bambi Lake, Sylvester's contemporary, recalls the public spectacle of his style:

NUBIAN GODDESS
I saw Sylvester one night at a party
(he was thin then) descending a staircase
He was wearing long Garbo slacks, a tropical vintage shirt,
fox coat, and a turban
He looked radiant and said, "I just had sex with Leon Russel."

I saw Sylvester getting off a bus at Market and Castro
He had an Afro, cutoff shorts, and platform shoes
He said, "Me and my girls the Pointer Sisters are going to London
with Rod Stewart"

I saw Sylvester at the Upper Market Street Gallery one afternoon
He had just gotten back from L.A. and was being escorted
everywhere in limousines
He showed me a vintage '20s gown he'd just bought
He said, "I just met Debra Walley from
. . . Beach Blanket Something."
(It was the Debra Walley, from *Gidget Goes Hawaiian.*)

I saw Sylvester in front of the Palace Theater one night
He was wearing a tropical print '30s rayon dress, a fox fur coat,
and six-inch cork wedgies
I asked where he got his dress and he said, "Oh, it was a gift."

I saw Sylvester in a big hat, in flowing robes, on Polk Street,
walking his two Borzoi dogs
He said, "We're looking for someone to buy us cocktails."

I saw Sylvester on Halloween night on Polk Street
in a blue sequin gown
with a huge cotton candy beehive wig, wrapped in blue tulle
And he didn't have to say anything.[63]

This amazing cavalcade of fashions conflates a dizzying number of specific references to styles and garments, illustrating Sylvester's ability
to shape his identity with costume. He appears to the author in each

instance, his extreme visibility mobilizing his transformative persona. In each stanza, a speech act by Sylvester himself, one that elevates his social status, caps the look, punctuating each identification with an utterance. That is, except in the final stanza, when he communicates more by saying nothing at all, his costume finally speaking for itself. Not only is there no coherent set of historical references made by these garments through which to understand Sylvester's identity, but this identity is taken out of time and spread across an array of anachronistic instances, unified only by the space of San Francisco. The title, "Nubian Goddess," also implies this possibility, imagining an ahistorical supernatural diva like Simone's "High Priestess of Soul," a figure through which incongruities in action and speech are assimilated. Sylvester's performed presence is the unifying element among these various signs and codes.

The Cockettes further deployed drag's ambivalent potential by inhabiting an ambivalent relationship to drag. Nudity and a mix of coded costumes often colluded to create an image of gender ambiguity. Importantly, these costumed performances were enacted both onstage and off, in theatrical contexts as well as the public and private spaces of the everyday. Sylvester himself was an innovator of a deconstructed gender appearance. As in several of the ensembles outlined in "Nubian Goddess," Sylvester's style of dress often incorporated a mix of gendered signifiers, purveying a drag of excessive androgyny rather than a drag of female impersonation. An enduring part of his public display, this androgynous presentation extended from the mid-sixties, when he attended underground clubs in Los Angeles, to the time of his death in 1988, when his performance had been experienced by a wide audience. Gamson describes the scene in which fellow Cockette Reggie first spotted Sylvester at the Whisky a Go Go, a Hollywood club where rock bands such as The Doors frequently played. According to Gamson, Reggie quickly forged a stylistic solidarity with Sylvester: "That night, Reggie was wearing a blond wig and a bandleader costume with big brass buttons. He saw, standing along the wall, a tall, dark, and handsome person with pierced ears, wearing a blunt-cut wig, men's pants, and a dress with the front cut open to make a smart little jacket. 'We both just like zoomed in on one another,' he recalled many years later, 'because we were like men with sort of female touches around the edges.'"[64] Sylvester's look incorporated men's and women's garments, adapted and altered to stylize a transgres-

Figure 4.5. "Lucille Higgins of Peoria Comes to See Miss Ruby Blue." Sylvester and
Rumi Missabu in the lobby of the Pagoda Palace Theater in San Francisco. Photo by
David Wise, courtesy of the Rumi Missabu Papers, New York Public Library for the
Performing Arts at Lincoln Center.

sion of the fidelity between dress and gender. Another of his contemporaries recalled, "He was more than just a drag queen or a gay guy or
a transsexual; he was all of that."[65] The use of different gender codes allowed Sylvester to exceed gender categories. The specific arrangements
of drag queen, gay guy, and transgender person each indicate an anti-
normative posture oriented around a subcultural set of practices. Each
of these categories stakes out a specific relationship to the presentation
of gender, to the body, and to sexual acts. Sylvester's excess is a subver-
sion of even these subversive categories, an excess forged in androgyny.
The combination of signs not only theatricalizes gender, but reinvents
its potential. The logic of the binary is left behind as Sylvester marks his
singularity with this creative multiplicity.

In considering Sylvester's singular yet multiple dress-up strategy, his
fascination with Josephine Baker is instructive: "I really believed for a
certain time that I *was* Josephine Baker. In my attitude, in my everything, I *was* Josephine Baker."[66] Sylvester, who eventually was able to

meet Baker when she performed in California, enacted an imagination of the black transnational entertainer, who crosses borders of all kinds.[67] Baker's own ambiguous drag performances signaled her own agile resistance to normative categories and her apparent transcendence of the racial and gender roles she was born into, but evaded through imaginative performances. This imagination was no doubt impressive to Sylvester, instigating his Baker fantasy. In addition to Baker, other outstanding images of black divas also filtered into Sylvester's imaginative repertoire. Gamson reports the impression Sylvester made on his San Francisco community with his impression of Billie Holiday: "Sylvester pulled out a little square hi-fi and put on a Billie Holiday album. 'Wait, no, hold on,' he said, 'I have to do it with a gardenia in my hair.' He found a white flower and put it in his hair, and restarted the record. 'Wait, no, hold on,' he said, 'I have to put on a cut-on-the-bias dress.' Finding just the right thing, he put it on, restarted the record, and sang with Billie."[68] Sylvester often claimed, as was reported in a 1971 *Rolling Stone* article, that he was in fact a relative of Holiday's. Though that claim is unsubstantiated, it is no less important if it is not factual. The assertion underscores an idea that transformative potential can be enacted through an imagination of black iconography. This iconography is recrafted by the specific configurations of costume. A white flower can stand in for Holiday's signature gardenia, doubly performative, as Holiday herself first used the flower to conceal an unfortunate hairstyle. Sylvester's drag does not invent an alternate identity to conceal a true identity, but rather reflects his own subjectivity by arranging specific signs of gender and race so that they read as the figure he imagines he will be. Through the radical expressivity of costume, Sylvester, like Baker, like Holiday, like Simone, constructs a persona. While the gendered, black *person* has difficulty assuming the position of a subject with agency, the diva *persona* assumes provisional power through this radical expressivity. More than constructing a gender, drag in this case constructs a lifeworld.

Sylvester's Transvocality

Sylvester was far more interested in professional singing that most Cockettes, and his proficiency in this regard led later to a professional career. *Rolling Stone* singled Sylvester out, claiming he had "the style, nuances, and command of Nina Simone, Bessie Smith, Billie Holiday. . . . [He] summons all the pride and dignity of ten thousand years of blackness."[69] This hyperbole again places Sylvester within a lineage of black women performers who revised other black materials and used a commanding present persona to manage differences. Again, this presence is described in mythical terms, imagined as part of an ahistorical ten-thousand-year span of difference, a kind of perpetual exclusion. The diva persona reworks this exclusion, turning marginality into powerful singularity. Aside from the press and audiences, the other Cockettes were impressed by Sylvester's singular ability as well; he would show off this aptitude on stage and in their communal house. Other Cockettes remember Sylvester at home by the piano: "He played the Mickey Mouse Club song as a gospel prayer, slowing down each letter and circling around it like he was spelling the name of Christ Himself."[70] Sylvester used the familiar black American technique of revision as an expressive mode. His voice, like Simone's, was ambiguously gendered; his consistent, soulful falsetto enunciated this ambiguity. This kind of transvocality, enacting a multiply gendered voice that assimilates diverse materials, resembles Simone's own practice. This voice also contributed to the group's popularity: a recording included in David Weissman's documentary film *The Cockettes* includes a thrilled outburst of audience approval when Sylvester breaks into the jazzy number "Jaded Lady" from the stage revue *Pearls over Shanghai*, lending a moment of assured technical proficiency to the production.[71] Sylvester, who had studied the history of blues singers, used these familiar techniques of revision, recombination, and virtuosity to bolster his expressive power. While his persona was an accumulation of signs, his transvocality enacted a reliable black presence that could speak performatively amid its ambivalent setting.

This vocal aptitude and these strategies of revision are evident in an enduring collection of recordings Sylvester made soon after leaving the Cockettes. Sylvester and the Hot Band released two albums on Blue Thumb Records in 1973. The first, eponymous record was also known as "Scratch My Flower," for the scratch-and-sniff gardenia on the cover, a campy tribute to Billie Holiday. The second was called *Bazaar*, and the cover resembled that fashion magazine's layout, with Sylvester taking the pose of the cover model, shown in a close-up with long wavy hair, subtle makeup emphasizing slightly parted red lips, and an abundance

Figure 4.6. Sylvester with phonograph, Mountain View, California, 1971. Photo by Peter Mintun, courtesy of the Peter Mintun Papers at the San Francisco Public Library.

of gigantic rings, earrings and bracelets. Both albums mix the era's rock and funk sounds into a pastiche of source materials, revising songs authored by popular artists Neil Young, James Taylor, Leonard Cohen, Ray Charles, and Otis Redding, alongside songs associated with Billie Holiday and Bessie Smith. Sylvester sings emphatically, wailing above guitars, drums, horns, funky bass grooves, and backup singers. Sometimes pretty, Sylvester usually arrives at a controlled belting sound with coarse edges by each song's finale. His voice signals blues-inflected rock, along the lines of Janis Joplin's hit recordings, and a black originality embedded in the abandoned devotion of church singing. Sylvester makes all of these references his own, extending his unique voice across these diverse materials, even radically revising the patriotic song "My Country, 'Tis of Thee" in his signature falsetto, intervening in that song's image of ideal citizenship. Using a variety of borrowed materials, Sylvester asserts a convincing ownership of his own voice. The transvocality of this voice, in which racial and gender differences are brought together and performed simultaneously, crystallizes within this performance medium the life as performance persona Sylvester adopted since before his time with the Cockettes.

Far beyond the the Cockettes period, Sylvester continued to record music into the eighties, reaching a broad audience with successful dance singles and touring outside of the United States. His most widely distributed performance was the song "You Make Me Feel (Mighty Real)," a disco anthem released in 1978 on the album *Step II*. The song reached the top 10 in the United Kingdom, the top 40 in the United States, and remained for several weeks at number one on *Billboard*'s U.S. dance/disco chart. In what has become a disco classic, Sylvester soulfully repeats the title as a mantra, suggesting a notion of reality formed in relation, where the subject is constituted syntactically in response to the force an object exerts on it. In "You Make me Feel (Mighty Real)," reality is not founded in the "I," but in the difference between "me" and "you." This notion of meaning in difference, which is understood through feeling, is further radicalized by the sexual relation imagined. As the repetitive groove drives an energetic physicality, the lyrics describe this relation coming into being in the act of dancing. That this dance hit dominated gay clubs of the era suggests the performativity of the emerging gay identity. It was enacted in queer spaces where disco dancing was a part of a physical repertoire that also included sexual contact. Rather than an *a priori* sense of self, this sexualized identity is actualized in physical relation. Following two verses and the repetitions of the chorus, Sylvester's vocal breakdown reasserts the imaginative sense of being enacted through gay identity, actualized by queer sexuality.

> I feel real when you touch me
> I feel real when you kiss me
> I feel real when you touch me
> I feel real when you hold me[72]

Finally, his voice breaks into sighs and breathy non-verbal exclamations, suggesting the ecstatic vocalizations of intercourse. Sylvester's voice speaks from the place of a subjectivity who is also a persona, one purposefully oriented around the bringing into being of identificatory categories prohibited in normative social life. Toward the end of his own life, Sylvester's popularity provided a platform for a growing gay subculture, taking pleasure in its sexuality, and forging spaces for its articulation.

Conclusion

While the Cockettes proposed liberation through life-as-performance drag, Sylvester's black American approach defined this liberation as a means of artistic, personal expression. While there are differences in these two approaches, they each informed the other within the space of differences the Cockettes created for a short time in San Francisco at the end of the sixties. While an interest in transcending racial and sexual categories motivated many of the troupe's members, they were always compelled to reenact those categories nonetheless, using the image of difference to satirize the disciplinary structures that dominated the experiences of public and private life. Queer sexuality mixed with iden-tificatory travesties, making a mockery of essentialist premises. These actors proved that performance can serve as a potent site of personal reinvention and social transformation. While the gay festive time of late-sixties San Francisco is long gone, these performances still provide an impressive model for provisional resistance.

Afterword

A History of Impossible Progress

The present is not enough.
—José Esteban Muñoz

Once we reject the view that claims that no political position can rest on performative contradiction, and allow the
performative function as a claim and an act whose effects
unfold in time, then we can actually entertain the opposite
thesis, namely that there can be no radical politics of change
without performative contradiction.
—Judith Butler

At this point I don't feel that gay guerillas can really match
with Afghani guerillas or PLO guerillas. But let us hope in
the future that they might.
—Julius Eastman

Throughout these pages, I have argued that the raising of different possibilities in performance can be a transformative act, though clearly
the sixties and its performances did not altogether revolutionize familiar powers. Economic exploitation, white supremacy, and patriarchy
endure. Their reprisals are as discouraging as ever. Whether this is a
failure of the sixties, as is sometimes asserted, or a failure of the present might be worth discussing. But the performances I have described
suggest that failure and success are not reliable measures. Possibility
confirms the co-occurrence of failure and success, and the way negativity is engendered even in a positive result. Here is a condition blackness
shares with the idea of possibility—among its iterations exists at least a
doubling of that which definitely is with that which simply cannot.

The antagonism so vexing to Dr. Du Bois has outlived him significantly. Race has cleaved its way into the twenty-first century, organizing disjunctions that have extended modernity's reach. Of special relevance to performance studies has been the expansion of representational technologies, their images distributed through an intensified sphere of visuality, which organizes authority and power around what is seen.[1] This sphere continues to affirm the immanence of blackness as commodity, narrative structure, and identification—it is exchanged as a volatile arrangement of values, it compels dramatic action around conflict and strife, and it activates a position from which to speak into discourse. By now, these processes have played out across a wide swath of historical time, and still today, blackness's performative repertoire is called upon as insistently as ever. Blackness is exhausting activity.

The idea of excess that I have drawn from a retrospective understanding of the sixties, a sense that order could be recuperated by declaring that the sixties were too much, resists that very recontainment. The hope that revolutionary self-determination or radically utopian outcomes are just around the corner may be more remote now than it was within the political movements of that time. Under different historical conditions, the volatility of black performance continues to destabilize categorical distinctions and radicalize its contexts. Importantly, the alienations, demands for multiplicitous production, global flows, and general ambivalences of contemporary capitalist life are well met by blackness, which has developed a language for addressing those very conditions. This resemblance between blackness and contemporary economic conditions should not be mistaken for collusion. Resistance, a force so evident in those performances of the sixties, still activates black performances that find themselves persistently interested in that history. Today, there is the opportunity to include among blackness's ambivalent techniques an ambivalent approach to the sixties and its politics. Within that, radical energy persists, and can be deployed apart from linear claims of historical progress that appear to disprove themselves. This concluding section reads that energy from the point of view of 2015, locating modes of resistant representations that have exceeded the sixties, offering a sense of resistance's reach and flexibility. Situated in this moment, I approach this concluding section from the subjective position of a black performer with the hope of intensifying the presence of black performance.

Babel

From spring to fall of 2015, inside a centuries-old brick watchtower backed against the historic port of Venice, Italy, ten black audio speakers were installed at ear level, surrounding the space. The speakers delivered the voices of ten singers singing the German national anthem in ten African languages. One voice began, and others joined, until a chorus surrounded the listener with overlapping languages, performing the same heavy tune, the "Song of the Germans" ("Lied der Deutschen") in Douala, Igbo, Lingála, Bamun, Kikongo, Yoruba, Sango, More, Twi, and Ewondo. Each time the song began again, a different voice, a different language, and again the others filled in the chorus.

I encountered this work by Emeka Ogboh in the exhibition organized for the 56th Venice Biennial, which in 2015 included an unprecedented number of black artists from the United States, Europe, and Africa. The biennial's curator, Okwui Enwezor, a Nigerian man who has held curatorial and academic posts in Europe and the United States, is the only black person ever to have been appointed to that job. I made the trip to see the show and to celebrate the occasion with friends and colleagues and my artist father, whose work was included. The Venice Biennial was founded in 1895 and still maintains a "world's fair" quality connected to that time, with its national art pavilions and international group exhibition, assembling a diversity of modernities and modernisms that have by now been assimilated into globalist exchange. While the art world's leading destinations are regular subjects of pilgrimage for the artists, curators, writers, collectors, and other professionals who do its work, this particular event, given its participants, was of anomalous interest as an object of "black study."[2] While there, I was enlisted to participate in a performance by musicians Alicia Hall Moran and Jason Moran. On my last day in Venice I worked through their piece from a central stage and then, with suitcase in tow, I set out to see the far reaches of the gigantic exhibition, and discovered there Ogboh's tower, and hearing those voices singing that song, I found myself moved.

Ogboh's piece is an example of music transporting historical resonances across time, troubling ontologies along the way. While emphasizing the place of song and of oral traditions in the making of black subjectivity, I do not wish here to romanticize sound as an unfettered force that necessarily leads to liberation, but rather wish to consider sound's flexible communicative powers within visuality, even when conscribed to the fixities of its disciplines. Following scholars of black musical production, this history suggests what Tavia Nyong'o has described as a demand to "listen to the black body as a musical and technical instrument that resound at frequencies that confound its routinized, racialized instrumentation."[3] The works discussed here elaborate on music as, in Shana Redmond's words, "a method of rebellion, revolution, and future visions."[4] Enwezor's exhibition was insidiously aural, carefully orchestrating its sounds around objects, video installations, and live interventions. His performance selections moved away from the body and toward its voice. A central Arena Stage built for readings and performances served as a platform for the voice of the biennial. This emphasis on sound, in a visual art context, offered modes that exceed the auspices of visuality.

Distributed across the spaces of the biennial, sound offered echoes of a resistant past while announcing possible futures. Emeka Ogboh's "Song of the Germans" raises important connections between history, nationalism, and performance, as in those unpacked by Judith Butler and Gayatri Spivak in their text *Who Sings the Nation-State?* The anthem, originally composed by Joseph Haydn for an imperial birthday, rises and falls in the manner of Western music's most satisfying melodic mode. It was used in the German unification effort in the 1840s, as various principalities were becoming a state. A nationalistic poem was set to the melody at that time, the third stanza of which is the anthem of today's reunified Germany. This is the stanza adapted by Ogboh and his singers, who are members of an Afro-German gospel choir based in Berlin. This stanza calls for the principles *"Einigkeit und Recht und Freiheit"* (unity and justice and freedom),[5] reflective of the Enlightenment terms that generally informed the development of the most orderly nation-states.

There are other original stanzas of the song that are no longer used. The second celebrates "German women, German loyalty, German wine and German song,"[6] offering a seemingly medieval premise for the modern project. These features are celebrated as elements of an essential past, which inspires future deeds, emanating from their *"alten schönen Klang"* (old beautiful tone).[7] Sound carries this historicity into the future, as in the song's self-reflexive reference to song itself, and never mind that Haydn was Austrian. The notion that women are either abstractions, like loyalty, or cultural products, like wine, rather than agents of a unified, just, and free history, is out of step with the Germany of Angela Merkel and partially accounts for this stanza's relegation to history.

A founding national identity also pushes through the other stanza that is never officially sung, the first, which begins "*Deutschland, Deutschland, über alles*" (Germany, Germany, above all)[8] and is closely associated in the imagination with the National Socialist regime. Its opening declaration is perhaps the most familiar aspect of this song to non-Germans, given the breadth of the conquering project it accompanied in the thirties and forties. For me at least, hearing the anthem's melody conjures those words more readily than unity, justice, or freedom. This content is accompanied by the melody's affective strength, its conveyance of beauty and resolution, reinforcing the rightness of that claim. It reminds me, in some ways, of "Dixie," the unofficial anthem of the Confederate States of America, which, using mannered sentimentality rather than courtly elegance, also conveys a melancholic past that underscores a desired future. That pretty tune romanticizes the Southern U.S. it describes through a longing that is something like what Germans call *Sehnsucht*, and never mind that "Dixie" was written in Chicago for a minstrel show.

In 2015, Germany's political strength, as economic arbiter for the European Union, was a tense political matter. Some German visitors to Venice described to me the resentment they sensed while traveling in southern Europe; an activist art action at the German pavilion referencing Greece's current debt crisis denounced Germany's austerity policies; the artist Hito Steyerl's video installation *Factory of the Sun* inside that same pavilion expressed a highly critical attitude toward the German financial sector, even offering a sarcastic gesture linking it to Nazism. While such a comparison may be hyperbolic, the problem of German power is again a European concern. The raciality of that national power resonates in Ogboh's tower. Sung in those ten languages, some of which come from former German colonial territory, the patriotic song is articulated in utterances that, to most Germans, may as well be Greek.

In *Who Sings the Nation-State?*, Butler describes protestors in California singing the American national anthem in Spanish as an instance of resistance. Reading Hannah Arendt and Giorgio Agamben, Butler keeps the nation-state's extraordinary ordering abilities in view, while imagining how the movement in and out of territory and citizenship choreograph challenges to state power.

> A certain distance or fissure becomes the condition of possibility of equality, which means that equality is not a matter of extending or augmenting the homogeneity of the nation. Of course, this might be no more than a pluralism which, as we know, reinstalls homogeneity only after a little complexity is admitted into the fold. But if we consider this both as plural act and as speech in translation, then it seems to me that we witness at least two conditions that are at work, not only in the assertion of equality but in the exercise of freedom. Both the ontologies of liberal individualism and the ideas of a common language are forfeited in favor of a collectivity that comes to exercise its freedom in a language or a set of languages for which difference and translation are irreducible.[9]

Butler recognizes (at least) two conditions in a common action that resists homogenizing state force in one move, while maintaining difference through translation in another. As Spivak observes in conversation, "the national anthem, unlike the International (or 'We shall overcome'), is untranslatable."[10] In this example, and in Ogboh's piece, we observe the loss of the nationalistic requirement in translation, and with it, its unifying demand. Patriotism lacks continuity without the authorizing and authenticating claim that would be laid by common use of the national language.

Ogboh, who was born in 1977 in Enugu, Nigeria, is a contemporary artist based in both Lagos and Berlin whose works have exploited sound's politicizing and affective powers. He is the winner of a German competition commissioning a public artwork for the planned African Union headquarters in Addis Ababa, Ethiopia, the construction of which is also backed by Germany. In his proposed work, Ogboh is to build a sound installation using the anthem of the African Union, "Let Us All Unite and Celebrate Together," as well as recordings of speeches delivered in 1963 at the opening of an older organization, the Organization of African Unity, at the highpoint of African independence. In her book *Anthem*, Redmond describes comparable political songs that resist nationalist participation in favor of extra-national affinities. "The Black and interracial organizations that these anthems represent serve to rebut, reorient, or reimagine the state's role in the lives of Black citizens,"[11] a strategy characteristic of black transnationalism in the sixties. "Let Us All Unite and Celebrate Together" announces this historic intention, and represents it as an occasion for festive pleasure, accessing an affect produced by collective singing in connection to new forms of belonging.

Reflecting the moment's utopian possibility, Ghanaian president Kwame Nkrumah's speech on that occasion called for a politically unified continent that would overcome the neo-colonial forces preventing African economic control over its vast natural resources. "So many blessings must flow from our unity; so many disasters must follow on our continued disunity, that our failure to unite today will not be attributed by posterity only to faulty reasoning and lack of courage, but to our capitulation before the forces of imperialism."[12] Nkrumah alludes to the American Constitutional Convention as a model for post-colonial organization, an image that recalls a founding democratic past while projecting great future power, and delivers a lengthy critique of the ways Africans have been deprived of their own capital, and how they may revolutionize that condition, articulating his African Marxist analysis. Nkrumah's extraordinary plan, which called for new cooperative bodies, a new common currency, common citizenship, common defense, and other major innovations, was not put into effect. Instead, the Organization of African Unity, which came to serve autocratic rather than cooperative states, was finally dissolved in 2002 and replaced with the African Union, which now looks to Germany to build its headquarters.

In both of these works by Ogboh, the problem of *Einigkeit* resonates, as sound carries, or is proposed to carry, presence, history, and possibility with ambivalence. The time between Nkrumah's predictions and today's past holds big disappointments that shadow political promises. In the case of the "Lied der Deutschen," the music unfurls the banners of globalist present, and by implication, fascist and imperial legacies that linger behind the voices. Even within this intractable history, African singularities surround the listener in possibility, confounding the meanings that confine it.

In Hortense Spillers's attention to expressive production, one is reminded that what happens in a field of representation is still very important, as it makes the meanings that support ways of living. Having provided as thorough a definition of race as any, Spillers explains:

> "[R]ace" marks both an in-itselfness and a figurative economy that can take on any number of different faces at the drop of a hat. Understanding how this mechanism works is crucial: "race" is not *simply* a metaphor and nothing more; it is the outcome of politics. For one to mistake it is to be politically stupid and endangered. It is also a *complicated* figure, or metaphoricity, that demonstrates the power and danger of difference, that signs and assigns difference as a way to situate social subjects. If we did not already have "race" and its quite impressive powers of proliferation, we would need to invent them. The social mechanism here is *difference in, and as, hierarchy*, although "race" remains one of its most venerable master signs.[13]

Everywhere we look, there is doubling (at least). Race is both the condition of social assignment and the economy that assigns. This multiplication creates ontological problems; it's difficult to imagine modernity without race and its power to situate being, and that being is situated through confounding difference. In the sphere of the racialized, status is precariously balanced in hierarchical arrangement. The historical is hounded by the contingent. In its multiplicity, race is outrageously anti-ontological, considering its incredible claims of definition. In the previous chapters, I have pursued the ways Du Bois's double consciousness had given way to radical proliferations of consciousnesses as politicized subjective modes by the sixties, when resolution was no longer a primary goal. These performances enacted a complicated set of positions, foregrounding the decentering powers of gender, sexuality, location, and other differences that productively multiplied racial categories in excess of the boundaries that might contain them. Distinct from the notion of unified consciousness, Spillers goes on to describe a kind of "interior intersubjectivity"[14] that more fully depicts a black psychic situation, shaped by the social positions made available to it. There is no recourse here to the discrete individual as agential being. There is rather ambivalent situation and intertextual arrangement, and in this sense, the utterance and the act are embedded in performative contradiction.

Attention to thinking about being reveals, beyond race, the pluralities that categories organize. As Arendt muses, "For all scientific thinking there is only *man*—in biology, or psychology, as in philosophy and theology, just as in zoology there is only *the* lion. Lions would be of concern only to lions."[15] The category of study is singular and general, while the singularities within each category raise differences of particular interest only to the subjectivities that are differentiated in the first place, the metaphorical plural lions. Reflecting that problem, Agamben refers to being as an unfixed process: "This is not, in the terms that dominate Western ontology, either an essence or an existence, but a *manner of rising forth*; not a being that is *in* this or that mode, but a being that is *its* mode of being."[16] In this plural manner, there remains the singularity within each thing that is distinct from general category to which it belongs, opening up multiple possibilities within each proper instance. Still, possibility itself is shown to contain the possibility of not; each thing that may occur may just as determinedly not occur. Possibility maintains substantial negative power. Tracing a Christian philosophical tradition, Agamben describes original sin as the retroactive organization of this negative possibility in an originary past, for which morality is a compensatory mode. Ethics, accordingly, returns possibility to the future where it may or may not happen and anticipates ways of moving toward those outcomes. Possibility is not the project of changing one totality into another. Possibility is an attunement to being's manner of being, which time does nothing to unify, and a consciousness of the impossible.

Curator Okwui Enwezor's writing for the Venice Biennial exhibition catalogue addresses capitalism's rapacity, a current state of political upheaval, and impending climate disaster, implying that at least one possible future is a non-future. "*All the World's Futures* are not presented in the affirmative key,"[17] he writes, distancing himself from the utopian premises that might be inferred from his exhibition title. Enwezor described himself in an interview with the activist American news program *Democracy Now!*, broadcast canal-side from Venice, as "deeply anti-utopia, simply because I believe that utopia is the end of politics. And I'm very much invested in the politics of the possible."[18] Here, Enwezor affirms the future's limitations. He departs from the kind of critical idealism described by José Muñoz in *Cruising Utopia: The Then and*

Figure A.1. Michelle Obama with Malia Obama and artist Joan Jonas in 2015 in Venice. Jonas, whose early performance works date to the late sixties, represented the United States in the 56th Venice Biennial. Photograph by Andreas Solaro (Getty).

There of Queer Futurity, which follows Agamben and Ernst Bloch to take possibility all the way to potentiality, a less indifferent, more promising futurity. Muñoz describes his critical utopianism in queer terms, critiquing "the autonaturalizing temporality we call *straight time*"[19] by offering a horizon of experience outside that temporality's reproductive order, and a collectivity founded in that experience. This vision looks past the negativity that disbands collective potential. Muñoz's unfinished work on the idea of the "brown commons" rethinks the pessimism that of-color critique has inherited from black study.

Enwezor's project, on the other hand, returns to that difficulty. In the *Democracy Now!* interview, Enwezor cites the sixties as an instigator of his project: "I came from a generation of the post-independence era in Nigeria in the sixties, born in the sixties, growing up in Nigeria with a sense of purpose, a sense of the fact that the world is round, the sense of the idea of the complex entanglement of destinies and processes. And arriving in the United States and, you know, seeing myself on the margins of that was not really what I thought my life should be."[20] Enwezor ends this anecdote with a classical invocation of double consciousness, out of which he developed inventive and multiplicitous production. Invoking this productive alienation, the program cuts away from Enwezor before a break as Nina Simone's version of "Strange Fruit," Billie Holiday's darkly ironic song about lynching, plays over a video montage of protests in Missouri. The protesters are responding to the shooting of African American teenager Michael Brown by a police officer. These protests formed the beginning of the Black Lives Matter movement, which has responded to the increased visibility of instances of police violence against black people, which have been distributed through new video technologies. Black futures perpetually reroute us to the here and now.

The question of time, as history and as a measure of action, was insistently posed by a months-long reading of the three books of Karl Marx's *Capital* in the center of the exhibition, a reading Enwezor describes as a main component of his curatorial premise. Importantly, the idea of reading *Capital* aloud placed performance squarely in the center of the biennial, with the construction of the square Arena Stage facing the audience on three sides, and many performances filling out discursive spaces around Marx's analysis: British artist Jeremy Deller offered a program of historic labor ballads, American musicians Alicia Hall Moran and Jason Moran responded to black American work songs (to which I will return shortly), my artist father, Charles Gaines, presented a composition that translated political speech into musical notation, and other performances and screenings enlivened the occasion. Marx's text looses fixity in Enwezor's context. The exhibition catalogue offers images of first-edition title pages of *Capital* published in Bengali, Arabic, Serbian, Croatian, Danish, Czech, French, English, Dutch, Italian, Yiddish, Polish, Russian, Persian, Thai, Indonesian, Kazakh, Uygher, and Telegu. While this suggests the internationalism of that influential writing, attention to the histories of the places where these languages are spoken diminishes a sense of uniformity in its reading.

Enwezor enlisted the British film and video artist Isaac Julien to direct the live reading. Julien's work has also circulated widely and has offered specific influence on black and queer art practices with pieces such as the 1989 film *Looking for Langston*, an ambivalent meditation on the legacy of Langston Hughes. Working with his partner Mark Nash, Julien's staging of *Das Kapital Oratorio* heightened dialogic processes: two readers alternated from either side of the stage; the readers spoke English with cumbersome Italian accents; the reading was accompanied by a projection of Marx's footnotes annotating the speech. The oratorio offered a concrete engagement with politics, while its performed difficulties kept multiplicity alive.

The *Capital* oratorio followed up on Julien's earlier piece, *Kapital*, a two-channel video presented in London in 2013 and also on view in Venice, in which Julien interviews the Marxist scholar David Harvey in a gallery space, surrounded by an attentive audience. Intermittently, video montages splash across the walls of the gallery, offering bits of economic information, scenes of commerce and trade, and enactments of political crisis. Meanwhile, Julien asks Harvey about capital's conditions. Answering the implicit question of whether or not *Capital* is still relevant, Harvey insists that Marx capably expresses contemporary crises, describing the ways capital's motion, acceleration, and precarity are as persistent as ever. Julien mentions Marx's idea that value, as an expression of capital, "brings forth living offspring, or, at the least, lays golden eggs,"[21] and suggests a resemblance in that image to contemporary art objects bought for outrageous amounts by billionaire oligarchs, ruling families, and the like. Harvey returns attention to the idea of the fetish, and reminds the audience that this produces jobs for no one but a few artists like Julien.

A couple of lucid questioners wonder if *Capital* is better suited to address large ontologies, such as capital and art, and less adept at analyzing the more detailed places of differentiation within those categories where much meaning can be found. Harvey turns attention to strata of analysis attributed to Marx: the universal, which includes a relationship to nature; the general, where capital's rules dominate; the particular, where variables like wages, rents, and interest rates fluctuate; and the singularity, the place of consumption, where we might recognize our own individual drives and "human passion."[22] Cultural theorist Stuart Hall, who is also in the audience, suggests that Harvey's strata do not go far enough to uncover contemporary conditions and calls for a stronger revisionism.

Hall asserts that a revisionist approach might better account for something in Marx's own writing that attends to the productive, the masculine, the factory, while paying less attention to reproduction and consumption, processes which have moved into the foreground of present capitalist life. Though Harvey disagrees, Hall insists that *Capital* does not depict current economic experience, which is ambiguous in that it lacks clear demarcations between classes. With the diminishment of factory production, the privileged proletariat class is no longer so contiguous or complete. Julien's video montages that appear within the video include a constructed cinematic scene of suited white-collar workers battling riot police, suggesting that perhaps hedge fund managers might form part of today's revolutionary class. Hall cautions, however, that simply expanding the idea of the proletariat to include different kinds of workers makes everyone proletariats, and is not at all a solution. Hall points finally to the fact that *Capital* does not account for gender or race, affirming that further revision to Marx's model is called for. Harvey, characteristically, sticks to his guns, replying that you cannot use race or gender to theorize economic crisis, "you can only look at the way capital is racialized and genderized."[23] This back and forth, set within a video that itself is an art commodity, reveals some of the differences Marx can bring us to. Crucially, Hall's intervention restages the kinds of revisions, adaptations, and interpretations black political projects have brought to Marxist analysis, including those of the sixties that I have discussed in depth.

While this exchange shows how *Capital* continues to productively shape political discourse, attention to black performance and its relationship to leftist projects shows the necessity of revision when thinking about social differences unarticulated in the figure of the European factory worker. Reflecting this tradition of revision, Hall, an influential figure in the British New Left, called for openness where it comes to Marx:

> This relative openness or relative indeterminacy is necessary to Marxism itself as a theory. What is "scientific" about the Marxist theory of politics is that it seeks to understand the limits to political action given by the terrain on which it operates. This terrain is defined, not by forces we can predict with the certainty of natural science, but by the existing balance of social forces, the specific nature of the concrete conjuncture. It is "scientific" because it understands itself as determinate; and because it seeks to develop a practice which is theoretically informed. But it is *not*

"scientific" in the sense that political outcomes and the consequences of the conduct of political struggles are foreordained in the stars.[24]

This reading, identifying a useful science of economics that ought not cross into prognostication, opens two important possibilities: first, an incorporation into Marxist theory of the value of different social configurations than those detailed by Marx himself; second, a resistance to the notion that Marxism, or all of politics for that matter, have come to fail, as made evident by the present lack of a world workers' government that ought to have been an historical inevitability. Hall's body of writing, which pays attention to race and colonialism, made an important contribution to this first result, helping to retain Marxist analysis as a critical tool for those marginalized by more than industrial class. By bringing historical material attention to blackness, Julien has argued that Hall ushered in "the end of the innocent essential black subject, and the freeing up of positions from which black artists and film-makers can speak."[25] The second matter—the retention of Marxist analysis in the twenty-first century, and its adaptability—is the proposition of the oratorio at the center of a world art exhibition that necessarily featured several "golden eggs."

Some news reports and online comments suggested there was a contradiction to the reading of *Capital* in the biennial's Giardini building while, outside, enormous yachts lined the waterfront.[26] And further, that the oratorio would have been better eliminated than the yachts.[27] This response said, perversely: Yachts are material; Marxism is a fantasy, like the sixties, like performance for that matter. I attended a party on a yacht while in Venice. I judged the yacht to be quite expensive. I was the guest of an artist friend who told me it was a birthday party for a young museum worker. That worker was the daughter of contemporary art collectors whose family fortune, I later discovered, derived from the dealing of weapons. Their big collection includes the work of several artists seen in the biennial, including Isaac Julien's. Class extremities frame contemporary art. If reading *Capital* does nothing to revolutionize this economy, it may at least propose a demystification of its fetishes.

Echoes

In black production, music allows for a kind of rising forth, a manner of being, played out in time, capable of managing performative contradiction, and open to revision. Music has served as a cultural and formal context that supports the kinds of multiplicitous expressions I have identified in performances of the sixties, expressions that refuse unification and represent possibility. Enwezor's exhibition laid claim to this black cultural practice and positioned it as a foundation of modernity. The biennial used music to transport past energies to the present, and to imagine and reimagine the future. This choice, in an art exhibition, put pressure on the status of the object, and in relation to that, of the social subject. I conclude with three final instances of music that used the multiplicities of black subjectivity to find a way toward futurity.

On the Arena Stage, four pianists played four grand pianos with large clocks set upon them, interpreting the composition "Evil Nigger" by Julius Eastman. Composed in 1979, the piece calls for a number of instruments of the same type, and is most often done using four pianos. The musicians work with two repeating themes, a vigorous repetition of sixteenth notes, and a set of specific time constraints, while improvising within those limitations. The piece produces a kind of quadruple consciousness (not unlike that expressed by Nina Simone in "Four Women"), as the same musical information moves through four very skilled pianists, coming apart and together, in ways that maintain difference, while fulfilling the intensity suggested by the composition's title. The first theme is made of a quick progression of three notes and then the aggressive repetition of the third, like a demand with the insistency of gunfire. The second theme, which is first played in unison by the four pianists, is a progression of notes ominously working their way down a minor scale, a simple, dark statement. A conductor, watching the time closely, guides the players from section to section. As new tones and overlapping key shifts enter this nearly thirty-minute piece, the repetitions begin to produce a soundscape of energy. Despite the music's simplicity, it required of the pianists nearly athletic determination to maintain the labor. "Evil Nigger" is not easy to perform.

Preceding this performance (by non-black Italian pianists), an audio clip was played, a recording of Eastman addressing the audience in 1980 at Chicago's Northwestern University, where the piece was presented along with the other works in its series, "Crazy Nigger" and "Gay Guerilla." In the run-up to that performance, the works' titles had stirred controversy. Eastman, who was black and gay, offers an assured explanation, saying he uses "nigger" to describe something "fundamental,"[28] as in the field labor that was fundamental to the American economy. This fundamental quality can be extended to the minimalist strategies contained within the piece, both its repetition of themes and the idea that most all of the musical information is immediately present, rather than introduced and developed in a progression throughout various movements. Presence, immediacy, and forcefulness all seem to reflect Eastman's claiming of the word. In the predominantly white world of difficult new music in which Eastman circulated, organized around a few schools, residencies, and music groups, the use of such contested, politicized language was not standard. "Since Eastman was African American," writes David Borden, "he could use the word with a certain freedom that is not appropriate for the rest of us. The word connotes racism, lynching, slavery, injustice, unimaginable suffering, and so on, and so forth. . . . Julius knew perfectly well what the word invoked and used it to make audiences come face to face with it. After all, he had to every day."[29] Eastman's use of the word was inevitably a reference to himself, very often the only black person in the room, a reference that radicalized his endeavor, connecting his authorship with the "so on, and so forth" of blackness. Eastman's music expressed this radicality. As a former lover describes: "he lived the titles of his music. He was the crazy nigger and the gay guerilla. He was fearsome. He played out those roles."[30]

Eastman's difficult position in his field brought him into legendary conflict with the influential composer John Cage, the leading figure in new music. Though Cage was also gay, his work did not support an idea of provocation founded in the politicized identity of the composer. His practice of reduction delimited the necessity of such positions. In an instance in 1975, Eastman introduced "virulent homosexual overtones" to a performance of a Cage work from 1970, filling out a limited set of instructions in the piece "Song Books" by, among other things, narrating and acting out an interracial sexual scenario with a young naked white man. According to Eastman biographer Renée Levine Packer: "Cage was furious. In his seminar the next morning, he was visibly agitated,

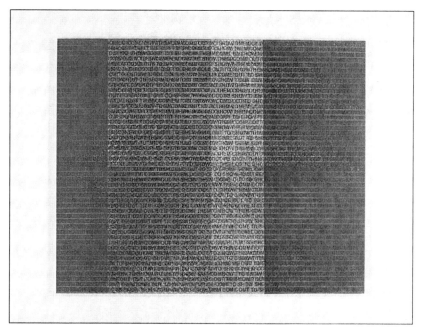

Figure A.2. Glenn Ligon, *Come Out #16*, 2015. Silkscreen on canvas, 95 1/8 x 120 inches (241.6 x 304.8 cm). © Glenn Ligon; courtesy of the artist, Luhring Augustine, New York, Regen Projects, Los Angeles, and Thomas Dane Gallery, London.

stamping around the room, breathlessly raising his voice in an uncharacteristic way, even pounding the piano with his fist."[31] Eastman's career was damaged by antagonizing Cage, who did not approve of sexual and racial specificity being connected to his work. Eastman died in 1990, at the age of forty-nine, alone and in near obscurity. Recent writing such as Levine Packer's has drawn renewed attention to his remarkable work.

Given the demands of "Evil Nigger," it is a challenge to mount live. Its performance spoke to the labor of transporting excessive production across time. Not only does the piece convey Eastman's persistence, but also reenacts the antagonism a black and queer subjectivity activates, even within avant-gardist spaces that are often understood to question normative positions and reject bourgeois expectations. Though the performance will not easily resolve. The labor time depicted cannot fully synthesize the black energy it articulates. Overlapping, repeated notes will not line up in order; they exceed both formal and historical conditions.

Strategies of repetition and reduction also resonate in the large silk-screen prints on canvas of American artist Glenn Ligon, on view in a gallery beside the Arena Stage. A musical scene related to Eastman's own acted itself out behind these works. Paired with an installation by conceptual artist Adrian Piper, Ligon's work pursued his established practice of appropriating and depicting texts associated with black cultural production. Ligon borrowed the phrase "come out to show them" from an early work of minimalist composer Steve Reich, who borrowed it for his 1966 piece "Come Out" from the recorded testimony of Daniel Hamm, who was arrested in 1964 in Harlem and suffered injuries from a beating by police. In an effort to make the wounds evident, Hamm describes pressing a bruise, so the blood would "come out to show them" the proof of extraordinary violence.

In Reich's piece, which involved manipulating a tape recording of Hamm's voice and playing it on two channels, a recorded phrase is introduced without alteration, then repeated, then shortened, and repeated in quick succession. Hamm's voice begins to divide across the channels, fragmenting and overlapping itself. As the channels move out of sync, the utterance is transformed into a sequence of sounds. The description of the action is literally instrumentalized, as the voice becomes material for abstraction. The piece has a complex effect: It introduces the fragment of political speech and multiplies it, amplifying a sense of subjectivity while removing the requirement to produce meaning. Performative speech becomes a speech object that is used performatively. Even though the signs are extracted, the music is still difficult, as the resulting rapid rhythm proves quite intense. By the end of twelve minutes, there is scarcely a sense of voice present, but rather a percussive mechanized whirl.

"Come Out" followed Reich's 1965 work "It's Gonna Rain," which also manipulated a recording of black speech, sampling fragments of a street preacher's sermon recorded by Reich in San Francisco. By isolating different syllables and combinations of syllables, a series of abstract patterns are produced, which, because of the speaker's musical oratory style, convey much tonality. These pieces attempt to hold on to something of their source materials. Reich maintains the original pitch of the voice, fragmenting and distributing it, but doing little else to mediate it. This suggests an interest in making connections among the compositional strategy, the recording technology, and the black social subject matter that underlies the sound. In the case of "Come Out," Reich had been hired by an activist to edit interviews with Hamm and others known as the Harlem Six, who, after a minor street altercation, were coerced into confessing to a white woman's murder, and whose case symbolized for many systemic police racism.[32] Reich took the job with the understanding that he could make work from that sound archive. He adapted not only the sound but the political event of which he was well aware, as Andrew V. Uroskie describes, "explicitly aligning the emerging interest in the possibilities of looped recording and feedback with the explosive social and cultural dynamics of the civil rights movement."[33]

In his act of retranslation, Ligon printed the original utterance as text, which he repeated in black layers across the surface of his imposing works. The words are translated from language to image and back, as they recede and return into legibility. The attempt to be seen that is invoked in the phrase is fulfilled in the materiality of the large-scale prints, which surround the viewer in their repetitive patterns. As in other Ligon works, the labor of applying layers of medium produces moments of unintelligibility in the text image, allowing the phrase to disappear and reappear under the work of representing it. And though no body literally appears, black or otherwise, a question of sexuality emerges around the racialized content, as the practice of "coming out," or making one's gay identity visible, appears to speak through the phrase when viewed in the context of 2015, proposing a collusion between that artist's voice, Reich's, and Hamm's. Ligon's work reappropriates an appropriation, and offers in that repetition a depiction of an intersubjectivity stretched through space and time. Returning to the question of revision raised by Hall, this text too expands its capacity as the voice of the accused testifies, multiplies, and transforms.

In these pieces and others, Ligon and Eastman have both used black historical conditions to revise the minimalist demands that shape their works' reception. Within influential music and visual art discourses since the sixties, a critical interest in repetition and reduction has worked against dramatic tendencies in order to free form from narrative structures that have been seen as coercive and illusionistic. Writing about Ligon's series of prints, Megan Ratner quotes the minimalist sculptor Richard Serra, who described his memory of Reich's work many years later: "I don't recall the structure or concise logic. What I retain is a feeling of alienation and discomfort. It might seem strange but this discomfort arises from a rethinking of form."[34] Stranger, perhaps, is to understand the racist violence to which Hamm's utterance responds as something distinct from the form of its recorded sound. That this distinction is received as "alienation," a term bound to Marx's analysis of labor, Brecht's politicized performance tactic, and Du Bois's critique of self-as-other, reorients the formal problem around one of content, and the radicalizing identities that animate these materials. In Ligon's "Come Out," as in Eastman's "Evil Nigger," the strategy of repetition, far from limiting politicized content, serves as a reiteration of subjectivity, an excessive layering of black narrative, offering flesh as the material of form. These works cleverly undermine the universalist sensibilities that have shaped the fields through which these artists' works have been distributed, and the art discourse to which the Venice Biennial itself responds. Further, these works' queer undercurrents unsettle even the black historical conditions to which they refer, flowing toward a horizon of ambiguous subjective pleasure.

Finally, I turn to *Work Songs*, the performance by Alicia Hall Moran and Jason Moran, which foregrounded an understanding of black performance as black labor. Hall Moran is a vocalist whose projects have included performing the role of Bess in the 2013 U.S. national tour of *The Gershwins' Porgy and Bess*, a retooling of the 1934 opera about black American life, which synthesizes classical, jazz, and theater music. Moran is a pianist and bandleader who presently serves as artistic director for jazz at the Kennedy Center in Washington, D.C., a post that places black music in close proximity to the machinery of the U.S. nation-state. The pair was invited by Enwezor to work through the idea of the work song on the Arena Stage, bringing that form into contact with the reading of *Capital*. This position proposes an alternate theory of labor to complement Marx's own, one founded in a collective vocalization that speaks back to the repetitious rhythms of work. In a series of performances throughout the run of the biennial, Moran and Hall Moran brought singers together in different solo, duo, and trio performances to work through an improvisatory structure that played against a thirty-eight-minute recording of rhythms, voices, and music in loops. The recording subtly referenced field work, chain gangs, spirituals, instrumental improvisation, the kind of tape music innovated by Reich, and electronic sampling found in popular idioms. The track, in combinatory form, created a progression upon which different voices could engage with the labor of the work song in regulated time. That labor never produced the same results. It was always both singular and collective. A diverse range of singers participated: Rashida Bumbray, Roosevelt Andre Credit, LaTasha N. Nevada Diggs, Lisa Harris, Steven Herring, Andrea Jones-Sojola, Anthony Mills, Jamet Pittman, Phumzile Sojola, and me. All of them associates of the artist pair, many of these are trained singers who work in classical, jazz, Broadway, and commercial contexts, though some, like myself, use music as part of art production outside of the professional field of music.

I saw a performance of *Work Songs* during the exhibition's opening days that included Moran seated at the grand piano, Hall Moran standing at a music stand, and dance artist and curator Rashida Bumbray standing at another music stand. Though the singers wore elegant gowns, the performance was a practice of restraint, offering a limited vocabulary of chords, voice, and movement, emphasizing work's regulated expression. While steeped in a history of work music, the performers made evident their negotiation of the present. In an unplanned moment, Hall Moran, having asked for water and having been brought a Coca-Cola instead, guzzled the drink with a kind of triumphant disdain. The action embodied the contradictions inherent in performing material rooted in American slavery for an international art audience in an old European capital of trade, and with only a global commodity to drink. The openness of the improvisatory mode exposed the pleasures and pains of black work.

Finding themselves in need of performer later that weekend, the Morans asked me to perform an iteration of *Work Songs*. Though I had come to Venice as a researcher, tourist, and supporter, I was excited to perform as well. A stricter series of instructions were delivered to singers who appeared later in the series; I, however, was given relative freedom to interpret the piece as best I could, having been told by Hall Moran only that I must repeatedly sing the word "work," and that I should focus on a couple of American folk songs she had been writing notes about: "John Henry," about a legendary figure whose incredible performance of power leads to his death at work, and the suppositional utopian affirma-

Figure A.3. Alicia Hall Moran and Jason Moran, *Work Songs*, 2015. Courtesy La Biennale di Venezia (Archivio Storico delle Arti Contemporanee). Photo by Isabella Balena.

tion of action "If I Had a Hammer." While I entered the process with a strong sense of the texts and the subjectivities they announce, performing in this piece taught me something about improvisation's instability. Structure and freedom indicate each other; compulsory regimes open up passages to imaginative interpretation. I played piano and sang at the same time, and though I would not call my performance virtuoso, I would say it communicated.

The following day, after having arrived in Lisbon, Portugal for a vacation, I wrote a summary email:

5/11/15

Alicia, Jason, I loved doing that performance. Thank you so much for inviting me in your hour of need. It reminded me that I need to more of that kind of thing. I'm a rehearser [*sic*] more than an improvisor [*sic*], but it was such a great challenge to bring those two parts together, it stretched me in a productive way to try to listen and express at the same time. You guys are inspiring and generous to let me do my thing. I heard from others that Rashida's solo turn was wonderful. Music, theater, and dance people all know how to collaborate and it's such a stretch for art people, I love that you brought that into the biennial, even by accident. The only person I knew there was a woman who runs the Montreal Biennial, she shot video on her phone and got at least 31 minutes of it. She hasn't sent it to me yet but she said she would. I'll send it along as soon as I get it.

I chanted 'work' for awhile, adding some 'work it' and 'do your thing,' references to RuPaul's 90s dance hit which I'm sure no one could notice. I worked through Nina Simone's 'Work Song,' the spirituals 'Hammering' and 'Gospel Plow.' I did a full version of 'John Henry' to that active piano section, delivering a lot of that to a small German child with thick glasses. I improvised with 'If I Had a Hammer,' imagining different things I'd hammer out. I played with Odetta's 'He Had a Long Chain On' and 'Your Son has Been Shot' from My Barbarian's Brecht songs. Concluded working through Elaine Brown's 'End of the Silence,' a complicated song from her 60s album of Black Panther propaganda. As you see, I decided I had to bring some of my familiar material to this in order to be able to improvise and still feel confident, but always connecting to your themes, and realizing how much spiritual, work, and political songs overlap in this music tradition, they are so often doing the same thing. I think it all worked well. Folks stuck around to watch it. The crew guys complimented my singing, which was nice.

Then I wandered to the back of the Arsenale and discovered that piece where different Afro-Germans are singing the German national anthem all at once in different African languages and I burst into tears. Then I came to Lisbon where my suitcase was lost but I think it's been found. But as of now I only have the clothes I performed in.

What a world. Love to you both and congratulations.[35]

Alicia Hall Moran responded hours later:

All I can really say in response to this email is I love you, and Welcome to jazz.[36]

To conclude with love is to return to resistance. Despite the world of constraints, despite history's exhausting claims, and all of the ways race punishes us all, black expressivity continues to draw on its contradictory traditions of defiance and affirmation, intensity and multiplicity, slavery and self-rule, antagonism and identification, ambivalence and commitment, to ideate life worth living, life imagined on the other side of impossibility. In the performances of the sixties I have considered, and in the works of *All the World's Futures* discussed here, blackness endures, not only as a mode of subjection, but as a deeply energetic position from which to communicate.

NOTES

INTRODUCTION

1 Copeland, *Bound to Appear.*
2 Roach, *Cities of the Dead*, p. 94.
3 Jameson, "Periodizing the 60s."
4 Ball, "Obama: Reagan Changed Direction."
5 McClure, "On the Subject of Rights," p. 112.
6 Laclau and Mouffe, *Hegemony and Socialist Strategy*, p. 2.
7 Wilderson, "Gramsci's Black Marx," p. 225.
8 Laclau and Mouffe, *Hegemony and Socialist Strategy*, p. 3.
9 Ibid., p. 4.
10 Foucault, *Discipline and Punish.*
11 Spillers, *Black, White, and in Color*, p. 18.
12 Toni Morrison quoted in DeFrantz, *Dancing Revelations*, p. 22.
13 Debord, "Decline and Fall," p. 154.
14 Ibid.
15 X and Haley, *The Autobiography of Malcolm X*, p. 178.
16 Ibid.
17 Said, *Orientalism.*
18 See Du Bois, *The Souls of Black Folk.*
19 Contee, "The Encyclopedia Africana Project of W.E.B. Du Bois," p. 78.
20 "W. E. B. DuBois Dies in Ghana."
21 Du Bois, "Application for Membership," p. 633.
22 Pierre de Regnier quoted in Baker and Chase, *Josephine*, p. 5.
23 Ibid., photo, p. 10.
24 Jules-Rosette *Josephine Baker in Art and Life*, p. 66.
25 Cohodas, *Princess Noire*, p. 306.
26 Papich, *Remembering Josephine*, p. 210.
27 Ibid.
28 Baker and Chase, *Josephine*, p. 370.
29 Ibid., p. 6.
30 Beyoncé, *I Am—Sasha Fierce.*
31 Appadurai, *Modernity at Large*, p. 7.
32 Brown, *A Taste of Power*, p. 21.
33 Stallings, *Funk the Erotic*, p. 11.

CHAPTER 1. NINA SIMONE'S QUADRUPLE CONSCIOUSNESS

1 Edwards, "W.E.B. Du Bois," p. xv.
2 Moten, *In the Break*; and Vogel, *The Scene of Harlem Cabaret.*
3 Brooks, "Nina Simone's Triple-Play," p. 178.
4 Simone and Cleary, *I Put a Spell on You*, p. 87.
5 Cohodas, *Princess Noire*, p. 137.
6 *Nina Simone Great Performances: College Concerts and Interviews.* Directed by Andy Stroud. New York: Andy Stroud, Inc., 2007. DVD.
7 Ibid.
8 Ibid.
9 Simone, *Nina Simone Sings the Blues.*
10 Nemiroff and Hansberry, *To Be Young, Gifted, and Black*, p. 256.
11 Simone and Cleary, *I Put a Spell on You*, p. 89.
12 Simone, *Nina Simone in Concert*, Phillips, 1964.
13 Ibid.
14 Cohodas, *Princess Noire* , p. 157.
15 Ibid.
16 Ibid.
17 Ibid., p. 106.
18 Ibid., p. 153.
19 Brecht, "On Gestic Music," p. 105.
20 Ibid.
21 Brooks, "Nina Simone's Triple Play," p. 182.
22 Lotte Lenya in Hilliker, "Brecht's Gestic Vision for Opera," p. 226.
23 Ibid., p. 227.
24 Simone, *Nina Simone Live.*
25 Yan, "Spheres of Feelings," p. 2.
26 Brecht, "Alienation Effects in Chinese Acting," pp. 91–93.
27 Yan, "Spheres of Feelings," p. 2.
28 Ibid., p. 7.
29 Ibid.
30 Benjamin, "The Author as Producer," p. 236.
31 Brooks, *Bodies in Dissent*, p. 5.
32 Ibid., p. 4.
33 Simone, *Live in Berkeley.*
34 Simone and Cleary, *I Put a Spell on You*, p. 117.
35 Simone, *Live in Berkeley.*
36 Ibid.
37 Fanon, *Black Skin, White Masks*, p. 112.
38 Wilderson, "The Position of the Unthought."
39 Robinson, "The Sense of Ritualizing," p. 334.
40 Spillers, *Black, White, and in Color*, p. 5.

41 Ibid., p. 3.

42 *Nina Simone Live in '65 & '68.*

43 Ibid.

44 Ibid.

45 Wilson, "Nina Simone Sings at Carnegie Hall" (1963).

46 Ibid.

47 Wilson, "Cosby Simone Concert a Hit."

48 Wilson, "Nina Simone Sings at Carnegie Hall" (1965).

49 Wilson, "Nina Simone Sings Stirring Program."

50 Sherman, "Nina Simone Casts Her Moody Spells."

51 Wilson, "Museums in Tune with Nina Simone."

52 Jahn, "Throng Welcomes Nina Simone."

53 Simone and Cleary, *I Put a Spell on You*, p. 92.

54 Ibid.

55 Wilson, "Nina Simone Sings at Carnegie Hall" (1963).

56 Wilson, "Singer Triumphs at Jazz Festival."

57 *Nina Simone Live.*

58 Cohodas, *Princess Noire*, p. 156.

59 Moten, *In the Break*, p. 1.

60 Ibid., p. 20.

61 Simone, *The Blues.*

62 *Nina Simone Live at Ronnie Scott's.*

63 Ibid.

64 Braunmuller, Introduction, p. 9.

65 Simone, *Nina Simone Live.*

66 Simone and Cleary, *I Put a Spell on You*, p. 138.

67 Ibid., p. ix.

CHAPTER 2. EFUA SUTHERLAND, AMA ATA AIDOO, THE STATE, AND THE STAGE

1 Hartman, *Lose Your Mother: A Journey along the Atlantic Slave Route*, p. 19.

2 Cohodas, *Princess Noire*, p. 123.

3 Lewis, *W.E.B. Du Bois*, p. 7.

4 Nnamdi Azikiwe, *Chicago Daily Defender*, September 4, 1963.

5 Lewis, *W.E.B. Du Bois: A Biography*, p. 5.

6 Aborampah, "Women's Roles," p. 261.

7 Enwezor, *The Short Century*, pp. 10–11.

8 Mudimbe, *The Invention of Africa*, p. 93.

9 Edwards, *The Practice of Diaspora.*

10 Jahn, *History of Neo-African Literature*, pp. 265–66.

11 Botwe-Asamoah, *Kwame Nkrumah's Politico-Cultural Thought*, p. 5.

12 Ibid., p. 190.

13 Ibid., p. 12.

14 Ibid.
15 Nketia, "Kwame Nkrumah and the Arts," pp. 144–45.
16 Lemly, "Hesitant Homecomings," p. 122.
17 Nketia, "Kwame Nkrumah and the Arts," p. 144.
18 Ibid., p. 143.
19 Adams and Sutherland-Addy, Legacy of Efua Sutherland, p. 12.
20 Sutherland and Lautre, "A Recorded Interview," p. 42.
21 July, "Here, Then, Is Efua," p. 160.
22 Enwezor, The Short Century, p. 13.
23 Ibid., p. 14.
24 Botwe-Asamoah, Kwame Nkrumah's Politico-Cultural Thought, p. 5.
25 July, "Here, Then, Is Efua," p. 160.
26 Cole, Ghana's Concert Party Theatre, p. 53.
27 Collins, "Comic Opera in Ghana," p. 50.
28 Cole, Manuh, and Miescher, Africa after Gender, p. 1.
29 Sutherland, Edufa, p. 14.
30 Ibid., p. 16.
31 Ibid., p. 27.
32 Ibid., p. 28.
33 Yan, Chinese Women Writers, pp. 245–46.
34 July, "Here, Then, Is Efua," p. 161.
35 X and Haley, The Autobiography of Malcolm X, p. 352.
36 Ibid., p. 356.
37 Hartman, Lose Your Mother, p. 35.
38 July, "Here, Then, Is Efua," p. 160.
39 Adams and Sutherland-Addy, Legacy of Efua Sutherland, p. 9.
40 "Rockefeller Foundation Annual Reports" (1961).
41 "Rockefeller Foundation Annual Report 1962."
42 Ibid.
43 Rockefeller Foundation, Annual Reports" (1964).
44 Sutherland, Edufa, p. 61.
45 Sutherland, Foriwa, p. ii.
46 Ibid.
47 Ibid.
48 Ibid.
49 Ibid.
50 Manuh, "Wives, Children," pp. 77–78.
51 Sutherland, Foriwa, p. 38.
52 Ibid., p. 51.
53 Hountondji, African Philosophy, p. 161.
54 Ibid., p. 154.
55 Ibid., p. 151.
56 Appiah, In My Father's House, p. 158.

57 Sutherland, *Foriwa*, p. 67.
58 Aidoo, "An Interrogation," p. 230.
59 Richards, "Dramatizing the Diaspora's Return," p. 113.
60 Aidoo, *The Dilemma of a Ghost*, p. 7.
61 Michael Walling, "Interview with Ama Ata Aidoo," Border Crossing video, 8:02. Posted on YouTube, www.youtube.com.
62 Aidoo, *The Dilemma of a Ghost*, p. 17.
63 Ibid.
64 Ibid.
65 Ibid., p. 18.
66 Ibid., p. 7.
67 Richards, "Dramatizing the Diaspora's Return," p. 120.
68 Aidoo, *The Dilemma of a Ghost*, p. 22.
69 Ibid., p. 28.
70 Richards, "What Is to Be Remembered?," p. 94.
71 Aidoo, *The Dilemma of a Ghost*, p. 25.
72 Ibid., p. 24.
73 Ibid., p. 47.
74 Ibid., p. 52.
75 Willey, "National Identities," p. 18.

CHAPTER 3. THE RADICAL AMBIVALENCE OF GÜNTHER KAUFMANN

1 Silverman, *Male Subjectivity*, p. 126.
2 Thomsen, "Five Interviews with Fassbinder," p. 93.
3 Dyer, "Reading Fassbinder's Sexual Politics," p. 55.
4 Iden, "Making an Impact," p. 18.
5 Barnett, *Fassbinder and the German Theatre*, p. 48.
6 Ibid., p. 51.
7 Ibid.
8 Ibid., p. 55.
9 Ibid., p. 31.
10 Ibid., p. 29.
11 Ibid.
12 Ibid., p. 27.
13 Malina, Beck, and The Living Theatre, *Paradise Now*, p. 6.
14 Fassbinder and Calandra, *Fassbinder: Plays*, p. 10.
15 Barnett, *Fassbinder and the German Theatre*, p. 46.
16 Fassbinder and Calandra, *Fassbinder: Plays*, p. 9.
17 Thomsen, "Five Interviews with Fassbinder," p. 92.
18 Case, *Performing Science*, p. 49.
19 Hoffmeister, *The Theater of Confinement*, p. 22.
20 Thomsen, "Five Interviews with Fassbinder," p. 83.
21 Ibid., p. 42.

22 Rainer Werner Fassbinder Foundation, *Rainer Werner Fassbinder: Werkschau* (Berlin: Argon, 1992), p. 82.

23 Ibid.

24 Ingrid Caven in Lorenz, *Chaos as Usual*, p. 45.

25 Stritzke, *Marieluise Fleißer*, p. 19.

26 Ibid., p. 141.

27 Finnan, "Versions of the Literary Self," p. 280.

28 Barnett, *Fassbinder and the German Theatre*, p. 45.

29 Case, *The Divided Home/Land*, p. 21.

30 Ibid., p. 25.

31 Finnan, "Versions of the Literary Self," p. 281.

32 Herzfeld-Sander, *Early 20th-Century German Plays*, p. xx.

33 Limmer, *Fassbinder, Filmmacher*, p. 17.

34 Campt, *Other Germans*.

35 "Our Father Was Cameroonian, Our Mother, East Prussian, We Are Mulattoes: Sisters Doris Reiprich and Erika Ngambi ul Kuo (Ages 67 and 70) Speak about Their Lives," in *Showing Our Colors: Afro-German Women Speak Out*, ed. May Opitz, Katharina Oguntoye, and Dagmar Schultz (Amherst: University of Massachusetts Press, 1992), p. 70.

36 Fassbinder, *Gods of the Plague*.

37 Ibid.

38 Katz, *Love Is Colder than Death*, p. 45.

39 Ibid., p. 44.

40 Fehrenbach, "Black Occupation Children," p. 37.

41 Ibid., p. 39.

42 Ibid., p. 33.

43 Tina Campt, *Other Germans*, p. 145.

44 Silverman, *Male Subjectivity*, pp. 134–35.

45 Ibid., p. 155.

46 Case, "Tracking the Vampire," p. 13.

47 Ibid., p. 11.

48 Silverman, "Fassbinder and Lacan," p. 67.

49 Lacan, *The Seminar*, p. 98.

50 Ibid., p. 99.

51 Ibid.

52 Ibid., p. 149.

53 Katz, *Love Is Colder than Death*, p. xxiii.

54 Fassbinder in Thomsen, "Five Interviews with Fassbinder," p. 89.

55 Ibid., p. 90.

56 Ibid., p. 96.

57 Mulvey, *Visual and Other Pleasures*, p. 47.

58 Freidrich Engels, "Why There Is No Large Socialist Party in America," in *Basic Writings on Politics and Philosophy*, ed. Lewis S. Feuer (London: Fontana, 1969), p. 458.

59 Fassbinder, *Whity*.
60 Ibid.
61 Fassbinder in Thomsen, "Five Interviews with Fassbinder," p. 82.
62 Raoul Walsh, dir. *Band of Angels*. Performed by Clark Gable, Yvonne De Carlo, Sidney Poitier. Warner Home Video, 2007 [1957]. DVD.
63 Dyer, "Reading Fassbinder's Sexual Politics," p. 63.
64 Case, "Tracking the Vampire," p. 12.
65 Dyer, "Reading Fassbinder's Sexual Politics," p. 62.
66 Ibid., p. 60.
67 Ibid., p. 63.
68 Ibid., p. 61.
69 Lorenz, *Chaos as Usual*, p. 38.
70 Kardish and Lorenz, *Rainer Werner Fassbinder*, p. 47.
71 Barnett, *Fassbinder and the German Theatre*, p. 139.
72 Harry Baer, *Schlafen kann ich, wenn ich tot bin* (Köln: Kiepenheuer & Witsch, 1982), p. 57.

CHAPTER 4. THE COCKETTES, SYLVESTER, AND PERFORMANCE AS LIFE

1 TV Legends, "Barbara Walters on Covering Tricia Nixon's Wedding." Posted on YouTube, www.youtube.com.
2 Cimons, "Edward Cox Weds Tricia," p. 1.
3 "Nixon Gives Wife," p. 12.
4 Bakhtin, *Rabelais and His World*, p. 307.
5 Ibid., p. 272.
6 Ibid., p. 296.
7 Stallybrass and White, *Politics and Poetics*.
8 Weissman and Weber, *The Cockettes*.
9 Douglas Crimp, *Before Pictures*, manuscript. Dancing Foxes Press.
10 Katz, *Love Is Colder than Death*, p. 92.
11 Gamson, *The Fabulous Sylvester*, p. 37.
12 Ibid.
13 Echols, *Shaky Ground*, p. 34.
14 Gamson, *The Fabulous Sylvester*, pp. 58–59.
15 Ibid., p. 58.
16 Ibid., p. 46.
17 Tent, *Midnight at the Palace*, p. 41.
18 Briggs and Bauman, p. 149.
19 Ibid., p. 158.
20 Brecht, *Brecht on Theatre*, pp. 86–87.
21 Ibid., pp. 147–48.
22 Gamson, *The Fabulous Sylvester*, p. 55.
23 Tent, p. 37.

24 Ibid.
25 Hardt and Negri, *Multitude*, p. 203.
26 Berlant and Warner, "Sex in Public," p. 559.
27 Ibid., p. 554.
28 Ibid., p. 558.
29 Gamson, *The Fabulous Sylvester*, p. 49.
30 Tent, *Midnight at the Palace*, p. 36.
31 Gamson, *The Fabulous Sylvester*, p. 50.
32 Lake and Orloff, *The Unsinkable Bambi Lake*, p. 26.
33 Scrumbly Koldewyn and Maude Mormon, "People's Theater," KPFA, Pacifica Radio Archives, 1977.
34 Debord, "On the Construction of Situations," p. 44.
35 Kalman, *Elevator Girls in Bondage*.
36 Weissman and Weber, *The Cockettes*.
37 Brown, *A Taste of Power*, p. 205.
38 Newton, "The Black Panthers," p. 126.
39 Davis, *An Autobiography*, p. 150.
40 Hardt and Negri, *Multitude*, p. 77.
41 Brown, *A Taste of Power*.
42 Angela Davis, *Angela Davis Speaks*, Folkways Records (1971).
43 Brown, *A Taste of Power*, p. 4.
44 Brown and Black Panther Party, *Seize the Time*.
45 Ibid.
46 Jennings, "Poetry of the Black Panther Party," p. 123.
47 Genet, *Here and Now for Bobby Seale*, p. 8.
48 Jones and Jeffries, "'Don't Believe the Hype,'" p. 35.
49 E. Patrick Johnson, *Appropriating Blackness*, (Durham and London: Duke University Press, 2003), pp. 55–57.
50 Gamson, *The Fabulous Sylvester*, p. 38.
51 Butler, "Performative Acts," p. 279.
52 Ibid.
53 Ibid.
54 Kelly, *Imaging Desire*, p. 231.
55 Muñoz, *Disidentifications*, p. 99.
56 Ibid.
57 Case, "Classic Drag," p. 318.
58 Ibid., p. 319.
59 Plautus and Richlin, *Rome and the Mysterious Orient*, p. 21.
60 Ibid., pp. 21–30.
61 Ibid., p. 20.
62 Ibid., p. 19.
63 Lake and Orloff, *The Unsinkable Bambi Lake*, p. 47.
64 Gamson, *The Fabulous Sylvester*, p. 41.

65 Ibid., p. 42.
66 Sylvester quoted in ibid., p. 58.
67 Ibid., p. 90.
68 Ibid, p. 43.
69 Quoted in Brian Chin, "Vissi D'Arte: Sylvester's Music on Blue Thumb," liner notes to the album *Slyvester and His Hot Band: The Blue Thumb Collection*, Geffen Records, 2009, p. 5.
70 Gamson, *The Fabulous Sylvester*, p. 45.
71 Weissman and Weber, *The Cockettes*.
72 Sylvester, *Sylvester: The Original Hits*, Fantasy Records, 1989.

AFTERWORD
1 See Mirzoeff, *The Right to Look*.
2 Harney and Moten, *The Undercommons*.
3 Nyong'o, "Afro-philo-sonic Fictions," 174.
4 Redmond, *Anthem*, p. 1.
5 August Heinrich Hoffman von Fallersleben, "Das Lied der Deutschen," 1841.
6 Ibid.
7 Ibid.
8 Ibid.
9 Butler and Spivak, *Who Sings the Nation-State?*, pp. 61–62.
10 Ibid., p. 73.
11 Redmond, *Anthem*, pp. 12–13.
12 Nkrumah, "Inauguration Speech of the First OAU Conference."
13 Spillers, "All the Things You Could Be," p. 380.
14 Ibid., p. 383.
15 Arendt, *The Promise of Politics*, p. 93.
16 Agamben, *The Coming Community*, p. 27.
17 Okwui Enwezor, "Exploding Gardens," in Enwezor, *All the World's Futures*, p. 93.
18 "Art, Politics, and 'All the World's Futures.'"
19 Muñoz, *Cruising Utopia*, p. 22.
20 "Art, Politics, and 'All the World's Futures.'"
21 Marx, *Capital, Volume I*, p. 154.
22 Isaac Julien, *Kapital*, 2013, two-channel video, 31 minutes.
23 Ibid.
24 Hall, "The Problem of Ideology," p. 45.
25 Julien and Nash, "Dialogues with Stuart Hall," p. 481.
26 Higgins, "Das Kapital at the Arsenale."
27 Gennocchio, "Enwezor's 56th Venice Biennial."
28 Julius Eastman, "Julius Eastman's Spoken Introduction to the Northwestern University Concert," on Eastman, *Unjust Malaise*.
29 Borden, "Evil Nigger," pp. 136–37.
30 R. Nemo Hill quoted in Packer, "Julius Eastman: A Biography," p. 55.

31 Packer, "Julius Eastman," p. 45.

32 Uroskie, *Between the Black Box*, p. 208.

33 Ibid., p. 209.

34 Richard Serra quoted in Ratner, "The Come Out Notebook," p. 15.

35 Malik Gaines, email to Alicia Hall Moran and Jason Moran, May 11, 2015.

36 Alicia Hall Moran, email to author, May 11, 2015.

BIBLIOGRAPHY

Aborampah, Osei-Mensah. "Women's Roles in the Mourning Rituals of the Akan of Ghana." *Ethnology* 38, no. 3 (1999).

Achebe, Chinua. "The Short Century: Independence and Liberation Movements in Africa, 1945–1994: An Introduction." Introduction to *The Short Century: Independence and Liberation Movements in Africa, 1945–1994*, by Okwui Enwezor. Munich: Prestel, 2001.

Adams, Anne V. and Esi Sutherland-Addy, eds. *The Legacy of Efua Sutherland: Pan-African Cultural Activism*. Banbury: Ayebia Clarke, 2007.

Agamben, Giorgio. *The Coming Community*. London and Minneapolis: University of Minnesota Press, 1993.

Aidoo, Ama Ata. *The Dilemma of a Ghost*. White Plains, NY: Longman, 1987.

Aidoo, Ama Ata. "An Interrogation of an Academic Kind: An Essay." In *The Legacy of Efua Sutherland: Pan-African Cultural Activism*, ed. Anne V. Adams and Esi Sutherland-Addy. Banbury: Ayebia Clarke, 2007.

Appadurai, Arjun. *Modernity at Large: Cultural Dimensions of Globalization*. Minneapolis: University of Minnesota Press, 1996.

Appiah, Kwame Anthony. *In My Father's House: Africa in the Philosophy of Culture*. Oxford and New York: Oxford University Press, 1992.

Arendt, Hannah, and Jerome Kohn. *The Promise of Politics*. New York: Schocken Books, 2005.

"Art, Politics, and 'All the World's Futures': Okwui Enwezor, First African Curator of Venice Biennale." *Democracy Now!*, August 11, 2015. www.democracynow.org.

Baker, Jean-Claude, and Chris Chase. *Josephine: The Hungry Heart*. New York: Random House, 1993.

Bakhtin, Mikhail. *Rabelais and His World*. Bloomington and Indianapolis: Indiana University Press, 1968.

Ball, James. "Obama: Reagan Changed Direction; Bill Clinton Didn't." YouTube. January 21, 2008. www.youtube.com.

Barnett, David. *Rainer Werner Fassbinder and the German Theatre*. Cambridge and New York: Cambridge University Press, 2005.

Benjamin, Walter. "The Author as Producer." In *Reflections: Essays, Aphorisms, Autobiographical Writings*, ed. Peter Demetz. New York: Schiken Books, 1978.

Berlant, Lauren, and Michael Warner. "Sex in Public." *Critical Inquiry*, no. 547 (1998).

Beyoncé. *I Am—Sasha Fierce*. Music World Music/Columbia, 2008, CD.

Borden, David. "Evil Nigger: A Piece for Multiple Instruments of the Same Type by Julius Eastman (1979), with Performance Instructions by Joseph Kubera." In *Gay Guerrilla: Julius Eastman and His Music*, ed. Renée Levine Packer and Mary Jane Leach. Rochester, NY: University of Rochester Press, 2015.

Botwe-Asamoah, Kwame. *Kwame Nkrumah's Politico-Cultural Thought and Policies: An African-centered Paradigm for the Second Phase of the African Revolution*. New York and London: Routledge, 2005.

Braunmuller, A. R. Introduction to *The Rise and Fall of the City of Mahagonny*, by Bertolt Brecht. Boston: David R. Godine, 1976.

Brecht, Bertolt. "Alienation Effects in Chinese Acting." In *Brecht on Theatre: The Development of an Aesthetic*, ed. John Willett. New York: Hill and Wang, 1964.

Brecht, Bertolt. "On Gestic Music." In *Brecht on Theatre: The Development of an Aesthetic*, ed. John Willett. New York: Hill and Wang, 1964.

Briggs, Charles L., and Richard Bauman. "Genre, Intertextuality, and Social Power." *Journal of Linguistic Anthropology* 2, no. 2 (1992): 131–72.

Brooks, Daphne. *Bodies in Dissent: Spectacular Performances of Race and Freedom, 1850–1910*. Durham: Duke University Press, 2006.

Brooks, Daphne A. "Nina Simone's Triple Play." *Callaloo* 34, no. 1 (2011): 176–97.

Brown, Elaine. *A Taste of Power: A Black Woman's Story*. New York: Pantheon Books, 1992.

Brown, Elaine, and Black Panther Party. *Seize the Time*. Water Records, 2006 [1969], CD.

Butler, Judith. "Performative Acts and Gender Constitution: An Essay in Phenomenology and Feminist Theory." Edited by Sue-Ellen Case. *Feminist Critical Theory and Theatre* 40, no. 4 (1988): 519.

Butler, Judith, and Gayatri Chakravorty Spivak. *Who Sings the Nation-State?: Language, Politics, Belonging*. London: Seagull Books, 2007.

Campt, Tina. *Other Germans: Black Germans and the Politics of Race, Gender, and Memory in the Third Reich*. Ann Arbor: University of Michigan, 2004.

Case, Sue-Ellen. "Classic Drag: The Greek Creation of Female Parts." *Theatre Journal* 37, no. 3 (1985): 317.

Case, Sue-Ellen, ed. *The Divided Home/Land: Contemporary German Women's Plays*. Ann Arbor: University of Michigan Press, 1992.

Case, Sue-Ellen. *Performing Science and the Virtual*. New York and London: Routledge, 2007.

Case, Sue-Ellen. "Tracking the Vampire." *Differences: A Journal of Feminist Cultural Studies* 3, no. 2 (1991).

Caven, Ingrid. "Curious in the Present." In *Chaos as Usual: Conversations about Rainer Werner Fassbinder*, ed. Juliane Lorenz. New York: Applause, 1997.

Cimons, Marlene. "Edward Cox Weds Tricia as Rain Drifts into Rose Garden." *Los Angeles Times*, June 13, 1971.

Cohodas, Nadine. *Princess Noire: The Tumultuous Reign of Nina Simone*. New York: Pantheon Books, 2010.

Cole, Catherine M. *Ghana's Concert Party Theatre*. Bloomington: Indiana University Press, 2001.

Cole, Catherine M., Takyiwaa Manuh, and Stephen F. Miescher, eds., *Africa after Gender*. Bloomington: Indiana University Press, 2007.

Collins, E. J. "Comic Opera in Ghana." *African Arts* 9, no. 2 (January 1976): 50–57.

Contee, Clarence G. "The Encyclopedia Africana Project of W. E. B. Du Bois." *African Historical Studies* 4, no. 1 (1971): 77–91.

Copeland, Huey. *Bound to Appear: Art, Slavery, and the Site of Blackness in Multicultural America*. Chicago and London: University of Chicago, 2013.

Davis, Angela Y. *Angela Davis—an Autobiography*. New York: Random House, 1974.

Debord, Guy. "The Decline and Fall of the Spectacle-Commodity Economy." In *Situationist International Anthology*, ed. Ken Knabb. Berkeley, CA: Bureau of Public Secrets, 1981.

Debord, Guy. "Report on the Construction of Situations and on the Terms of Organization and Action of the International Situationist Tendency." In *Guy Debord and the Situationist International: Texts and Documents*, trans. Tom McDonough. Cambridge, MA: MIT Press, 2002.

DeFrantz, Thomas. *Dancing Revelations: Alvin Ailey's Embodiment of African American Culture*. Oxford: Oxford University Press, 2004.

"Dialogues with Stuart Hall." In *Stuart Hall: Critical Dialogues in Cultural Studies*, ed. David Morley and Kuan-Hsing Chen, 476–83. London: Routledge, 1996.

Du Bois, W.E.B. "Application for Membership in the Communist Party of the United States of America." In *W.E.B. Du Bois, a Reader*, ed. David Levering Lewis. New York: Henry Holt & Co., 1995.

Du Bois, W.E.B. *The Souls of Black Folk*. Oxford and New York: Oxford University Press, 2007.

Dyer, Richard. "Reading Fassbinder's Sexual Politics." In *Fassbinder*, ed. Tony Rayns. London: British Film Institute, 1980.

Eastman, Julius. *Unjust Malaise*. New World Records, 2005. CD.

Echols, Alice. *Shaky Ground: The Sixties and Its Aftershocks*. New York: Columbia University Press, 2002.

Edwards, Brent Hayes. *The Practice of Diaspora: Literature, Translation, and the Rise of Black Internationalism*. Cambridge, MA: Harvard University Press, 2003.

Edwards, Brent. "W.E.B. Du Bois." Introduction to *The Ordeal of Mansart: The Black Flame Trilogy, Book One*, by W.E.B. Du Bois. Oxford and New York: Oxford University Press, 2007.

Enwezor, Okwui. *All the World's Futures: La Biennale Di Venezia, 56th International Art Exhibition*. Venice: Marsilio, 2015.

Enwezor, Okwui, ed. *The Short Century: Independence and Liberation Movements in Africa, 1945–1994*. Munich, London, and New York: Prestel, 2001.

Fanon, Frantz. *Black Skin, White Masks*. New York: Grove Press, 1967.

Fassbinder, Rainer Werner, dir. *Gods of the Plague*. Performed by Hanna Schygulla, Margarethe Von Trotta, Harry Bär, Günther Kauffmann, Carla Aulaulu, Ingrid

Caven, Jan George, Lilo Pempeit, Marian Seydowski, Micha Cochina, Yaak Karsunke, Hannes Gromball. Criterion Collection, 2013 [1970]. DVD.

Fassbinder, Rainer Werner, dir. *Whity*. Produced by Ulli Lommel and Kurt Raab. Written by Rainer Werner Fassbinder, Michael Ballhaus, Peer Raben, Franz Walsh, and Thea Eymèsz. Performed by Ulli Lommel, Günter Kaufmann, Ron Randell, and Hanna Schygulla. Fantoma, 2003 [1971]. DVD.

Fassbinder, Rainer Werner, and Denis Calandra. *Rainer Werner Fassbinder: Plays*. New York: PAJ Publications, 1985.

Fehrenbach, Heide. "Black Occupation Children and the Devolution of the Nazi Racial State." In *After the Nazi Racial State: Difference and Democracy in Germany and Europe*, by Rita Chin, Heide Fehrenbach, Geoff Eley, and Atina Grossman. Ann Arbor: University of Michigan Press, 2009.

Finnan, Carmel. "Versions of the Literary Self in Texts by Marieluise Fleißer." In *Practicing Modernity: Female Creativity in the Weimar Republic*, by Christiane Schönfeld and Carmel Finnan. Würzburg: Königshausen & Neumann, 2006.

Foucault, Michel. *Discipline and Punish: The Birth of the Prison*. Translated by Alan Sheridan. New York: Vintage Books, 1978.

Gaines, Malik. Email to Alicia Hall Moran and Jason Moran, May 11, 2015.

Gamson, Joshua. *The Fabulous Sylvester: The Legend, the Music, the Seventies in San Francisco*. New York: H. Holt, 2005.

Genet, Jean. *Here and Now for Bobby Seale: Essays*. Committee to Defend the Panther, 1970.

Gennocchio, Benjamin. "Okwui Enwezor's 56th Venice Biennial Is Morose, Joyless, and Ugly." *Artnet*, May 8, 2015. https://news.artnet.com.

Hall, Stuart. "The Problem of Ideology: Marxism without Guarantees." In *Critical Dialogues in Cultural Studies*, ed. David Morley and Kuan-Hsing Chen. London and New York: Routledge, 1996.

Hardt, Michael, and Antonio Negri. *Multitude*. New York: Penguin, 2004.

Harney, Stefano, and Fred Moten. *The Undercommons: Fugitive Planning & Black Study*. Wivenhoe, New York, and Port Watson: Minor Compositions, 2013.

Harrison, Paul Carter, Victor Leo Walker II, and Gus Edwards. "The Sense of Ritualizing New Performance Spaces for Survival." In *Black Theatre: Ritual Performance in the African Diaspora*. Philadelphia: Temple University Press. 2002.

Hartman, Saidiya V. *Lose Your Mother: A Journey along the Atlantic Slave Route*. New York: Farrar, Straus and Giroux, 2007.

Hartman, Saidiya V. "The Position of the Unthought." Interview by Frank Wilderson, III. *Qui Parle* 13, no. 2 (2003).

Herzfeld-Sander, Margaret. *Early 20th-Century German Plays*. New York: Continuum, 1998.

Higgins, Charlotte. "Das Kapital at the Arsenale: How Okwui Enwezor Invited Marx to the Venice Biennial." *Guardian*. May 7, 2015.

Hilliker, Rebecca. "Brecht's Gestic Vision for Opera: Why the Shock of Recognition Is More Powerful in the Rise and Fall of the City of Mahagonny than in The Three

Penny Opera." In *Essays on Twentieth-Century German Drama and Theater: An American Reception, 1977–1999*, by Hellmut H. Rennert, 225–35. New York: Peter Lang, 2004.

Hoffmeister, Donna L. *The Theater of Confinement: Language and Survival in the Milieu Plays of Marieluise Fleisser and Franz Xavier Kroetz*. Columbia, SC: Camden House, 1983.

Hountondji, Paulin J. *African Philosophy: Myth and Reality*. Bloomington: Indiana University Press, 1983.

Iden, Peter. "Making an Impact—Rainer Werner Fassbinder and the Theatre." In *Fassbinder*, ed. Tony Rayns. London: British Film Institute, 1980.

Jahn, Janheinz. *A History of Neo-African Literature*. Translated by Oliver Coburn and Ursula Lehrburger. London: Faber, 1968.

Jahn, Mike. "Throng Welcomes Nina Simone, Back after Long Absence." *New York Times*, May 11, 1971.

Jameson, Fredric. "Periodizing the 60s." *Social Text* 9/10 (1984): 178–209.

Jennings, Regina. "Poetry of the Black Panther Party: Metaphors of Militancy." *Journal of Black Studies* 29, no. 1 (1998): 106–29.

Johnson, E. Patrick. *Appropriating Blackness: Performance and the Politics of Authenticity*. Durham, NC: Duke University Press, 2003.

Jones, Charles E., and Judson L. Jeffries. "'Don't Believe the Hype': Debunking the Panther Mythology." In *The Black Panther Party (reconsidered)*, ed. Charles E. Jones. Baltimore: Black Classic Press, 1998.

Jules-Rosette, Bennetta. *Josephine Baker in Art and Life: The Icon and the Image*. Urbana: University of Illinois Press, 2007.

Julien, Isaac. *Kapital*, 2013, 2-channel video, 31 minutes.

Julien, Isaac, and Mark Nash. "Dialogues with Stuart Hall." In *Critical Dialogues in Cultural Studies*, ed. David Morley and Kuan-Hsing Chen. London and New York: Routledge, 1996.

July, Robert. "Here, Then, Is Efua." In *The Legacy of Efua Sutherland: Pan-African Cultural Activism*, ed. Anne V. Adams and Esi Sutherland-Addy. Banbury: Ayebia Clarke, 2007.

Kalman, Michael, dir. *Elevator Girls in Bondage*. Buffalo Pictures, 1972.

Kardish, Laurence, and Juliane Lorenz, eds. *Rainer Werner Fassbinder*. New York: Museum of Modern Art, 1997.

Katz, Robert. *Love Is Colder than Death: The Life and Times of Rainer Werner Fassbinder*. New York: Random House, 1987.

Kelly, Mary. *Imaging Desire*. Cambridge, MA: MIT Press, 1996.

Lacan, Jacques. *The Seminar of Jacques Lacan*. New York: Norton, 1998.

Laclau, Ernesto, and Chantal Mouffe. *Hegemony and Socialist Strategy: Towards a Radical Democratic Politics*. Translated by Winston Moore and Paul Cammack. London: Verso, 1985.

Lake, Bambi, and Alvin Orloff. *The Unsinkable Bambi Lake: A Fairy Tale Containing the Dish on Cockettes, Punks, and Angels*. San Francisco: Manic D Press, 1996.

Lemly, John. "Hesitant Homecomings in Hansberry's and Aidoo's First Plays." In *The Legacy of Efua Sutherland: Pan-African Cultural Activism*, ed. Anne V. Adams and Esi Sutherland-Addy. Banbury: Ayebia Clarke, 2007.

Lewis, David L. *W.E.B. Du Bois: A Biography*. New York: Henry Holt and Co., 2009.

Limmer, Wolfgang. *Wolfgang Limmer, Rainer Werner Fassbinder, Filmmacher*. Hamburg: Spiegel-Verlag, 1981.

Lorenz, Juliane, ed. *Chaos as Usual: Conversations about Rainer Werner Fassbinder*. New York: Applause, 1997.

Malina, Judith, Julian Beck, and the Living Theatre. *Paradise Now: Collective Creation of the Living Theatre*. New York: Random House, 1971.

Manuh, Takyiwaa. "Wives, Children, and Intestate Succession in Ghana,." In *African Feminism: The Politics of Survival in Sub-Saharan Africa*, ed. Gwendolyn Mikell, 77–96. Philadelphia: University of Pennsylvania Press, 1997.

Marx, Karl. *Capital, Volume I*. New York: International Publishers, 1967.

Marx, Karl, and Friedrich Engels. *Basic Writings on Politics and Philosophy*, ed. Lewis Samuel. Feuer. London: Fontana, 1969.

McClure, Kristie. "On the Subject of Rights: Pluralism, Plurality and Political Identity." In *Dimensions of Radical Democracy: Pluralism, Citizenship, Community*, ed. Chantal Mouffe, 108–28. London: Verso, 1992.

Mirzoeff, Nicholas. *The Right to Look: A Counterhistory of Visuality*. Durham and London: Duke University Press, 2011.

Moran, Alicia Hall. Email to author. May 11, 2015.

Moten, Fred. *In the Break: The Aesthetics of the Black Radical Tradition*. Minneapolis: University of Minnesota Press, 2003.

Mudimbe, Valentin Y. *The Invention of Africa: Gnosis, Philosophy, and The Order of Knowledge*. Bloomington: Indiana University Press, 1988.

Mulvey, Laura. *Visual and Other Pleasures*. Bloomington: Indiana University Press, 1989.

Muñoz, José Esteban. *Cruising Utopia: The Then and There of Queer Futurity*. New York: New York University Press, 2009.

Muñoz, José Esteban. *Disidentifications: Queers of Color and the Performance of Politics*. Minneapolis: University of Minnesota Press, 1999.

Nemiroff, Robert, and Lorraine Hansberry. *To Be Young, Gifted, and Black: Lorraine Hansberry in Her Own Words*. New York: Vintage Books, 1995.

Newton, Huey P. "The Black Panthers," in *The Black Revolution: An Ebony Special Issue* (Chicago: Johnson Publishing Company, 1970), p. 126 (originally published in *Ebony*, August 1969).

Nina Simone Live. Directed by Al Schackman, Chris White, and Bobby Hamilton. Performed by Nina Simone. West Long Branch: Kultur, 2004. DVD.

Nina Simone Live at Ronnie Scott's. Performed by Nina Simone. Oaks, PA: Music Video Distributors, 2003. DVD.

Nina Simone Live in '65 & '68. Directed by David Peck, et al. Performed by Nina Simone. San Diego: Reelin' in the Years Productions, 2008. DVD.

"Nixon Gives Wife, Daughters Fur Coats." *Los Angeles Times*, December 23, 1968.

Nketia, J. H. Kwabena. "Kwame Nkrumah and the Arts." In *Gender: Evolving Roles and Perceptions*, ed. Ghana Academy of Arts and Sciences. Accra: Ghana Academy of Arts and Sciences, 2006.

Nkrumah, Kwame. "Inauguration Speech of the First OAU Conference in Addis Ababa Ethiopia, 1963." *GhanaWeb*, May 26, 2013. www.ghanaweb.com.

Nyong'o, Tavia. "Afro-philo-sonic Fictions: Black Sound Studies after the Millennium." *Small Axe: A Caribbean Journal of Criticism* 18, no. 2 (2014): 173–79.

Packer, Renée Levine. "Julius Eastman: A Biography." In *Gay Guerilla: Julius Eastman and His Music*, ed. Renée Levine Packer and Mary Jane Leach. Rochester, NY: University of Rochester Press, 2015.

Papich, Stephen. *Remembering Josephine*. New York: Bobbs-Merrill Company, 1976.

Plautus, Titus Maccius, and Amy Richlin. *Rome and the Mysterious Orient: Three Plays by Plautus*. Berkeley: University of California Press, 2005.

Ratner, Megan. "The Come Out Notebook." In Glenn Ligon, *Come Out*. London: Ridinghouse and Thomas Dane Gallery, 2014.

Redmond, Shana L. *Anthem: Social Movements and the Sound of Solidarity in the African Diaspora*. New York: New York University Press, 2013.

Richards, Sandra. "Dramatizing the Diaspora's Return: Tess Onwueme's The Missing Face and Ama Ata Aidoo's The Dilemma of a Ghost." In *The Legacy of Efua Sutherland: Pan-African Cultural Activism*, ed. Anne V. Adams and Esi Sutherland-Addy. Banbury: Ayebia Clarke, 2007.

Richards, Sandra. "What Is to Be Remembered?: Tourism to Ghana's Slave Castle-Dungeons." In *Critical Theory and Performance*, ed. Janelle G. Reinelt and Joseph R. Roach. Ann Arbor: University of Michigan Press, 1992.

Roach, Joseph R. *Cities of the Dead: Circum-Atlantic Performance*. New York: Columbia University Press, 1996.

Robinson, Beverly. "The Sense of Ritualizing New Performance Spaces for Survival." In *Black Theater: Ritual Performance in the African Diaspora*, ed. Paul Carter Harrison, Victor Leo Walker II, and Gus Edwards. Philadelphia: Temple University Press, 2002.

"The Rockefeller Foundation Annual Report, 1961." New York: Rockefeller Foundation, 1961. www.rockefellerfoundation.org.

"The Rockefeller Foundation Annual Report for 1962." New York: Rockefeller Foundation, 1962. www.rockefellerfoundation.org.

"The Rockefeller Foundation Annual Report for 1964." New York: Rockefeller Foundation, 1964. www.rockefellerfoundation.org.

Said, Edward W. *Orientalism*. New York: Vintage Books, 1979.

Sherman, Robert. "Nina Simone Casts Her Moody Spells." *New York Times*, November 23, 1966.

Silverman, Kaja. "Fassbinder and Lacan: A Reconsideration of Gaze, Look, and Image." *Camera Obscura: Feminism, Culture, and Media Studies* 7, no. 1 (1989): 54–85.

Silverman, Kaja. *Male Subjectivity at the Margins*. New York: Routledge, 1992.

Simone, Nina. *The Blues*. RCA, 1970. LP/CD.

Simone, Nina. *Live in Berkeley*. Stroud, 1973. LP.

Simone, Nina. *Nina Simone in Concert*. Phillips, 1964. LP.

Simone, Nina. *Nina Simone Live*. Phillips, 1964. LP.

Simone, Nina. *Nina Simone Sings the Blues*. BMG, 2001. CD.

Simone, Nina, and Stephen Cleary. *I Put a Spell on You: The Autobiography of Nina Simone*. New York: Pantheon Books, 1991.

Spillers, Hortense J. "'All the Things You Could Be by Now, If Sigmund Freud's Wife Was Your Mother': Psychoanalysis and Race." In *Black, White, and In Color: Essays on American Literature and Culture*, 376–427. Chicago: University of Chicago Press, 2003.

Spillers, Hortense J. *Black, White, and in Color: Essays on American Literature and Culture*. Chicago: University of Chicago Press, 2003.

Stallings, L. H. *Funk the Erotic: Transaesthetics and Black Sexual Cultures*. Urbana, Chicago, and Springfield: University of Illinois Press, 2015.

Stallybrass, Peter, and Allon White. *The Politics and Poetics of Transgression*. Ithaca, NY: Cornell University Press, 1986.

Stritzke, Barbara. *Marieluise Fleißer "Pioniere in Ingolstadt."* Frankfurt A.M. and Bern: Verlag Peter Lang, 1982.

Sutherland, Efua. *Edufa*. London: Longmans, Green and Co., 1967.

Sutherland, Efua Theodora Morgue. *Foriwa*. Accra: State Pub., 1967.

Sutherland, Efua Theodora Morgue, and Maxine Lautre. "A Recorded Interview with Efua Sutherland of the Drama Studio, Accra, and the Institute of African Studies, University of Ghana, on the Current Theatre Movement in Ghana." *Cultural Events in Africa* 42, 1968.

Tent, Pam. *Midnight at the Palace: My Life as a Fabulous Cockette*. Los Angeles: Alyson Books, 2004.

Thomas, John Patrick. "Julius Eastman: A Biography." In *Gay Guerrilla: Julius Eastman and His Music*, ed. Renée Levine Packer and Mary Jane Leach. Rochester, NY: University of Rochester Press, 2015.

Thomsen, Christian Braad. "Five Interviews with Fassbinder." In *Fassbinder*, ed. Tony Rayns. London: British Film Institute, 1980.

TV Legends. "Barbara Walters on Covering Tricia Nixon's Wedding." YouTube. August 2009. www.youtube.com.

Uroskie, Andrew V. *Between the Black Box and the White Cube: Expanded Cinema and Postwar Art*. Chicago: University of Chicago Press, 2014.

Vogel, Shane. *The Scene of Harlem Cabaret: Race, Sexuality, Performance*. Chicago: University of Chicago Press, 2009.

"W. E. B. DuBois Dies in Ghana; Negro Leader and Author, 95." *New York Times*, August 28, 1963. www.nytimes.com.

Wedekind, Frank, Ödön von Horváth, and Marieluise Fleißer. *Early 20th-Century German Plays*, ed. Margaret Herzfeld-Sander. New York: Continuum, 1998.

Weissman, David, and Bill Weber, dirs. *The Cockettes*. Produced by David Weissman. Grandelusion, 2002. DVD.

Wilderson, Frank. "Gramsci's Black Marx: Whither the Slave in Civil Society?" *Social Identities* 9 (225th ser.), no. 2 (2003): 225–40.

Wilderson, Frank. "The Position of the Unthought: An Interview with Saidiya V. Hartman Conducted by Frank B. Wilderson III." *Qui Parle* 13, no. 2 (Spring/Summer 2003): 183–201.

Willey, Elizabeth. "National Identities, Tradition, and Feminism: The Novels of Ama Ata Aidoo Read in the Context of the Works of Kwame Nkrumah." In *Interventions: Feminist Dialogues on Third World Women's Literature and Film*, ed. Bishnupriya Ghosh and Brinda Bose. New York: Garland, 1997.

Wilson, John S. "Cosby Simone Concert a Hit at Philharmonic." *New York Times*, February 20, 1967.

Wilson, John S. "Museums in Tune with Nina Simone." *New York Times*, February 5, 1969.

Wilson, John S. "Nina Simone Sings at Carnegie Hall." *New York Times*, April 13, 1963.

Wilson, John S. "Nina Simone Sings at Carnegie Hall." *New York Times*, January 16, 1965.

Wilson, John S. "Nina Simone Sings Stirring Program." *New York Times*, April 16, 1965.

Wilson, John S. "Singer Triumphs at Jazz Festival." *New York Times*, July 4, 1966.

X, Malcolm, and Alex Haley. *The Autobiography of Malcolm X*. New York: Ballantine Books, 1992.

Yan, Haiping. *Chinese Women Writers and the Feminist Imagination, 1905–1948*. London and New York: Routledge, 2006.

Yan, Haiping. "Spheres of Feelings: Theatricality in Chinese Aesthetics and Beyond." In *Theatricality*, ed. Tracy C. Davis and Thomas Postlewait. Cambridge, UK: Cambridge University Press, 2003.

INDEX

42–43; Baker's disruption of binaries, 11–16; Black Panther Party and, 162–67; California's sixties scene, 135–77; class struggle and, 4–5; drag and cross-gender performances, 12–14, 135, 138–42, 144, 146–51, 156–58, 165, 167–73, 177; in Fassbinder's works, 107–33; jazz and, 51; performance and, 2–3; Simone's transvocality and, 47–48; in Sutherland's plays, 68, 69–71, 73, 79–83; visibility and, 39–40, 42, 83, 165

Genet, Jean, 1, 31, 135; *The Blacks*, 128; defense of Black Panthers, 165; *Querelle*, 96, 128

Gershwins' Porgy and Bess, The (adapted musical), 198

Ghana: Anglo-Christian education system in, 62; assimilation challenges in, 83–93; change *vs.* tradition as portrayed by Sutherland, 76–83; dilemma genre storytelling tradition, 83–84, 87–88; Du Bois's gravesite in, 16; funeral tradition in, 57–58; as imaginative space, 17, 56–57, 93–94; independence of, 58, 74–75; Marxism in, 5; National Theater Movement in, 55–56, 62–64, 69, 73; Nkrumah's pan-African movement, 55, 58, 60–66; PANAFEST in, 16–17; post-independence nationalism, 62–65, 73–75, 82–83; Rockefeller Foundation's arts funding, 75; slavery and, 56, 74, 82–83, 85, 87–89

Ghana Drama Studio, 65, 75, 84

Ghana Writers Society, 65–66, 73

Gilroy, Paul, 10

Ginsburg, Allen, 155

Giovanni, Nikki, 164

Glitters, Goldie, 139, 143

Glover, Danny, 16–17

Gods of the Plague (film), 112–20, *116*, 121, 133

Goldoni, Carlo: *The Coffeehouse*, 133

Gone with the Showboat to Oklahoma (Cockettes musical), 149–51, 153, 154, 167

Gone with the Wind (film), 126

Habermas, Jürgen, 155

Haley, Alex, 73

Hall, Stuart: "The Problem of Ideology," 190–91, 197

Hamm, Daniel, 196, 197, 198

Hampton, Deborah, 161

Hampton, Fred, 131, 161

Hansberry, Lorraine: collage by, 40, *41*, 42; death of, 26; *A Raisin in the Sun*, 24, 63, 76; Simone and, 23, 24–25; "To Be Young, Gifted and Black," 24, 26, 40, 42

Hardt, Michael: *Multitude* (with Negri), 135, 155, 162

Harlem Six, 197

Harris, Lisa, 199

Hartman, Saidiya: *Lose Your Mother*, 38, 39, 50, 74, 88

Harvey, David, 190–91

Hauser, Fayette, 147

Haydn, Joseph: *Deutschland, Deutschland über alles*, 181–82

Hegel, G.W.F., 55

Hermann, Irm, 108–9

Herring, Steven, 199

Herzfeld-Sander, Margaret: *Early 20th-Century German Plays*, 108

heteronormativity, 156–57

Hibiscus, 147–48, 155, 157, 158, 167

Hitler, Adolf, 114

Holiday, Billie: death of, 26; performance of "For All We Know," 48–49; "Strange Fruit," 189; Sylvester compared to, 174; Sylvester influenced by, 173

Hountondji, Paulin: *African Philosophy*, 55, 80–82

Huggins, Ericka, 163, 165

ABOUT THE AUTHOR

Malik Gaines is Assistant Professor of Performance Studies in New York University's Tisch School of the Arts and a member of the performance group My Barbarian.

CPSIA information can be obtained
at www.ICGtesting.com
Printed in the USA
LVOW11s1515070318
568992LV00001B/83/P